Muslim Family Law in Western Courts

Edited by
Elisa Giunchi

Routledge
Taylor & Francis Group
LONDON AND NEW YORK

First published 2014
by Routledge
2 Park Square, Milton Park, Abingdon, Oxfordshire OX14 4RN

and by Routledge
711 Third Avenue, New York, NY 10017

First issued in paperback 2016

Routledge is an imprint of the Taylor & Francis Group, an informa business

British Library Cataloguing in Publication Data
A catalogue record for this book is available from the British Library

Library of Congress Cataloging in Publication Data
A catolog record for this book has been requested

ISBN 13: 978-0-415-78800-7 (pbk)
ISBN 13: 978-0-415-81977-0 (hbk)

Typeset in Times New Roman
by Taylor & Francis Books

Muslim Family Law in Western Courts

This book focuses on Islamic family law as interpreted and applied by judges in Europe, Australia and North America. It uses court transcriptions and observations to discuss how the most contentious marriage-related issues – consent and age of spouses, dower, polygamy, and divorce – are adjudicated. The solutions proposed by different legal systems are reviewed, and some broader questions are addressed: how Islamic principles are harmonized with norms based on gender equality, how parties bargain strategically in and out of court, and how Muslim diasporas align their Islamic worldview with a Western normative narrative.

Elisa Giunchi is an Assistant Professor of History and Institutions of Muslim Countries at the University of Milan, Italy.

Durham Modern Middle East and Islamic World Series

Series Editor: Anoushiravan Ehteshami, University of Durham

1. **Economic Development in Saudi Arabia**
   Rodney Wilson, with Abdullah Al-Salamah, Monica Malik and Ahmed Al-Rajhi

2. **Islam Encountering Globalization**
   Edited by Ali Mohammadi

3. **China's Relations with Arabia and the Gulf, 1949–99**
   Mohamed Bin Huwaidin

4. **Good Governance in the Middle East Oil Monarchies**
   Edited by Tom Pierre Najem and Martin Hetherington

5. **The Middle East's Relations with Asia and Russia**
   Edited by Hannah Carter and Anoushiravan Ehteshami

6. **Israeli Politics and the Middle East Peace Process, 1988–2002**
   Hassan A. Barari

7. **The Communist Movement in the Arab World**
   Tareq Y. Ismael

8. **Oman – The Islamic Democratic Tradition**
   Hussein Ghubash

9. **The Secret Israeli-Palestinian Negotiations in Oslo**
   Their success and why the process ultimately failed
   Sven Behrendt

10. **Globalization and Geopolitics in the Middle East**
    Old games, new rules
    Anoushiravan Ehteshami

11. **Iran-Europe Relations**
    Challenges and opportunities
    Seyyed Hossein Mousavian

12. **Islands and International Politics in the Persian Gulf**
    The Abu Musa and Tunbs in strategic perspective
    Kourosh Ahmadi

13. **Monetary Union in the Gulf**
    Prospects for a single currency in the Arabian Peninsula
    Emilie Rutledge

14. **Contested Sudan**
    The political economy of war and reconstruction
    Ibrahim Elnur

15. **Palestinian Politics and the Middle East Peace Process**
Consensus and competition in the Palestinian negotiation team
Ghassan Khatib

16. **Islam in the Eyes of the West**
Images and realities in an age of terror
Edited by Tareq Y. Ismael and Andrew Rippin

17. **Islamic Extremism in Kuwait**
From the Muslim Brotherhood to Al-Qaeda and other Islamic political groups
Falah Abdullah al-Mdaires

18. **Iraq, Democracy and the Future of the Muslim World**
Edited by Ali Paya and John Esposito

19. **Islamic Entrepreneurship**
Rasem N. Kayed and M. Kabir Hassan

20. **Iran and the International System**
Edited by Anoushiravan Ehteshami and Reza Molavi

21. **The International Politics of the Red Sea**
Anoushiravan Ehteshami and Emma C. Murphy

22. **Palestinian Christians in Israel**
State attitudes towards non-Muslims in a Jewish state
Una McGahern

23. **Iran–Turkey Relations, 1979–2011**
Conceptualising the dynamics of politics, religion and security in middle-power states
Suleyman Elik

24. **The Sudanese Communist Party**
Ideology and party politics
Tareq Y. Ismael

25. **The Muslim Brotherhood in Contemporary Egypt**
Democracy defined or confined?
Mariz Tadros

26. **Social and Gender Inequality in Oman**
The power of religious and political tradition
Khalid M. Al-Azri

27. **American Democracy Promotion in the Changing Middle East**
From Bush to Obama
Edited by Shahram Akbarzadeh, James Piscatori, Benjamin MacQueen and Amin Saikal

28. **China-Saudi Arabia Relations, 1990–2012**
Marriage of Convenience or Strategic Alliance?
Naser M. Al-Tamimi

29. **Adjudicating Family Law in Muslim Courts**
Edited by Elisa Giunchi

30. **Muslim Family Law in Western Courts**
Edited by Elisa Giunchi

31. **Anti-Veiling Campaigns in the Muslim World**
Gender, Modernism and the Politics of Dress
Edited by Stephanie Cronin

Contents

Acknowledgements

I am grateful to Daniel Atzori and Prakash Shah for their advice in the planning phase of the book; to Peter Snowden of Routledge for believing in this project; to the publishing team for its practical support; to the copyeditor Janet MacMillan for doing an excellent job, and to the authors of the volume for enriching my knowledge.

Contributors

Abed Awad is an attorney, expert witness and consultant on Islamic law and legislation in Arab countries. His practice in the New Jersey-New York area focuses on general civil litigation, including matrimonial law, Islamic law and international law. He is also an Adjunct Law Professor at Rutgers Law School, Newark, Pace Law School, New York, and Seton Hall Law School, Newark.

Ann Black (BA, B. Soc Wk, LLB (Hons), LLM, SJD) is a senior lecturer in law at The University of Queensland and is the deputy director of the Centre for Public International and Comparative Law.

Andrea Büchler is professor of law at the University of Zurich. She founded the Center for Islamic and Middle Eastern Legal Studies at the University of Zurich and is the on-site director of the Law Summer School in Cairo. She is currently a fellow at the Collegium Helveticum ETH/UZH.

Pascale Fournier is Associate Professor at the Faculty of Law of the University of Ottawa. She holds a PhD in law from Harvard University and has published extensively on multiculturalism and women rights, and on Islamic family law as applied in Europe and North America.

Katja Jansen Fredriksen is a PhD fellow at the Faculty of Law, University of Bergen. She has taught at the University of Bergen and currently is a research assistant for the project 'The Shari'a in the Modern World: Faith, Norms, and State Power'.

Elisa Giunchi teaches history and institutions of Islamic countries at the University of Milan, Italy. She is senior research fellow at the Italian Institute for International Political Studies (ISPI), where she co-ordinates the programme on South Asia. Her research focuses on Islamic law and gender in Pakistan.

Denise Helly is a senior researcher at the Institut National de Recherche Scientifique. She was trained in anthropology (PhD La Sorbonne), and has specialized in ethnic minorities, citizenship, nationalism, policies of cultural pluralism and of immigration, discrimination and Islam in the West.

Amira Latif earned an MSc in Geography and Islamic Studies from the University of Berne and is a BLaw candidate. She works as a research assistant at the Center for Islamic and Middle Eastern Legal Studies and as a coordinator of the Law Summer School Cairo at the University of Zurich

Ana Quiñones Escámez is a Professor of Private International Law at Pompeu Fabra University in Barcelona, Spain. She has also been an expert consultant in Project Development ADL Morocco-Spain (2005–09)

Al-Rahim Moosa worked as a legal research associate at the National Institute of Scientific Research in Montreal, researching the treatment of Islamic family law in the courts of the United Kingdom. He is currently Program Officer for Refugees and Internally Displaced Persons at Focus Humanitarian Assistance Canada.

Prakash Shah is a senior lecturer at Queen Mary, University of London, where he teaches several courses. He has published and lectured extensively on legal pluralism, religion and law, ethnic minorities and diasporas in law, immigration, refugee and nationality law, and comparative law with special reference to South Asia.

Acronyms and Abbreviations

ADR	alternative dispute resolution
APH	Appellationshof [Switzerland]
ATA	Arrêt du Tribunal Administratif [Switzerland]
BE	Canton Bern [Switzerland]
BStPra	Basellandschaftliche Steuerpraxis [Switzerland]
ECHR	European Convention on Human Rights
FLA	Family Law Act 1986 [UK]
FSO	Federal Statistical Office
GE	Canton Geneva [Switzerland]
GER	Grundsätzliche Entscheide des Regierungsrates, Kanton Solothurn [Switzerland]
GVP	Gerichts-und Verwaltungspraxis [Switzerland]
ISC	Islamic Shari'a Council [Britain]
Iranian CC	Civil Code of the Islamic Republic of Iran of 23 May 1928, as amended
JdT	Journal des Tribunaux [Switzerland]
LGVE	Gerichts und Verwaltungsentscheide, Kanton Luzern [Switzerland]
MAT	Muslim Arbitration Tribunal [UK]
MCA	Matrimonial Causes Act 1973 [UK]
MFC	Moroccan Family Code
MFLO	Muslim Family Laws Ordinance [Pakistan]
PIL	Private international law
PILA	Federal Act on Private International Law of 18 December 1987 [Switzerland]
Pra	Die Praxis [Switzerland]
RBOG	Rechenschaftsbericht des Obergerichts des Kanton Thurgau [Switzerland]
SJ	Semaine Judiciaire [Switzerland]
SR	Systematische Sammlung des Bundesrechts [Switzerland]
Swiss CC	Swiss Civil Code of 10 December 1907, as amended
VD	Canton Vaud [Switzerland]
VPB	Verwaltungspraxis der Bundesbehörden [Switzerland]

Preface

An expanding literature has analysed the way in which Western societies address pluralizing pressures in the legal field, focusing on the coexistence of shari'a-based laws and Western normative orders, particularly in the field of family law.[1] Increasing attention has also been devoted to arbitration of family disputes in Europe and North America through religious-based alternative dispute resolution (ADR) mechanisms.

Academic work on 'shari'a in the West' has been stimulated by proposals to recognize existing Muslim forms of arbitration and to create a parallel system for adjudicating personal status law disputes concerning Muslims. The outcry following a speech by the Archbishop of Canterbury in 2008, widely interpreted as an endorsement of shari'a, and the debate on faith-based arbitration in Canada in 2004–05 have, in particular, prompted new academic reflections on legal pluralism and on judicial practices by informal Muslim channels in the west.[2]

This book contributes to this growing body of literature by assessing recent legal developments in European, North American, and Australian court judgments and the ways in which the courts use their discretion and balance competing values when addressing Islamic law in the family realm. Contributors are legal experts and anthropologists whose research focuses on multiculturalism, legal pluralism, and Islam in the West, and all chapters are based on extensive research and expertise. Countries analysed include some with a consolidated and homogeneous Muslim community, such as Britain and Spain, and others where their presence is more recent and heterogeneous, such as Australia.

An introductory chapter sketches some of the issues arising from the penetration of Islamic family law in the West through official and unofficial means.

In the second and third chapters some broad issues are tackled, concerning the trends emerging from the contact between Western and Islamic law and the strategies used by Muslim women to further their interests. Prakash Shah observes that the West – influenced by its religious roots – constrains through various means the penetration of shari'a in the official legal systems. At the same time, particularly in Britain, Muslim diasporas increasingly refer to informal faith-based institutions to settle their disputes. By doing so they attempt to respond to the need for cultural authenticity and sense of belonging. But rather than preserving their identity, Shah argues, Muslim diasporas may contribute to the metamorphosis of their religious references by aligning their ideal marriage practices with the Western ethical and normative account. Illustrated through the analysis of 'forced marriage', an issue that has attracted increasing attention in Europe, the adoption by Muslims of an allogenous narrative is seen by the author as an example of 'colonial consciousness', a construction that owes much to Western interests and culture despite its religious framework and terminology.

While adapting to Western legal narratives, Muslim diasporas also pursue concrete interests. In a most thought-provoking analysis, Pascale Fournier deconstructs common notions of religious law and religious minorities in the West by presenting an empirical study of Muslim and Jewish women who went through divorce in Canada. On the basis of socio-legal fieldwork in Toronto, Ottawa, and Montreal, and by employing the economic language of costs/benefits, interwoven with a storytelling narrative, she illustrates the ways in which men and women navigate between legal systems and bargain strategically upon divorce.

In the following chapters the judicial practice of various Western countries is analysed. Andrea Büchler and Amira Latif explore in detail the way in which Swiss judicial and administrative authorities assess whether foreign court decisions and documents on Islamic marriage and divorce can be recognized in Switzerland. The chapter analyses, in particular, legislation and court practice in relation to under-age and forced marriages, marriages by proxy, temporary marriages, polygamy, and divorce by *talaq* (unilateral repudiation by the husband), and *khul'* (divorce by mutual consent at the initiative of the wife).

In the next chapter, Katja J. Fredriksen focuses on the recognition of transnational Muslim marriages and divorces by Norwegian courts. Particular attention is given to arranged, forced, proxy, and polygamous marriages, and to *talaq* and *khul'*. The chapter emphasizes the importance of so-called religious marriages and divorces to Muslim immigrants and their descendants and analyses how the Norwegian legal system meets the challenges that these informal marriages and divorces pose.

With Ana Quiñones Escámez's chapter we move to the position of Spanish judges with regard to the 2004 Family Code of Morocco, which is the country of origin of most Muslim immigrants to Spain. Her contribution focuses on court practice concerning polygamy, a woman's age at marriage and consent, dower (*mahr*), talaq, *kafala* (guardianship of children), and inheritance, and gives an overview of the new European Union regulations that are replacing each Member State's private international law. In the following chapter, Denise Helly and Al-Rahim Moosa look at the British judicial treatment of divorces obtained in jurisdictions under Islamic law, with one party to the divorce attempting to enforce his/her marital status or rights in the United Kingdom.

The last two chapters look at the non-European West. Ann Black analyses the position of Australian judges vis-à-vis registration of Muslim marriages, age of marriage, consent, *mahr*, divorce, polygamy, and *kafala*, in the context of the 'one law for all' approach traditionally followed by the Australian legal system. In the concluding chapter, Abed Awad surveys several published and unpublished cases from the United States involving Islamic family law issues, and focuses on religious recognition of *mahr*, marriages and divorces. The cases analysed, by Awad as well as by the other authors, indicate a diverse and evolving jurisprudence and a pragmatic approach that is guided by the attempt to safeguard women's rights and 'the best interests of the child'. This approach is followed also by the courts of many Muslim countries, as recent studies reveal (Giunchi 2013a). Whether a case of 'colonial consciousness' or a coincidence of sociocultural developments cloaked by a Western terminology, judicial practices in the West and in the Muslim world may not be as different as often imagined.

Note on transliteration

To make the volume accessible to non-specialists, a simplified transliteration has been adopted, without diacritical marks. A glossary is provided at the end of the book. To indicate plurals the Arabic singular is pluralized according to the English language, by adding a final 's', with the exception of plurals that are commonly used in Western texts, such as *'ulama'* (pl. of *'alim*). The article al- and the letters *hamza* and *ayn* are disregarded in the alphabetical ordering in the bibliography and index.

Shari'a, Islamic law, and state Islamic law: some notes on terminology

Consistently with a previous volume on family law as adjudicated in Muslim courts (Giunchi 2013a), when I use the term shari'a I mean God's will as known through revelation (the Qur'an) and the Sunna – while the term *fiqh* indicates the human constructions resulting in a pluralistic legal literature developed between the 8th and 13th centuries on the basis of various sources besides the Qur'an and Sunna, primarily consensus (*'ijma*) and analogy (*qiyas*). For a detailed analysis of Islamic law, its sources, and historical development, the reader should refer to Vikør (2005) and Hallaq (2005). I use Islamic law as a synonym of *fiqh*, with its evolving nature preventing it from being identified with shari'a. By using the term Islamic law I do not imply, as other authors do, that it is a unified code. Islamic law has always accommodated diversity, despite attempts in the last centuries, particularly under Saudi-led wahhabization, to reconstruct it as a uniform and decontextualized set of laws. I borrow Arabi's term 'state Islamic law' (Arabi 2001: 193) to refer to the elements of Islamic law that have been absorbed by legislation, while Muslim law means to me the religious law as actually practised by Muslims.

The distinction between Islamic law and state Islamic law is important as Western judges are concerned with the latter only, while shari‘a councils and other informal channels of arbitration refer to the former, considered as the correct embodiment of shari‘a. The authors' terminology may of course slightly differ from my own.

Notes

1 Among the most recent literature are Büchler (2011), looking at family adjudication in Germany, Switzerland, France, England, and Spain, and, on the specific issue of *mahr*, Fournier (2010), and Mehdi and Nielsen (2011), and Shah, with Foblets and Rohe (eds) (2014).

2 See for example Ahdar and Aroney (2010); Korteweg and Selby (2012); Robin Griffith-Jones (2013).

1 Muslim family law and legal practice in the West

An introduction

Elisa Giunchi

At the beginning of the twentieth century, the scholar James Bryce, in the context of discussing the introduction in India of British-influenced codes, predicted that 'European ideas ... will sink deeper and deeper until the old native life dies out [and] will come to prevail everywhere' (1914: 2). In the face of the 'rising tide of European law', he added with evident satisfaction, 'both Hinduism and Islam may ... begin within a century or two to show signs of approaching dissolution' (ibid.: 131, 129). Completing a process that had been initiated in the previous century, under the 'beneficial influence of the British, rationalization and uniformity would prevail over chaos and plurality' (ibid.: 118, 133), the hallmarks of the 'irrational Orient'.

Back then, most Europeans would have agreed with him on the inevitability of the expansion and ultimate success of the European legal model. And yet, colonialism could not, in India or elsewhere, completely dislodge native customs and laws, but rather it added a new layer of pluralism to the existing one. Family law remained largely outside the purview of colonial intervention. When it was reformed after independence, codes on personal status retained some aspects of classical *fiqh*, rethought others along modernist lines, and added new concepts and procedures. The hybridization of the legal system was further complicated by the process of Islamization in the 1970s and 80s. Through this process, relevant segments of Muslim societies expressed the desire to distance themselves from the Western legal model and replace it with 'authentic' Islam, seen as a panacea for all social and economic ills. In the name of authenticity, concepts and norms of *fiqh*, selectively picked and transformed, entered the penal and financial fields in several countries, coming to coexist with legal procedures and concepts of European origin as well as with previous, modernist interpretations of shari'a. The ideas that inspired the Islamization of laws were in many ways a product of the very globalization this process wished to reverse, and 'Islamist' reformists were undoubtedly under the spell of Western influence despite their anti-Western rhetoric. Besides using concepts and terms that were foreign to classical Islam, the quest for 'authenticity' – a primordial essence freed from any historical and local contamination – is itself a modern idea. Be that as it may, the Islamization of laws added a new exegetical model to pre-existing ones, with the effect of furthering the heterogeneity of state Islamic law in those countries in which the criminal and fiscal system have been 'Islamicized'.

Today, one century after Bryce and contrary to his predictions, Islamic law, far from dissolving, remains part of the legislation on personal status, albeit transformed from its classical model, and it has increasingly penetrated the West itself. This has occurred through official and unofficial means. On the unofficial level, faith-based mechanisms for dispute settlement have been thriving, particularly in countries with an established Muslim population and multicultural policies. In Britain, in particular, Muslim diasporas increasingly refer their marital disputes to these alternative channels, which tend to be part of mosques and cultural centres. On the official level, Western legal systems have come, to some extent, to recognize Islamic rules and institutions, although they have adopted slightly different methods of incorporating them and/or recognizing the validity of their results. When addressing family disputes concerning citizens of other countries, some legislators, such as those of Germany and Italy, have decided to apply the laws of the foreigner's country through international private law norms, as long as they neither contravene the concept of '*ordre public*' – that is, the fundamental principles of the prevailing system – nor violate international conventions to which the host country is a party. Other countries, such as Switzerland, Denmark, Norway and Britain, have decided to adhere to the principle of domicile or residence unless a contrary bilateral agreement exists. Even in such cases, state Islamic law is taken into account when authorities are called upon to assess the effects of changes in civil status that have been undertaken in a Muslim country and to balance these changes with '*ordre public*'. Religious family practices are also often recognized in the West unless they clash with fundamental principles of the 'hosting' legal system or, as in Britain, are deemed 'unreasonable'. Some countries, such as France, recognize for example *kafala*, a form of guardianship of children that does not create a full parental relationship between child and guardian. In other countries, such as Britain and Norway, Islamic marriage ceremonies celebrated at registered mosques are recognized as having legal validity.

It should be stressed that when Western judges apply foreign norms, or recognize their effects, Islamic law is relevant only inasmuch as it has been absorbed by the national law of the litigants, or by the law of the country in which certain acts were performed. Islamic law therefore reflects one understanding of shari'a, rather than shari'a per se, and it stems from legal devices and doctrinal developments that depart from *fiqh* on several points. The Western judge needs not be aware of the plurality of Islamic sources and exegetical methods, though his limited knowledge of the nuances and meaning of Islamic law may hinder his understanding of state Islamic law, an issue we will return to later on.

Irrespective of the methods used, and of the varying degrees of flexibility displayed, when accommodating aspects of Islamic law all Western systems face similar dilemmas, such as how to balance gender parity – the core of '*ordre public*' – with other valued principles, such as freedom of religion and equality. As Büchler observes, *ordre public* is an elusive concept that confers great discretionary power on the judiciary (Büchler 2011: 41) as well as hiding, as she and Latif point out in Chapter 4 of this book, culture-specific ideals of marriage that have an underpinning of Christian morality. The aspects of Islamic family law most at odds with the concept of *ordre public*, and which are, with few exceptions (such as Turkey, Tunisia and the Central Asian republics) part of state Islamic law, are polygyny and the unilateral right of the man to repudiate his wife (*talaq*). While polygyny is apparently fairly rare outside Gulf countries, *talaq* is probably the most common form of divorce in the Muslim world, though reliable statistics are hard to come by, as *nikah* (religious marriage) and *talaq* are not often registered. According to *fiqh*, the husband desiring to repudiate his wife needs neither grounds nor her consent, although legislation in the contemporary Muslim world has made *talaq* dependent on a series of conditions, which are regulated by the state, in order to limit the practice. The wife, according to Islamic law, can divorce in limited circumstances only. One of them is through *khul'*, i.e. at her initiative with the consent of the husband, provided she forfeits the deferred portion of the *mahr* (dower) to which she is entitled. However, in some countries the requirement of the husband's consent has been dropped through legislation (Egypt) or via the judiciary (Pakistan). *Mubarat* is a rarely practised no-fault option which, if initiated by the husband with his wife's consent, does not entail the loss of her financial rights. Another infrequent option is that of delegated divorce (*talaq-i tafwid*), i.e. the delegation to the wife, in the marriage contract, of the right to pronounce *talaq* on behalf of her husband. Neither of these options is usually included in legislation. The wife can divorce by means of the court's intervention in case of breach of licit contractual clauses or in some other cases that vary from school to school. While the only valid grounds that the Hanafi school accepts are the husband's apostasy, his impotence and prolonged absence, at the opposite end of the spectrum thc Maliki school provides women with several ways to escape from an unhappy marriage, including claims of desertion and harm (*darar*). Legislation in the Muslim world has often extended women's rights to divorce by referring to the Maliki *madhhab* (legal school), even in countries where another *madhhab* is prevalent, and the judiciary has in some countries often expanded the concept of *darar* to cover the psychological sphere (Giunchi 2013a).

Another problematic aspect of Islamic law, from the point of view of the Western legal system, concerns agency in contracting the marriage. The guardianship powers of the male legal representative (*wali*) of the bride, particularly if she a minor, are central to Islamic law and are today widely recognized in legislation in the Muslim world, as are the duty of the woman to obey her husband, the legal inequality of male and female heirs and the distinction between the mother's custody (*hadana*) and the father's guardianship (*wilaya*). Reflecting a consensus among classical jurists, most laws in Muslim countries, despite increasing attention paid by legislators and judges alike to the 'best interests of the child', establish that women are entitled to the custody of children only up to a certain age and under certain conditions, one of them being that they do not remarry outside their husband's family. Custody can also be revoked if the mother leaves Islam as an apostate or is deemed *nusyuz* (disobedient).

An issue often arising in divorce cases, in the Muslim world and in the West, is that of *mahr*. According to Islamic law and most legislation in Muslim countries, following the divorce the wife must refrain from remarrying for a period of time, the *'idda*. At its expiration, she must be given the part of the *mah*r that she has not already received, unless the marriage has not been consummated or has been dissolved at her request through *khul'*. The question of who initiated separation and/or divorce is therefore crucial. However, women often forfeit *mahr* in exchange for the right to *hadana*, or for her husband divorcing her or consenting to her request for divorce through *khul'*.

Maintenance of divorced women is limited by Islamic law and most Muslim legislation to only a few months or until delivery if they are pregnant. Another critical issue, from a Western perspective, is the prohibition of inter-religion marriages between Muslim females and non-Muslim males, which is found in most present-day legislation in the Muslim world. Underage marriages are also common, despite the fact that most legislation in the Muslim world now prescribes a minimum marriage age of 18 for females, although exceptions can be authorized by judges under certain circumstances. Another customary practice in some areas of the Muslim world is that of forced marriages, despite the fact that laws in most Muslim countries require that the bride must consent to the marriage. It needs to be stressed here that the fact that a *wali* can voice her consent or that the marriage has been arranged does not necessarily mean that the bride was coerced into it. Finally, 'proxy marriages', which the laws of several Muslim countries recognize, provided that there is the consent of both spouses, are considered by several western countries as invalid.

This brief overview indicates that, with the exception of Turkey and Central Asian republics, which have eliminated all references to Islamic law in their laws on personal status, codification in the Muslim world has softened but not eliminated the *fiqh* construction of the marital bond as an asymmetrical relationship that is based on what Ziba Mir-Hosseini, using Chiba's (1986) tripartite model of legal systems, calls 'the *qiwwama* postulate' (Mir-Hosseini 2013: 11), whereby submission (*tamkin*) is given in exchange for maintenance (*nafaqa*). All elements of inequality that characterize Islamic law stem from this postulate, which recent legislative reforms (such as the 2004 Moudawana in Morocco, eliminating the duty of obedience), as well as judicial practice in several Muslim countries, is eroding.

It is quite obvious that by contravening the concept of gender parity the elements of Islamic law summarized above are contrary to *ordre public*. Any faith-based discrimination is also considered as unacceptable. For example, whether a parent is lax in his/her adherence to religion should have no bearing on the parenting orders given by judges; similarly, the adherence to a specific religion cannot be a requirement for marriage. The Western judicial approach is, however, guided by a certain amount of pragmatism, as all the contributions in this volume indicate. Even though poligyny is not allowed in any Western country, for example, some of the legal effects of polygamous unions are usually recognized, provided that the unions are validly contracted in a country that formally allows them. A similar pragmatism is evident with regard to *talaq* and to informal religious marriages.

These accommodations are no doubt *ad hoc* concessions made in certain circumstances and on a limited scale. As such, they do not subvert Western legal systems or their narrative of Muslim 'otherness'. It is the 'hosting' system of law that, on the basis of its perception of what is acceptable, sets the boundaries of accommodation or, in the case of recognition of informal mechanisms for dispute resolution, defines the categories of instances in which its own institutions will refrain from acting (Woodman 2008: 35). These 'gracious concession[s]' to diversity (Ahdar and Aroney 2010b: 24) result, some have argued, in a haphazard and at times discriminatory process as different religious communities are subject to differential treatment (Menski 2009: 31–32).[1] Secularism, often invoked as a benchmark and central to Western self-perception, barely masks the priority given by the 'hosting' systems to the religion of the majority – be it Christianity or other 'acceptable' faiths (Bradney 1993: 160–61; see also Sayyid 2009).

Some scholars advocate the introduction in the West of a 'personalized' system of laws similar to that prevailing in many Muslim countries and in India, where the laws of other major religious communities concerning personal status are recognized by the state and are applied by courts headed by members of those communities (Menski 2009). Others have argued against this approach on various grounds (Pearl 1999). The most common concern is that the recognition of faith-based forms of adjudication would threaten the secular nature of the states in which adjudication takes place and challenge state hegemony while, at the same time, restricting individual freedoms. The diversity of Islamic legal doctrine and of Muslim societies is another important element to be considered: Muslim diasporas originate from different sociocultural contexts and thus express an extreme variety of religious practices and conceptions. To this should be added that not all immigrants who are nominally Muslim are motivated by religion. The danger is therefore to force immigrants to abide by religious rules, giving religious identity precedence over other identities. As to practising Muslims, they may be forced to live by the majority definition of religion or by that which is advanced by the group that has the most resources and influence. In either case, this means – today at least – sanctioning a conservative reading of shari'a and an asymmetrical family structure. Paradoxically, formalizing or creating a parallel judicial system in the name of diversity would thus run the risk of homogenizing interpretations of Islamic law to the benefit of dominant groups and of states that fund a specific vision of Islam, and to the detriment of women.

Recognizing faith-based bodies may also, it could be argued, contribute to setting Muslim diasporas apart from the rest of the population as 'irrational' beings motivated by religious feelings rather than interests, thus confirming their perceived inherent difference. As many contributors to this book stress, litigants, in the Muslim world as elsewhere, are moved not only by the desire to comply with their values, but also to further their interests and maximize their rights. Islamic law is often twisted by litigants to obtain the desired outcome, and even the choice of the venue where they bring their disputes is strategic: they will choose, whether in the West or in the Muslim world, the venue that will yield them the greatest benefit, in both psychological and practical terms. On one hand, it may be in the divorced woman's interest, for example, to apply to a Western state court to get financial support beyond the *'idda* period and property settlement, irrespective of who initiated the divorce or who was 'at fault'. On the other hand, a 'proper' religious avenue may allow for her remarriage to be acceptable and her children to be considered legitimate, which is of vital importance if she intends to maintain transitional relationships. Both avenues can be, and often are, pursued, giving rise to complex and at times contradictory cases.

We have seen that Islamic law, far from dissolving, is penetrating into the West through official and unofficial means, contributing to a diversified and evolving law and jurisprudence that defies Bryce's prediction of uniformity. Despite the preeminence of the 'hosting' legal system, legislation, court practice and the practices of diasporas affect that system, forcing it to react and arrive at compromises. Islamic law itself is being transformed in the process, thus becoming increasingly hybrid. This is not a new phenomenon. *Fiqh* is a composite doctrine that offers different solutions to everyday problems, all of them legitimate, and that has built-in mechanisms that ensure its flexibility and adaptability to changing circumstances. Heterogeneity and flexibility have been partially lost through codification, which has simplified an extremely rich jurisprudence and done away with inconsistencies. At the same time, however, codes in the Muslim world have created, as mentioned above, new hybrids by mixing classical legal principles, modernist and 'Islamist' reinterpretations and Western concepts and procedures. Hybridization is most evident at the judicial level: courts show that, in the course of the interaction of state-made law, different 'ideas of shari'a', and customs, the ensuing reconstruction of the Islamic legal doctrine reflects the adaptation to changing socio-economic circumstances, particularly in urban settings, and the adoption of a human rights discourse. The instruments – such as *talfiq* (combination of opinions from different schools) and *ijtihad* (individual juristic reasoning) – and the principles – such as *maslaha* (common good) and *darura* (necessity) – that guide – some would say justify – this reconstruction are inherited from tradition, albeit transformed in today's very different context of adjudication (Giunchi 2013a).

Hybridization is particularly evident among Muslim diasporas, who reconstruct their legal world as 'skilled cultural navigators' across legal systems searching for concrete solutions that adapt their practices and ideals to their new setting (Ballard 1994; Pearl and Menski 1998). It is the members of the younger generation who most easily navigate cross-culturally and have multiple senses of belonging (Büchler 2011: 9), facilitated by their access to the new media and thus to wider discourses. This creates a 'legal porosity, multiple networks of legal orders forcing us to constant transitions and trespassing' (Santos 1987: 279). This 'interlegality', as Santos calls it, does not only include customary laws, national and international law but also concrete interests and what we have called above 'ideas of shari'a'. The interpenetration of various normative orders, religious interpretations, values and interests is heightened by the diversity of the origins of Muslim diasporas. An immigrant of Turkish nationality, for example, has a family code that does not refer to shari'a, but he may in his private sphere follow religious provisions derived from the prevailing Hanafi *madhhab* as well as customs that are contrary to this *madhhab* or to *fiqh* in general; he may marry, for example, in a religious ceremony, without registering his marriage officially, but fail to provide in writing for a specific *mahr* or disinherit his daughters despite Hanafi rules. An immigrant of Iranian origins may not abide by Islamic law in his everyday life, or follow a progressive reading of shari'a, but find himself/herself bound by the strict norms of his/her country of nationality. Thus, among Muslim diasporas the state law of the country of origin – when applicable – and of the new country, different *madhhabs*, customs, and ideas of shari'a, all coexist, creating a complex arena of expectations and references.

The heterogeneity of Islamic doctrine is a thorny issue when it comes to dispute settlement in the Muslim world, as it brings up the issue of what Islamic source must be referred to and applied, or rather, according to which school and exegetical method. This is particularly so in informal dispute-solving mechanisms where imams are not constrained by codified norms and are therefore have much greater flexibility than judges. When adapting Islamic principles to the context of family disputes, imams refer to *fiqh*, usually without sticking to only one *madhhab*, as Yilmaz (2001) notes with regard to the Islamic Shari'a Council (ISC) in Britain. The fact that they practise *talfiq* does not tell us, however, which opinion within a specific *madhhab* they refer to. Would they be sufficiently familiar with all *madhhabs* and the intricacies of *fiqh* to qualify as *mujtahids*? Or would they instead tend to abide by the *madhhab* or opinions with which they are most familiar? The same kinds of problems arise from internet *fatwas*, increasingly used by young elements of Muslim diasporas. Self-taught Salafis tend to reject altogether the sophisticated constructions of *fiqh* and search for 'authentic' shari'a in primary sources; but even then they selectively choose what to apply and make exegetical decisions, influenced by several factors – religious knowledge, personal background and ideological orientation, source of funding and exposure to different understandings of religion.

The tendency of imams in the West to propose solutions to marital problems on the basis of *fiqh* expresses, it has been held by some, an outdated understanding of Islamic law that ignores legislative reforms and judicially innovative rulings which, in recent decades, have reinterpreted Islamic law in the Muslim world. Faith-based bodies neglect, for example, the fact that in some countries judges do not require that *khul'* be accompanied by the husband's consent, contrary to the majority opinion of classical jurists. They also ignore traditional concepts, such as those of *darar* or *shiqaq* (discord), that in many countries, in the last decade, have allowed a significant degree of legislative and judicial innovation aimed at extending women's rights to divorce (Warraich and Balchin 2006: 66–79).

The diversity of Islamic law results in mixed gender implications. There seems to be little doubt that most faith-based bodies are dominated by (male) conservatives, and that many mosques and associations of Muslims in the West are run according to neo-traditionalist or Wahhabi lines. It is thus not far-fetched to believe, as some women's associations do, that the formal recognition of shari'a councils and the like would work to the disadvantage of women, threatening the rights they enjoy under the 'hosting' system (WLUML 2003; Warraich and Balchin 2006). Research has confirmed these fears and points to the fact that arbitration services offered to Muslim women in Britain may reflect patriarchal assumptions and asymmetric power relations (Bano 2008). Media reports have also indicated that informal Muslim faith-based councils tend to rule in favour of abusive husbands and enforce female obedience. These concerns are not shared by all academics, and are undermined by the fact that women activists paradoxically find themselves in company with conservatives who use gender-equality arguments to justify their Islamophobic vision, in the same fashion as colonial officers such as Lord Cromer opposed women's rights in their home country while using feminist discourses in order to advocate women's empowerment in colonized Muslim countries – thus trying to justify their moral superiority and, ultimately, their occupation.

Some works on informal adjudication and mediation actually indicate that faith-based bodies may play a positive function. A 2001 report noted that women applying to the Islamic Shari'a Council, an independent organization based in west London and aimed at offering 'services for dispute resolutions … regarding social, family and matrimonial issues', reported that the organization met their demands by helping them dissolve their marriages (Shah-Kazemi 2001: 64). Warraich and Balchin (2006: 73) argue that studies such as that of Shah-Kazemi may be flawed in their methodology; nevertheless these studies remind us that gender implications of faith-based councils are not clear-cut and that despite the bias of the imams these councils may indeed provide psychological relief to some women, as well as socially acceptable solutions to their marital problems. As mentioned above, recourse to these channels may be a necessary prerequisite for further 'acceptable' actions: an Islamic divorce may be necessary, for example, if a divorced woman wishes to remarry in an Islamically 'proper' way. A remarriage outside the acceptable religious limits would be seen by her community as adulterous and any children would be considered illegitimate, a problem that the husband would not have as his marriage can be polygamous. There is also some evidence that imams try to align Islamic law with the prevailing normative order. For example, by following the Maliki *madhhab* in relation to custody, they comply with British law and its principle of 'the best interests of the child' (Bano 2012: 94–95). Alternative dispute resolution (ADR) can thus be a way to facilitate diasporas' acceptance of the official legal system and its underlying values. Similarly, Internet *fatwas*, despite usually expressing one variant or the other of the *qiwama* postulate, enable women to raise questions and issues that could not be expressed in more traditional face-to-face encounters and, by acknowledging exigencies of time and space, allow them to adapt to new realities.

Also in the Muslim world, Islamic precepts are at times invoked to reinforce unequal power relations within the family and society at large, but in other cases to subvert them and expand women's rights. Written laws, which tend to be inelastic due to political factors, are in fact often circumvented by more progressive readings of religions, usually supported by an extensive reference to extra-*madhhab fiqh* or to *ijtihad* and guided by concepts such as *darura* and *maslaha* (Giunchi 2013a, 2013b). Unfortunately, these kinds of cases are generally unknown to legal practitioners in the West who focus on the written legislation of foreign countries, despite the fact that the most innovative legal changes in recent decades within the Muslim world have occurred via the judiciary.

As already mentioned, the issue of 'what shari'a' may not seem particularly relevant when we address the attitude of Western judges towards Islamic precepts, as courts are not called upon to express an opinion as to what is 'correct' shari'a or to take sides for any interpretation. Judges need 'simply' to apply the state law of the country of origin of the litigants, mitigated by considerations of *ordre public*, or to recognize, or not, the validity of family-related steps that have been taken abroad according to state Islamic law. They are thus apparently untouched by the problem of what *madhhab* or intra-*madhhab* opinion, or what exegetical method should guide them in cases that are not addressed satisfactorily by legislation of the country of origin. Legislation on personal status in the Muslim world usually refers to a specific *madhhab* to fill the legal lacunae of the codes, and in some countries, such as Pakistan, the judges may go so far as to refuse to apply written norms, on the basis of the norms' supposed un-Islamic character, and, as a consequence, to replace them with uncodified Islamic law. The references to *fiqh* in the codes open the gates of adjudication to the heterogeneous realm of medieval jurisprudence and to a considerable degree of judicial discretion (Giunchi 2013a). While Muslim judges can, and do, refer to some extent to that intellectual background, Western judges are neither allowed nor qualified to do so. Nor are they familiar with legal practice in the Muslim world or its cultural context, which is what gives meaning to the law. They have a very limited knowledge, or none at all, of Islamic law and the way in which it is 'lived', perceived and concretely applied. This limits their understanding of the norms of the state Islamic law they enforce and has led to rulings that are more conservative and literalist than judicial practices in the Muslim world. For example, as Helly and Al Rahim tell us in Chapter 7, British judges believe that a *talaq* pronounced in Pakistan and not followed by notice to the chairman on the basis of the Muslim Family Laws Ordinance is invalid, while Pakistani courts have in many instances, particularly when doing so could save women from criminal liabilities connected to *zina* cases, considered the registration of *talaq* as irrelevant to establishing the existence of marriage and they have justified these decisions by invoking uncodified Islamic law and its superiority vis-à-vis man-made legislation.

One could argue that judges in the Muslim world, who are mostly lay, have a poor knowledge of *fiqh* and that even when exercising *ijtihad* they do not have the conceptual instruments to practise it correctly. However, their religious knowledge, which increases at the appellate level, finds its origins in the fact of taking part in a common cultural milieu where there is a shared idea of what the spirit and objectives of shari'a are. How do Western judges, then, interpret vague norms of Islamic state law or fill legal lacunae? Are they aware of the disconnect between 'living law', judicial practice and codified law in the Muslim world? And what is their attitude towards practices that are more cultural than religious in their origin and that may not be backed by the written codes of the immigrants' country of origin?

These issues are far too complex to be addressed in any detailed or systematic manner by this book. What the authors have done here is to highlight how different legal systems in the West interpret state Islamic law and balance competing demands and values. What emerges is the lack of consistency between and even within countries, with judges exercising wide discretion in applying and interpreting foreign norms and recognizing their effects. Another common trend that emerges is the lack of understanding by Western judges of some concepts evoked in Muslim legislation, such as that of *khul'*, and their lack of knowledge on judicial practice in the Muslim world. In all countries analysed, there is also the tendency to legally recognize facts 'on the ground', whether or not in conformity with *ordre public*, if doing so protects the interests of women and minors. Thus some fundamental principles of the 'dominating' legal system, such as monogamous marriage, are bent so as to protect the interests of the second wife and her children in a polygamous union. If, for instance, as Friediksen tells us in Chapter 5, a Norwegian resident who is married to more than one spouse passes away, the inheritance of the deceased will be equally divided among the spouses and the children of the polygamous marriages. The same can be said about marriage by proxy: in Switzerland, as Büchler and Latif tell us in Chapter 4, marriage by proxy, contrary to what happens in Norway, is recognized as valid in order to safeguard the wife's claim to legal protection, provided it is proved that the consent of the spouses was free of coercion or deception. In both of these instances, women's interests in specific cases are paramount vis-à-vis general principles of *ordre public*, which include that of gender parity.

A similar pragmatism can be found in Muslim countries such as Turkey where religious norms and institutions that do not find a place in the secular statutes are still de facto followed, particularly in rural areas, and are often recognized as having valid legal effects (Yilmaz 2013). Also in Muslim countries that have remained anchored to Islamic law there is the increasing tendency of judges to follow general principles and objectives of religion, often via *ijtihad*, particularly those in favour of minors and women. In many cases judicial practice in the Muslim world appears, in fact, to be far more advanced than Western judges infer from Muslim statute books.

The attempt by Muslim courts to defend or improve women's rights may be seen as an element of 'colonial consciousness' that consolidates the Western hegemonic narrative. For example, Prakash Shah convincingly argues in Chapter 2 that the current Muslim critique of forced marriage largely responds to a Western narrative. Yet, the fact that Western terminology intersects with traditional Islamic concepts and autochthonous developments, as unearthed by 'Islamic feminists' and studies on adjudication in Muslim history, makes it difficult to consign the human rights narratives in the Muslim world to internalized 'otherness' alone. The 'victims' – Edward Said's 'orientalized Orientals' – may speak a language other than their own, but the objectives and meaning of their speech may not be out of sync with the attention traditionally given by *qadis*, albeit within the *qiwama* postulate, to vulnerable groups or with the autochthonous reformist rethinking of that postulate since the nineteenth century. Most importantly, rather than a sheer imitation of the Western discourse, the current court practice in the Muslim world may be seen as the continuation of a legal tradition of flexibility and openness. Despite the West being 'everywhere … in structures and minds' (Nandy 1983: xi), the non-West may retain more of its own pre-colonial realities than we may be willing to concede. As to the Western legal system, through its 'gracious concessions' it opens itself up, albeit reluctantly, to diverse legal frameworks and social facts, and may ultimately come to reconsider its positivist assumptions and the long-cherished goal of uniformity expressed by Bryce.

Note

1 For a review of the pros and cons of Menski's proposal see Büchler 2011.

References

Ahdar, R. and Aroney, N. (eds) (2010a) *Shari'a in the West*, Oxford and New York: Oxford University Press.

——(2010b) 'The topography of shari'a in the western political landscape', in R. Ahdar and N. Aroney (eds), *Shari'a in the West*, Oxford and New York: Oxford University Press.

Ballard, R. (ed.) (1994) *Desh Pradesh. The South Asian presence in Britain*, London: C. Hurst and Co.

Bano, S. (2008) 'In pursuit of religious and legal diversity: a response to the archbishop of Canterbury and the "sharia debate" in Britain', *Ecclesiastical Law Journal*, 10(3): 283–309.

——(2012) *Muslim Women and Shari'ah Councils: Transcending the boundaries of community and law*, Basingstoke: Palgrave Macmillan.

Bradney, A. (1993) *Religions, Rights and Laws*, Leicester: Leicester University Press.

Bryce, J. (1914) *The Ancient Roman Empire and the British Empire in India. The diffusion of Roman and English law throughout the world. Two historical studies*, London: Oxford University Press.

Büchler, A. (2011) *Islamic Law in Europe? Legal pluralism and its limits in European family laws*, Farnham: Ashgate.

Chiba, M. (1986) *Asian Indigenous Law: in interaction with received law*, London and New York: KPI.

Fournier, P. (2010) *Muslim Marriage in Western Courts. Lost in transplantation*, Farnham: Ashgate.

Giunchi, E. (2010) 'The reinvention of the sharī'a under the British Raj: In search for authenticity and certainty', *Journal of Asian Studies*, 68(4): 1119–42.

——(ed.) (2013a) *Adjudicating Family Law in Muslim Courts*, London: Routledge.

——(2013b) 'Islamization and judicial activism in Pakistan: what šarī'ah?', *Oriente Moderno*, 93(1): 188–204.

Griffith-Jones, R. (ed.) (2013) *Islam and English Law Rights, responsibilities and the place of shari'a*, London: Cambridge University Press.

Grillo, R., Ballard, R., Ferrari, A., Hoekema, A.J., Maussen, M., Shah, P. (eds) (2009) *Legal Practice and Cultural Diversity*, Farnham: Ashgate.

Hallaq, W. (2005) *The Origins and Evolution of Islamic Law*, Cambridge: Cambridge University Press.

Korteweg, A.C. and Selby, J.A. (eds) (2012) *Debating Sharia. Islam, gender politics, and family law arbitration*, Toronto: University of Toronto Press.

Menski, W. (2009) 'India's secular pluralism and its relevance for Europe', in R. Grillo *et al.* (eds), *Legal Practice and Cultural Diversity*, Farnham: Ashgate.

Mir-Hosseini, Z. (2013) 'Justice, equality and Muslim family laws: new ideas, new prospects', in Z. Mir-Hosseini, K. Vogt, L. Larsen, and C. Moe (eds), *Gender and Equality in Muslim Family Law. Justice and ethics in the Islamic legal tradition*, London: I.B. Tauris

Nandy, A. (1983) *The Intimate Enemy. Loss and recovery of self under colonialism*, 3rd edn, New Delhi: Oxford University Press.

Pearl, D. (1999) 'Islamic family law and its reception by the courts in the West: the English experience', in C. von Bar (ed.), *Islamic Law and its Reception by the Courts in the West*, Koln: Carl Heymanns.

Pearl, D. and Menski, W. (1998) *Muslim Family Law*, London: Sweet and Maxwell.

Santos, B. de Sousa (1987) 'Law: a map of misreading. Towards a postmodern conception of law', *Journal of Law and Society*, 14(3): 279–99.

Sayyid, S. (2009) 'Contemporary politics of secularism', in G. Levery and T. Modood (eds), *Secularism, Religion and Multicultural Citizenship*, Cambridge: Cambridge University Press.

Shah-Kazemi, S.N. (2001) *Untying the Knot. Muslim women, divorce and the shariah*, London: Nuffield Foundation.

Vikør, K. (2005) *Between God and the Sultan: a history of Islamic law*, Oxford: Oxford University Press.
Warraich, S.A. and Balchin, C. (2006) *Recognizing the Un-Recognized: inter-country cases and Muslim marriages and divorces in Britain*, London: WLUML.
Woodman, G.R. (2008) 'The possibilities of co-existence of religious laws with other laws', in R. Mehdi, H. Petersen, E. Reenberg Sand, and G.R. Woodman (eds), *Law in Multicultural Societies*, Copenhagen: DJØF Publishing.
WLUML (2003) *Knowing our Rights: women, family, laws and customs in the Muslim world*, London: WLUML.
Yilmaz, I. (2001) 'Law as Chameleon: the question of incorporation of Muslim personal law into the English law', *Journal of Muslim Minority Affairs*, 21(2): 297–308.
——(2013) 'Islamic family law in secular Turkish courts', in E. Giunchi (ed.), *Adjudicating Family Law in Muslim Courts*, London: Routledge.

2 *Shari'a* in the West

Colonial consciousness in a context of normative competition

Prakash Shah

Theoretical background

Western legal systems do not seek to incorporate shari'a. Those that have a minimal reference to shari'a, usually via private international law, increasingly resent it and find ways to override its effects. Only Eastern Thrace in Greece applies Islamic law as a personal law system in family matters, a situation that is regarded as outdated for contemporary European legal systems. This does not mean that the widespread presence of Muslims throughout Western countries is not having an impact. It is, and it raises some of the most contentious and morally charged issues within Western law today, issues that are normally resolved in accordance with the ethos of the dominant legal order. What legal pluralist scholar Masaji Chiba (1989: 166–67) referred to as the 'identity postulate of a legal culture' rears its head most visibly in its brushing up against a competing legal order, that of Islamic law, in the encounter forcing its actors to decide how far they will accept its transformation. Chiba (1989: 157) pointed out that competition between different postulates, whether in space or in theory, is unavoidable, and that these postulates must reach accommodation or integration under a more inclusive one: 'This means that each people must not only cherish their own identity postulate of indigenous law, but also they must constantly endeavour to reformulate its content, so that it can maintain itself in this competition as circumstances change.' However, the more Western legal systems brush up against Islamic law, the more we find evidence of the former's Christian inheritance, which is discomforting to convinced secularists who predicted a divorce from religion as inevitable. Like the 'secularization thesis', the much touted 'return of religion' or 'post-secular' always relied on a faking of the identity of Western culture that, as some scholars have shown (Berman 1983; Balagangadhara 1994), retained its structure of thought deep in the Christian religious roots of that culture.

This chapter relies on work on the comparative science of cultures as pioneered by S. N. Balagangadhara and tests it in the diasporic Western Muslim context. In the process of building a theory of religion in *The Heathen in his Blindness*, Balagangadhara (1994) shows that the Semitic religions are exemplary instances of 'religions' and that worldviews are best exemplified by religions. In so doing he points out that the transmission of worldviews requires certain sociological conditions as the absolute prerequisites for guaranteeing the identity of these entities. These conditions are: the codification of these religions; a standard whereby transformations to the worldview can be measured; and doctrinal and organizational authorities to constrain such transmission, to resolve interpretive disputes, to denounce those who challenge its legitimacy, and to ensure that it is not lost or transformed in its entirety when transmitted (Balagangadhara 1994: 371–73). Certain consequences that flow from these insights are useful for a discussion of the interaction between Western and Islamic laws. Given that Western culture is constituted by religion, efforts to limit the role of shari'a in Western countries can be seen as countermeasures designed to preserve the domain of 'secular' Western law, while seeking to constrain transmission of shari'a and limit interpretive possibilities within the former's jurisdictional range. With the growing presence of Muslims in Western countries some legal measures are also taken by Muslims in order to preserve and transmit their worldview. This chapter will include illustrations of attempts to preserve the transmission of the worldviews of both Western and Muslim cultures. Further, given that the Western and Islamic cultures are both religious cultures that treat each other as rivals, a certain level of mutual resistance between them is inevitable. However, given also that Muslims live as members of a non-dominant, religious population we can also point, first, to certain 'instructional' initiatives within Western countries aimed at Muslims and, second, subtle shifts within Muslim law that attempt to preserve the Islamic *grundnorm*, while adjusting interpretations of Islamic law to align with the results produced by Western ethical and legal norms.

In *Reconceptualizing India Studies*, Balagangadhara (2012) writes that Edward Said suggested the existence of a pattern in Orientalism. If Orientalism is the structuring in the experience of one culture – the West – of the experiential entity which is the Orient, then it picks out particular aspects of a different culture in such a way that, rather than telling us about the other's culture, it tells us something about the Western culture. Therefore, attempts to adjust or correct Orientalism by adducing empirical evidence does not affect its basic structure and way of ordering experience. Balagangadhara also describes colonialism as the attempt to replace the experience of the colonised with the account of the experience of the coloniser. That attempt is made through the imposition of violence because the coloniser's account cannot be imposed on grounds of its reasonableness. The colonised thus ends up accepting the coloniser's account – which Balagangadhara refers to as 'colonial consciousness' – which leads to the colonised being unable to access his own experience. Studying the various attempts to reform Muslim cultures in the Western diasporas might also show that they do not occur randomly. Those attempts may reflect the individuality of decision-makers and the particular institutional and national contexts in which those attempts occur. However, those individual instances may reveal a pattern. This pattern should provide further evidence that the West continues to operate from its religious background, even if that background has now receded and the obvious references to the religion that constitutes it have been dropped. Only a few examples are mentioned here to start a conversation about the possibility of a pattern similar to the Edward Said's Orientalism. Such a pattern would show us that particular aspects of Muslim cultures are picked upon as offensive to Western reason and requiring reform, and that these elements of culture are structured through Christian theology and Christian anthropology. As with Orientalism, empirical information cannot dislodge the selection for reform of those aspects of Muslim cultures because these reforms are grounded in the Western experience of other cultures. Studying them should therefore tell us about how the West structures its legal experience and something about Western legal culture itself. Going a step further, this chapter also provides some evidence of how the West assumes the role of an 'instruction culture' (Malik 2004: 4) The assumption of such a role amounts to a variation of colonialism because of the attempt to replace the experience of the non-dominant group with the experience of the dominant culture. It results in a form of 'colonial consciousness' whereby members of the non-dominant group accept the dominant group's account of their culture as their own experience. While Muslim diasporic cultures in Western countries also change in accordance with the critique founded on the Western normative ethical system, the distinguishing feature of this process is that that change in culture is covered up because an Islamic framework is maintained.

Official exclusions and distortion

No Western country – apart from Western Thrace in Greece—accepts shari'a as a personal law system in the manner found in Afro-Asian countries like India or Kenya, where Muslims are also a non-dominant group. However, looking through a Western legal prism, we can see that Islamic law is present in the West in a variety of ways. At the 'highest' level, it is incorporated in official legal systems in perhaps unexpected ways. It is more apparent in those Western jurisdictions, like France or Germany, that have a civil law background and a reputedly more hostile approach to multiculturalism. Islamic law is least institutionalised in the countries of the 'Anglosphere' that have more well-developed models of toleration and multiculturalism. However, in this latter set of countries we see more 'action' in terms of the development of unofficial Muslim fora apparently dedicated to solving marital problems and usually set up to facilitate Islamic divorces.

Many continental European countries institutionalise shari'a as a matter of foreign law that is applied through rules of private international law. Rohe, for instance, points out that in the areas of family law and inheritance, the application of legal norms in Germany and in other European countries are often determined on the basis of nationality of the persons involved rather than by their domicile. ‘In this respect it may generally be stated that Islamic law has a strong position especially within these areas’ (Rohe 2007:19; similarly see Rohe 2007: 90; Büchler 2011: 27–34). The maintenance, through the principles of private international law, of the rule that the law of one’s nationality is to be applied in court cases therefore often means a version of shari‘a is used. In that sense, the formal assumptions of courts in many continental European countries may effectively be more legally pluralistic than the British application of the *lex loci* or the Swiss application of the law of residence. As Rohe (2007: 115) notes further, ‘the application of Islamic family law – within the limits of public policy – has become everyday business in German courts’. Rohe’s reference to public policy concerns has very real consequences. European courts regularly have recourse to rules of *ordre public*, e.g. to avoid recognizing the effects of the *talaq* if they feel strongly enough about the asymmetrical right to divorce between men and women (Fulchiron 2010 for France; Rohe 2007: 115–25 for Germany). Therefore, although there is a formal adherence to the principle that a foreign law should be applied to cases concerning foreigners, in practice the use of public policy principles may frustrate such an application.

European courts’ contact with shari‘a is not new and one can trace back court judgments that indicate the presence of Muslims in European legal systems and the attitudes of the courts in earlier generations, particularly when applying their view of public policy requirements. In a 29 October 1948 judgment concerning a unilateral divorce in Syria, the Appeals Court of Rome refused to recognise the legal effects of repudiation on the grounds that ‘it is abhorred by the moral and legal mentality of the peoples who have reached a higher degree of civilisation, and who have a far more advanced ethical and social concept of marriage than Eastern peoples’. Although British courts may not ‘apply’ shari‘a rules as a matter of applying the law of nationality, they still often need to decide whether they will recognise an act that has occurred in another jurisdiction. Thus, in a 1984 English Court of Appeal judgment, Cumming-Bruce LJ said: ‘Pronouncement of *talaq* three times finally terminates the marriage in Kashmir, Dubai, and probably in other unsophisticated peasant, desert or jungle communities which respect classical Muslim religious tradition.’[1] While European courts may more rarely adopt such language today, the kind of sentiments expressed by these courts continue to disfigure European legal systems in their approach to alterity. A sanitisation of language itself does not make the underlying attitudes disappear. An interesting phenomenon occurs when judges ‘receive’ or recognise an Islamic norm within a Western legal system manifesting what Fournier (2010) refers to as a ‘loss in transplantation’. Fournier is concerned with the *mahr* (Islamic dower) as applied in the case law of Canada, France, Germany, and the United States. Reworded, her characterisation of such application can be seen as depicting a form of ‘distortion’ that occurs when a Western court attempts to apply a foreign legal institution, norm or rule. The work by Fournier and, in the Netherlands, by Hoekema and van Rossum (2010; also Hoekema 2009) suggests that often litigants or judges convert a foreign legal institution to one that is familiar within Western practice. How instrumental the religious background of Western law is in creating distortions remains a question for further research.

We have seen that, in addition to stereotyping and distorting Muslims laws, European courts have developed ways to circumvent recognition, often on the basis of the incompatibility of European and Islamic values, and notably around the issue of gender equality. Very few, if any, of the conventions on private international law arrived at through the Hague Conference on Private International Law have non-Western countries as states parties or guarantee recognition of shari‘a rules.[2] This indicates that there is little willingness to accept rules or norms of a Muslim legal order in a Western one at least at the multilateral level. Since the 1970s, legislation on private international law in Britain has also steadily moved to prevent reliance on overseas laws (Pearl and Menski 1998: 86–104). This can often create trouble for the recognition of transnational family relations, with much confusion about the recognition of foregin legal acts among officials, lawyers, and judges, as well as the individuals caught up between laws (Menski 2011; Shah 2011). Private international law activity and law enforcement, whether on the part of individual European parliaments, European courts, or through international conventions, is characterised by unilateralism and, one might say, chauvinism.

Unofficial reconstruction of Islam and Western legal responses to it

While the formal mechanisms of its reception in Western countries constitute one structural dimension of how Muslim law is framed, another significant dimension is the background and activities of Muslims, and their attitudes to Islam. The background of Muslims in particular countries of origin is linked to the sorts of questions that come up in Western courts. Migrants from Turkey, and their descendants, constitute a substantial proportion of the Muslim population in Western Europe today (Çiçekli 1998). Turkey has a history of living with civil law in family matters; the shari‘a was officially ‘abolished’ in the 1920s (Yilmaz 2005: 97–99; Bayır 2013: 119–20).[3] This has an inevitable impact in private international law cases concerning Muslims with a Turkish background because they will tend not to directly raise shari‘a questions in a way that poses a direct challenge to Western legal systems. Turkish political parties that ran on a platform for the resurrection of religious personal law have been closed down. The European Court of Human Rights’ decision in the *Refah Partisi* case[4] is well known and much discussed in European legal circles (Griffith-Jones 2013). It followed the closure of the Refah party by Turkey’s Constitutional Court on the ground that the party’s programme of establishing a plurality of legal systems in which each group would be governed by a system in conformity with its members’ religious beliefs was in conflict with the constitutional principle of secularism (*laiklik*) (Kogacioglu 2004; Yavuz 2009: 65–69). The *Fazilet Partisi* case[5] is less well known. That party was closed down by the Turkish Constitutional Court on the ground that it offended the secular nature of the Turkish Constitution (Yavuz 2009: 71–77). This chain of events could explain the cautious strategy being followed by the Turkish proponents of reform along Islamic lines (Yavuz 2009: 114).

Besides the formal invocation of Islamic law principles and rules in Western legal systems, a less clear, though perhaps more interesting development is the emergence of bottom-up pressure from sections of the Muslim populations as they reconstruct their legal universes in Western countries. This movement is in tandem with whatever official mechanisms are in place for the recognition of shari'a rules or otherwise. This involves the continuation and adaptation of known Muslim practices in the diasporic sphere as part of the process of adjustment to the Western country of settlement. Therefore, an *angrezi shariat* (Pearl and Menski 1998: 74–80) and an *amrikan shariat* (Zaman 2009) develop as a wide set of unofficial practices largely below the official radar, but which are becoming increasingly better known. The British parliament took notice of the concept of *angrezi shariat* more than a decade ago.[6] Thinking about shari'a as 'hard law' may also occlude a wider development more generally taking place among Western Muslims. In a recent interview, writer, publisher and public intellectual, Yahya Birt, noted:

> The most important development … does not lie in the development of shari'a courts. The most important development will lie in the intellectual framework and public and theological language that Muslims use to frame and present their religion in the public sphere. That will be of more importance. For instance, in people like Tariq Ramadan, Hamza Yusuf or even some of the most traditional scholars, there is a shift in the language from law to ethics. In other words, stop talking about what is lawful and what is unlawful, stop talking about what is religion in terms of rules. Start talking about religion in terms of virtues, in terms of ethics, in terms of values, in terms of qualities of the heart. The Aristotelian tradition of Islamic ethics. That kind of language will fit more in a secular national public sphere than a language that sounds like you want to set up a parallel legal system.[7]

Rohe (2007: 93–94) has noted that while Turkey is the state of origin of the Muslim majority in many parts of Europe, the vast majority of Turks would reject the introduction of shari'a rules in European countries. Muslims in Turkey and the diaspora may therefore see shari'a as set of personal or social ethics, but which are not expected to be recognised in state courts (Yilmaz 2003; cf. Çarkoğlu 2004). This evidently has a bearing on how ethnic minorities with a Turkish background reconstruct their legal universe in European countries. Taş's (2012) research among London Kurds shows that dispute settlement models reinventing customary approaches predominate, but with scant reference to Islam as a source of law. However, the fact that a significant number of Kurds in London are Alevis who tend to distance themselves from shari'a (Shankland 2003: 84–86) also has had an impact on how reconstruction of their legal universe in London has occurred.

Notwithstanding the emphasis on shari'a as a system of ethics rather than a set of hard rules, a contrast that appears to resemble the distinction made by Chiba (1989: 139–40, 178) between legal postulates and legal rules, countries in the Anglosphere appear to show more development of institution-building explicitly around Islamic law. This higher profile could be just a function of the greater academic focus and the availability of research on Anglosphere countries which in turn depends on research cultures, funding and so on. However, it is likely that there are other specific reasons why such countries have implicitly or explicitly encouraged such developments. While it may be too early to come to definite conclusions on the matter, the reasons may include the above-mentioned, differently premised operation of private international law in these countries, which provides minimal space for the official application of shari'a rules which are largely confined to the recognition of legal acts occurring abroad. Officially encouraged multiculturalism may also have a role to play in Britain (Bano 2012) and Canada (Macklin 2012). As mentioned, the specific types of legal reconstruction the diasporas from Turkey engage in show that a shari'a that involves a set of legal rules and institutions is not a priority. Bowen (2010: 417–18) argues that the colonial backdrop influences contemporary British and French developments, while Brett (1988) shows how, in nineteenth-century colonial Algeria, French citizenship became linked to giving up claims on Islamic jurisdiction. In other words, citizenship and claims to live under Islamic personal law were regarded as incompatible, and extending that argument may explain the contemporary reticence about shari'a among Muslims in France. British policy, in India and elsewhere, was characterised by a recognition of religion and personal status law, which is echoed in the British post-colonial diasporic context (also Rohe 2007: 93).

Menski (in Pearl and Menski 1998) sees the emergence of shari'a councils in Britain as part of the wider set of practices he refers to as *angrezi shariat*. Demands for official recognition of shari'a were made as far back as the early 1970s (Nielsen 1993) but rejected by the government. Menski argues that shari'a councils aspired for the recognition of *angrezi shariat* without claiming it as a right or vigorously lobbying for it. Instead, 'by the creation of social facts, a quiet process of legal restructuring is being achieved from within the community' (Pearl and Menski 1998: 80). Ahmad Hajj Thomson, a barrister and convert to Islam who is often called upon to speak publicly on Islamic issues, is quoted as saying: 'In fact the various UK Shari'a Councils are the precursors of what will eventually become shari'a courts, *insh'Allah* – but they need to be improved and unified' (in Ameli *et al.* 2006: 81). In February 2008, the then Archbishop of Canterbury, Dr Rowan Williams, made a widely publicised speech at the Royal Courts of Justice in London, stating that English law would inevitably have to pay greater attention to Islamic law. The speech had international reverberations, forcing discussions on the compatibility of Western and Islamic law and the prospects for the recognition of shari‘a (Ahdar and Aroney 2010).

By 2008 it was more widely known that alternative Muslim legal institutional structures had operated across Britain at least since the early 1980s (Pearl and Menski 1998: 74–80; Shah 2010). The work of such institutions remains concentrated on the issuance of Islamic divorces for Muslim women (Badawi 1995; Shah-Kazemi 2001; Keshavjee 2007; Douglas *et al.* 2011; Bano 2012). Established according to the various segments of Islam, including Barelwi, Deobandhi or Salafi, Ahmadiyya, and various Shia groups, Muslim legal institutions are often linked to mosques which may refer questions to those bodies. Not all institutions refer to themselves as shari‘a councils, and the popular press tends to use ‘shari‘a law courts’, ‘shari‘a courts’ or ‘Islamic courts’. Some have more formalised structures, procedures, websites, record-keeping, form-filling, and a panel of ‘*ulama*’ who can consult each other, sometimes across *madhhab* lines. They tend to be run on a voluntary basis and charge minimal fees, especially when compared to the costs involved in going to official courts, although the level of demand and rising running costs may lead to increasing fees. Lawyers and official courts may be seen by clients as too expensive and as not capable of understanding or responding to their problems. This is particularly so if a marriage is not registered or it is a case of enforcing the terms of a *nikah* (Islamic marriage contract), which English courts do not regard as binding. Similar reasons are reported by Bunting (2009: 84–89) for Canadian Muslims opting out of official family law.

The establishment of a network known as the Muslim Arbitration Tribunal (MAT), just some months prior to Dr Williams’ speech, excited additional interest. European press reports have referred to MAT as capable of delivering shari‘a-compliant decisions enforceable in English law,[8] and some legal scholars are of the same impression (e.g. Witte and Nichols 2010: 123), thus leading to a wider than warranted reading of the accommodation of unofficial tribunals under English law. Reinforcing the ambiguity, MAT’s own website announces that ‘any determination reached by MAT can be enforced through existing means of enforcement open to normal litigants’.[9] According to English law, if the parties to a dispute agree to a binding arbitration the outcome may be enforceable under the Arbitration Act 1996. Binding arbitration is already well-established among the Jewish *Battei Din*, and is used by Ahmadiyyas and Ismailis. Such agreements only apply to disputes outside the jurisdictional range of family courts and are thus used in inheritance or business cases. In fact, English law mirrors the situation in Ontario since its passing of the Family Statute Law Amendment Act, 2006, which stipulates that only those family arbitration decisions that are made in accordance with Ontario and Canadian laws can be enforced in official courts (Bunting 2009: 80–84; and in detail Korteweg and Selby 2012). Even if some kind of official structure existed to allow Muslim religious arbitrations, mediations, etc., to gain the imprimatur of official courts, it is questionable to what extent Muslims might use such opportunities. Evidence collected by Macfarlane (2012) in Canada indicates that Muslims, unlike Jews, tended not to use the arbitration procedures available under the official law in Ontario before the 2006 Act, and Macfarlane doubts whether procedures for divorce adopted by most *imams* would be considered 'arbitrations' at all. The possibility that family courts in England will in future accept agreements arrived at in non-state fora is, however, flagged up in the cas of *AI v MT*, concerning an award given by a New York *Beth Din*.[10]

In the UK, Baroness Cox introduced a Private Member's Bill in the House of Lords that would legislate against certain activities of shari'a councils and similar bodies. The Arbitration and Mediation Services (Equality) Bill targets shari'a councils, MAT and similar bodies by bringing the Equality Act 2010 to bear down on their activities so as to make discrimination, harassment, or victimization on grounds of sex unlawful. The Bill also aims to make it a criminal offence where a person:

> (a) falsely purports to be exercising a judicial function or to be able to make legally binding rulings, or (b) otherwise falsely purports to adjudicate on any matter which that person knows or ought to know is within the jurisdiction of the criminal or family courts.

The proponents of the legislation do not appear interested in details of practice within shari'a councils and, to the extent that they are interested, their various statements and publications provide stereotyped impressions of practice. A report published by the think tank Civitas (MacEoin 2009) prior to the Bill gives examples of unacceptable practice from the more than 85 shari'a courts in the UK, and it is widely cited in the context of discussions about the Bill. The press release accompanying the report states:

> [S]haria courts operating in Britain may be handing down rulings that are inappropriate to this country because they are linked to elements in Islamic law that are seriously out of step with trends in Western legislation that derive from the values of the Enlightenment and are inherent in modern codes of human rights.[11]

The Bill is concerned primarily with making practices unlawful in so far as they are *assumed* to be founded on offending principles such as gender inequality. Because its proponents typically presuppose that practices embody or express beliefs, the battleground, so to speak, is a terrain of principles, while practice shifts to the background. If it is passed into law, shari'a councils will be subject to legal action on the basis that they have breached the legislation. It could limit their activities or bring them to an end altogether, which seems to be the intended aim of at least some of the proponents of the legislation.

In the United States there is a spate of legislative activity based on the understanding that the spread of shari'a into official legal institutions should be stopped (Elsayed 2013). In Oklahoma, an initiative seeking to amend that state's constitution stated in part: 'The courts shall not look to the legal precepts of other nations or cultures. Specifically, the courts shall not consider international law or Sharia Law.' On 10 January 2012, a Federal Appeals Court concluded that by singling out Islam for unfavourable treatment in state courts, the law was likely to violate the Establishment Clause of the First Amendment to the United States Constitution, and it therefore upheld a preliminary injunction against bringing the amendment into force.[12] The Appeals Court noted that the appellants could not identify any compelling interest behind the law, noting that:

> [they] do not identify any actual problem the challenged amendment seeks to solve. Indeed, they admitted at the preliminary injunction hearing that they did not know of even a single instance where an Oklahoma court had applied Sharia law or used the legal precepts of other nations or cultures, let alone that such applications or uses had resulted in concrete problems in Oklahoma.

As with the Ontario and (proposed) British legislation, the Oklahoma amendment responds to situations assumed to exist, but is without without empirical foundation. Although the Appeals Court upheld the injunction against it, the Oklahoma initiative is part of a wider campaign being pursued in several other states to prevent shari'a rules from being considered by courts those states. Much fractious litigation can be expected to take place. Therefore, we seem to find processes of distortion or exclusion taking shape, especially in those situations where shari'a appears in forms perceived to openly challenge norms entrenched within Western official legal systems. Besides the evident clashing, distorting and driving underground of Muslim laws, we find that the pressures placed upon non-dominant groups such as Muslims result in another more insidious development. As discussed below, this occurs when a Western normative account comes to replace the experience of the non-dominant group's members.

Forced marriage as an example of colonial consciousness

Legislation and court practice in Western countries is now often directed to ensuring that consent is present in both marriage and divorce cases. This re-emphasis on ensuring consent is attributable to the presence in Western countries of non-Christian minorities who are alleged to practise forced marriage. The norm requiring consensual marriage is found in ancient Christian legal sources and has been part of the Christian inheritance of the West for many centuries. Harold Berman, a historian of the Western legal tradition, mentions that in the early centuries of Christianity, among the Germanic peoples there continued to remain a tension in that, '[t]he church preached marriage by consent of the spouses, but many parents continued to have their offspring married in childhood' (1983: 75). In the same work (1983: 168) he writes:

> The Christian emperors of Byzantium considered it their Christian responsibility to revise the laws, as they put it, 'in the direction of greater humanity'. Under the influence of Christianity, and also under the influence of Stoic and neo Platonic ideas adopted by Christian philosophy, changes were made … in family law, giving the wife a position of greater equality before the law, requiring mutual consent of both spouses for the validity of a marriage.

The idea of free consent in marriage was further developed by the Christian theologians in the Middle Ages and eventually accepted as one of the core aspects of Christian marriage (Antokolskaia 2006: 106–08) and has become a key component of Western legislation on the formation of marriage.

Although its historical roots have now become obscured, the contemporary focus on forced marriage, which is used to discipline Muslims, among other groups, from overriding such consent is consistent with the ancient formulations of consent to marry. In English law, the Forced Marriage (Civil Protection) Act 2007 enables English courts to make orders to prevent forced marriages or to remove persons from a situation of forced marriage.[13] The ability to consent to marriage is seen as part of a person's autonomy and, as Ballard (2008) explains, legislating on this basis means that consent is founded on a value defended within Western culture, disregarding the fact that families of south-Asian Muslim origin, who continue the practice of arranging marriages *seemingly* against the will of one or both of the marriage partners, have their own framework concerning marriage. This legislation imposes an asymmetrical burden on such families, while potentially subjecting their members to court orders.[14] A year after the Forced Marriage (Civil Protection) Act 2007 came into force, social workers were unable or unwilling to act as its enforcers and the police were often used as enforcers (Ministry of Justice 2009). Therefore, even though the legislation is civil, it has, in effect, criminalised a section of the population. There are plans in England to introduce criminal legislation to tackle forced marriages, which is a way of adding legislative imprimatur to an already growing practice of criminalising Muslim and other minority families.

Evidence of non-enforceability leads the state to introduce more menacing tactics to enforce the age-old notion of consent to marriage. The fact that Muslim families continue to enter marriage in the ways they consider appropriate and the fact that the phenomenon appears to be intractable may be thought to constitute empirical 'facts' that should cause a rethink of legal strategies. Introducing criminal sanctions against forced marriage could result in a greater number of family members being criminalised, exacerbating the situation of an already over-criminalised population group. As mentioned above, however, empirical evidence does not dislodge the normative structure of Western culture from its confrontation with an other; that normative structure is merely reproduced through the deployment of further measures, taking Muslims and other groups 'in the direction of greater humanity'.

Bridget Prentice, at the time Parliamentary Under Secretary at the Ministry of Justice, reminded Muslims and others that no religious or cultural foundation exists for forced marriage:

> It is worth reiterating that across the board there is absolutely no religious or cultural foundation for forced marriage. Freely given consent is a prerequisite of all Christian, Jewish, Hindu, Muslim and Sikh marriages. Forcing someone to marry is widely recognised as a human rights abuse and is simply unacceptable within our society, and our common culture of values based on equality and respect between men and women. We must not excuse any practices which compromise or undermine the basic rights of all people.
>
> (Ministry of Justice 2009: 4)

This appears to be a hark-back to colonial times when the British rulers of India, working within a framework of Christian liberal toleration, looked for doctrinal justifications to uphold a traditional practice. In the absence of good foundations in native religious texts, the British rulers used secular law to justify reforming such practices (Roover 2011).

I would like to suggest that, as with the Orient of which Edward Said wrote, 'forced marriage' does not correspond to a real entity outside the experience of Western culture. It is, however, an experiential entity that is falsely assumed to exist in the world. In a real sense, therefore, it is an imagined construct.[15] And yet, the kind of official action and general pressure in Western society affecting Muslims appears to be leading to another development. That is, the beginnings of an alignment among diasporic Muslims to the kind of norms imposed from the top down. Among the effects of such official nudging, which is far wider than only the domain of 'forced marriage', is to oblige Muslims to speak out against practices considered offensive to the Western culture on the ground that those practices are 'not Islamic', to attribute errant practices to ignorance and a lack of Islamic education and to advocate reform of those practices (Glenn 2010: 224–25). The account of their culture produced by the West is thus partly reflected in the discourse of Western Muslims, who mimic the Western critique which depicts their culture as being immoral. Balagangadhara (2012: 95–120) refers to such mimicry as 'colonial consciousness'. However, this mimicry is conducted in such a way that it allows the preservation of an Islamic framework but within which custom and convention becomes the object of critique. As in Western jurisprudence, Islamic jurisprudence has only reluctantly acknowledged custom (Libson 1997).[16] In an Islamic framework, custom is always regarded as a potential repository of pagan culture, and Islamic reform should take the direction of conformity to the prescriptions of written texts. For instance, this is subtly reflected in Yilmaz's summary of Fethullah Gülen's advice to Alevis in Turkey: 'he … encourages the Alevis to transition to a written culture from an oral culture in order to preserve their identities' (Yilmaz 2003: 224).

The critiques of custom advocated by Muslim thinkers are reflected in the everyday attitudes among, say, British Pakistanis. In her recent study of second-generation British Pakistanis travelling to Mirpur, Bolognani (2013: 12–13) reports how they might think of themselves as bearers of stereotypical notions of Britishness, such as decency, honesty and equality, or practitioners of a superior brand of Islam as compared to their Pakistani counterparts. Not untypically, one of her respondents refers to how 'culture gets labelled as religion and vice versa' in the Mirpuri mindset (Bolognani 2013: 9). A report issued by the Muslim Arbitration Tribunal, *Liberation from Forced Marriages*, shows that MAT has taken up the cudgels in the fight against forced marriage and explains how MAT could offer its services and advice to prevent such marriages. A paragraph (p. 5, para. 3.1) from its report reads:

> Background in Culture:
> The institution of marriage in the Asian sub-continent is largely based on custom and practice that has been handed down from generation to generation. This culture has been infused with true Islamic practises where the faith was deemed important. The practises have largely remained entrenched in local cultural and traditional values. The conflicts within the Islamic practises and the culture have, to a large extent, remained unchallenged. This is primarily due to the lack of institutionalisation of the Islamic faith, either in the times of the Muslim Kingdoms or in the modern Islamic Republics. Therefore issues such as forced marriages on the pretext of religion or absolute arrangement have largely remained unchecked.

Forced marriage is here depicted as something that is not only a phenomenon intelligible to Muslims, but also one that can be attributed to the persistence of non-Islamic ancestral traditions or customs. The way to counter it is to subdue these practices as taught by Islam. The adoption of such a position basically completes the circle. The Western secular state advocates the suppression of a practice intelligible to those who share the assumptions of its theological framework. Muslims in a non-dominant position then take up the account provided of the offending practice and develop a discourse agreeing with the undesirability of the practice and justifying its abolition, but do so in Islamic terms. The dominant account is accepted but also hidden at the same time under an Islamic framework. Given that there is an extension of the Islamic framework to cover areas that it may not have previously touched, we might also consider whether the secular state here succeeds, as I argue more fully elsewhere (Shah 2013), in spreading Islam through a process of 'shariatisation'.

Conclusion

In this chapter I have tried to indicate some of the tendencies occurring in the contact between Islamic and Western law in the context of Muslim diasporas in the West. While there is a general acceptance of the role of Islamic law in the limited contexts of private international law, there is also evidence of its practical limitation through the invocation of public policy or more diffuse forms of distortions – the 'loss in transplantation' of the kind Fournier identifies – within Western legal fora. Particularly in the countries of the Anglosphere it can be seen that Muslims, as part of their unofficial practice, have built institutions designed with legal ends in mind. A swathe of legislation has recently been enacted, or is in the process of being passed, as a way of limiting the interaction of official organs with the activities of these Muslim bodies, and restricting the activities of Muslim institutions, thereby ensuring the integrity of Western law and their principles. Consistent with Balagangadhara's theorisation of religion, Muslim legal institution building as a means of catering to Muslim legal demands, as well as Western resistance to accepting an interface with Muslim legalities, can be seen as arising out of and manifesting the religious rivalry of the Western and Islamic legal cultures. The pressures upon Muslims to conform to Western ethical and legal goals are manifest in a variety of ways upon institutions and individuals. We have seen how the insinuation of forced marriage creates pressure upon Muslims to enact a critique of their marriage practices by adopting the Western account of the undesirability of those practices. In the change thereby engendered, evidence is found that Muslim cultures in the diaspora, where they are in a non-dominant position, remain prone to developing a variant of what Balagangadhara identifies as 'colonial consciousness'. The difference that we see, however, is that an Islamic framework is maintained, as the pagan within becomes the target of reform. The effect of this framework is to mask the fact that a variant of colonial consciousness is at play in the reformulation of Muslim practice.

Notes

1 *Chaudhary v Chaudhary* [1985] Fam. 19, at 38.
2 An exception to the non-participation of Western countries is the Hague Convention on Jurisdiction, Applicable Law, Recognition, Enforcement and Co-operation in Respect of Parental Responsibility and Measures for the Protection of Children of 19 October 1996, recognising the *kafala* (the Islamic institution of adoption without inheritance), acceded to by Morocco.
3 The extent to which Islamic norms were expelled from the legal system in Turkey is debateable. The Civil Code of Switzerland was transplanted during the early years of the Republic only after changes adapting that code to pre-existing understandings of family relations (see Miller 2000); custom is generally placed in a more prominent position in the Turkish legal system than in Western countries. A lack of attention to such features often results in an exaggerated evaluation of the secularisation of the Turkish legal system.
4 *Refah Partisi (Welfare Party) and others v Turkey*, Application nos. 41340/98, 41342/98, 41343/98 and 41344/98, judgment of 13 February 2003.
5 *Fazilet Partisi and anor v Turkey* [2006] ECtHR 488, Application no. 1444/02, 27 April 2006. The case was formally struck out by the European Court after the

party withdrew it on the grounds that how the European Court dealt with the *Refah* case showed its bias.

6 Lord Lester, House of Lords Debates, 30 Jun 2000, cols. 1246–47.

7 Interviewed for the RELIGARE project by Ashraf-ul Hoque, 12 April 2011.

8 See e.g. Katja Gelinsky, 'Deutsche Gerichte wenden die Scharia an', *Frankfurter Allgemeine Zeitung*, 29 December 2010, noting: 'The arbitrations of MAT are enforceable in court, unlike the decisions of the informal Shari'a councils, which conduct mediations on Islamic marriage contracts or settle family disputes.' Translation by writer. For another case of misreporting, see, Abul Taher, 'Revealed: UK's first official shari'a courts', *The Sunday Times*, September 14, 2008.

9 Available online at www.matribunal.com/ (accessed 16 February 2013).

10 *AI v MT* [2013] EWHC 100 (Fam).

11 Available online at www.civitas.org.uk/press/prcs91.php (accessed 22 February 2013).

12 *Muneer Awad v Paul Ziriax, Oklahoma State Board of Elections, et al.* 670 F.3d 1111; 2012 U.S. App. LEXIS 475.

13 The Forced Marriage (Civil Protection) Act 2007 Act applies in England and Wales and in Northern Ireland. The Scottish legislation is the Forced Marriage etc. (Protection and Jurisdiction) (Scotland) Act 2011.

14 This process involves a multi-level set of steps as explained by Balagangadhara (2012: 159–165). Adapting these steps to the situation at hand, we get the attribution of certain premises which appear to explain Muslim practices on the basis of an explanation which presupposes the truth of a theory that structures the nature of the phenomena requiring explanation.

15 Balagangadhara (2012: 51–55) argues as much for constructs such as the 'caste system' and 'Hinduism'. Ballard (2008) sheds further light on the different concerns regarding marriage in South-Asian Muslim families and the Western approach.

16 Glenn (2010: 212–13) describes custom as 'tolerated' and as not being an independent source of Islamic law.

References

Ahdar, R. and Aroney, N. (eds) (2010) *Shari'a in the West*, Oxford: Oxford University Press.

Ameli, S.R., Faridi, B., Lindahl, K. and Merali, A. (2006) *Law & British Muslims: domination of the majority or process of balance?* London: Islamic Human Rights Commission.

An-Na'im, A.A. (2009) *Islam and the Secular State: negotiating the future of Shari'a*, Cambridge, MA: Harvard University Press.

Antokolskaia, M. (2006) *Harmonisation of Family Law in Europe: a historical perspective*, Antwerp: Intersentia.

Badawi, Z. (1995) 'Muslim justice in a secular state' in M. King (ed.), *God's Law Versus State Law*, London: Grey Seal.

Balagangadhara, S.N. (1994) *"The Heathen in his Blindness … ". Asia, the West, and the dynamic of religion*, Leiden and New York: E.J. Brill.

——(2012) *Reconceptualizing India Studies*, Oxford: Oxford University Press.

Ballard, R. (2008) 'Inside and outside: contrasting perspectives on the dynamics of kinship and marriage in contemporary South Asian transnational networks', in R. Grillo (ed.), *The Family in Question: immigrants and minorities in multicultural Europe*, Amsterdam: University of Amsterdam Press.

Bano, S. (2012) *Muslim Women and Shari'ah Councils: transcending the boundaries of community and law*, Basingstoke: Palgrave Macmillan.

Bayir, D. (2013) *Minorities and Nationalism in Turkish Law*, Farnham: Ashgate.

Berman, H.J. (1983) *Law and Revolution: the formation of the western legal tradition*, Cambridge, MA: Harvard University Press.

Bolognani, M. (2013) 'Visits to the country of origin: how second generation British Pakistanis shape transnational identity and maintain power asymmetries', *Global Networks*. Available online at http://dx.doi.org/10.1111/glob.12015 (accessed 15 January 2013)

Bowen, J.R. (2010) 'How could English courts recognize Shariah?' *University of St. Thomas Law Journal*, 7(3): 411–35.

Brett, M. (1988) 'Legislating for Inequality in Algeria', *Bulletin of the School of Oriental and African Studies*, 51(3): 440–61.

Büchler, A. (2011) *Islamic Law in Europe? Legal pluralism and its limits in European family laws*, Farnham: Ashgate.

Bunting, A. (2009) 'Family law's legal pluralism: private "opting-out" in Canada and South Africa', in A. Breton, A. Des Ormeaux, K. Pistor and P. Salmon (eds), *Multijuralism: manifestations, causes, and consequences*, Farnham: Ashgate.

Çarkoğlu, A. (2004) 'Religiosity, support for şeriat and evaluations of secularist public policies in Turkey', *Middle Eastern Studies*, 40(2): 111–36.

Chiba, M. (1989) *Legal Pluralism: toward a general theory through Japanese legal culture*, Tokyo: Tokai University Press.

Çiçekli, B. (1998) *The Legal Position of Turkish Immigrants in the European Union*, Ankara: Karmap.

Douglas, G., Doe, N., Gilliat-Ray, S., Sandberg, R. and Khan, A. (2011) *Social Cohesion and Civil Law: marriage, divorce and religious courts*, Report of a Research Study Funded by the AHRC. Cardiff: Cardiff Law School. Available online at www.law.cf.ac.uk/clr/Social%20Cohesion%20and%20Civil%20Law%20Full%20Report.pdf (accessed 10 January 2013).

Elsayed, M. (2013) 'Contracting into religious law: anti-Sharia enactments and the free exercise clause', *George Mason Law Review*, 20(3): 937–78.

Fournier, P. (2010) *Muslim Marriage in Western Courts: lost in transplantation*, Farnham: Ashgate.

Fulchiron, H. (2010) 'The French family judge encounters cultural pluralism', in M.-C. Foblets, J.-F. Gaudreault-DesBiens, A.D. Renteln (eds), *Cultural Diversity and the Law: state responses from around the world*, Brussels: Bruylant.

Gelinsky, K. (2010) 'Deutsche Gerichte wenden die Scharia an', *Frankfurter Allgemeine Zeitung*, 29 December, p. 32.

Glenn, H.P. (2010) *Legal Traditions of the World*, 4th edn, Oxford: Oxford University Press.

Griffith-Jones, R. (ed.) (2013) *Islam and English Law: rights, responsibilities and the role of Sharia*, Cambridge: Cambridge University Press.

Hoekema, A. (2009) 'Does the Dutch judiciary pluralize domestic law?' in R. Grillo *et al.* (eds), *Legal Practice And Cultural Diversity*, Farnham: Ashgate.

Hoekema, A.J. and van Rossum, W. (2010) 'Empirical conflict rules in Dutch cases of cultural diversity', in M.-C. Foblets, J.-F. Gaudreault-DesBiens, A.D. Renteln (eds), *Cultural Diversity and the Law: state responses from around the world*, Brussels: Bruylant.

Keshavjee, M. (2007) 'Alternative dispute resolution in a diasporic Muslim community', in P. Shah (ed.), *Law and Ethnic Plurality: socio-legal perspectives*, Leiden: Martinus Nijhoff.

Kogacioglu, D. (2004) 'Progress, unity, and democracy: dissolving political parties in Turkey', *Law & Society Review*, 38(3): 433–62.

Korteweg, A.C. and Selby, J.A. (eds) (2012) *Debating Sharia: Islam, gender politics and family law arbitration*, Toronto: University of Toronto Press.

Libson, G. (1997) 'On the development of custom as a source of law in Islamic law', *Islamic Law and Society*, 4: 131–55.

MacEoin, D. (2009) *Sharia Law or 'One Law For All'?* London: Civitas.

Macfarlane, J. (2012) 'Practising an Islamic imagination: Islamic divorce in North America', in A.C. Korteweg, and J.A. Selby (eds), *Debating Sharia: Islam, gender politics and family law arbitration*, Toronto: University of Toronto Press.

Macklin, A. (2012) 'Multiculturalism meets privatization: the case of faith based arbitration', in A.C. Korteweg, and J.A. Selby (eds), *Debating Sharia: Islam, gender politics and family law arbitration*, Toronto: University of Toronto Press.

Malik, J. (2004) 'From the margin to the centre: Muslims in Europe – Introduction', in J. Malik (ed.), *Muslims in Europe: from the margin to the centre*, Münster: LIT Verlag.

Menski, W. (2011) 'Life and Law: advocacy and expert witnessing in the UK', in L. Holden (ed.), *Cultural Expertise and Litigation: patterns, conflicts, narratives*, London: Routledge.

Miller, R.A. (2000) 'The Ottoman and Islamic substratum of Turkey's Swiss Civil Code', *Journal of Islamic Studies*, 11(3): 335–61.

Ministry of Justice (2009) *One year On: the initial impact of the Forced Marriage (Civil Protection) Act 2007 in its first year of operation*, Ministry of Justice.

Muslim Arbitration Tribunal (n.d.) *Liberation from Forced Marriages*, MAT.

Nielsen, J.S. (1993) *Emerging Claims of Muslim Populations in Matters of Family Law in Europe*, Birmingham: Centre for the Study of Islam and Christian–Muslim Relations.

Pearl, D. and Menski, W.F. (1998) *Muslim Family Law*, London: Sweet and Maxwell.

Rohe, M. (2007) *Muslim Minorities and the Law in Europe: chances and challenges*, New Delhi: Global Media Publications.

Roover, J. De (2011) 'Secular law and the realm of false religion', in W.F. Sullivan, R.A. Yelle and M. Tausig-Rubbo (eds), *After Secular Law*, Stanford, CA: Stanford University Press.

Shah-Kazemi, S.N. (2001) *Untying the Knot: Muslim women, divorce and the Shariah*, London: Nuffield Foundation.

Shah, P. (2010) 'Between God and the Sultana? Legal pluralism in the British Muslim diaspora', in J.S. Nielsen and L. Christoffersen (eds), *Shari'a as Discourse: legal traditions and the encounter with Europe*, Farnham: Ashgate.

——(2011) 'When South Asians marry trans-jurisdictionally: some reflections on immigration cases by an "expert"', in L. Holden (ed.), *Cultural Expertise and Litigation: patterns, conflicts, narratives*, London: Routledge.

——(2013) 'In pursuit of the pagans: Muslim law in the English context', *Journal of Legal Pluralism*, 45(1): 58–75.

Shankland, D. (2003) *The Alevis in Turkey: the emergence of a secular Islamic tradition*, London: Routledge Curzon.

Taş, L. (2012) 'Kurds in the UK: legal pluralism and alternative dispute resolution', unpublished PhD thesis, Queen Mary, University of London.

Taher, A. (2008) 'Revealed: UK's first official shari'a courts', *The Sunday Times*, September 14, p. 2.

Witte, J. Jr. and J.A. Nichols (2010) 'Faith-based family laws in Western democracies?' *Fides et Libertas: The Journal of the International Religious Liberty Association*, 122–35.

Yavuz, M.H. (2009) *Secularism and Muslim Democracy in Turkey.* Cambridge: Cambridge University Press.

Yilmaz, I. (2003) 'Ijitihad and tacdid by conduct', in M.H. Yavuz and J.L. Esposito (eds), *Turkish Islam and the Secular State: the Gülen movement*, Syracuse, NY: Syracuse University Press.

——(2005) *Muslim Law, Politics and Society in Modern Nation-States,* Aldershot: Ashgate.

Zaman, S. (2008) 'Amrikan Shari'a: the reconstruction of Islamic family law in the United States' *South Asia Research*, 28(2): 185–202.

3 Please divorce me!

Subversive agency, resistance and gendered religious scripts*

Pascale Fournier

Introduction

In Canada, the use of religious arbitration recently sparked public outcries and gave rise to an ongoing discussion on the limits of multiculturalism. Proposed solutions to this phenomenon have varied from a complete ban[1] to a form of state-supervised legal pluralism.[2] Despite the varied political positions presented along the spectrum, both supporters and critics of the use of religious law in family law matters tend to adopt a dichotomous view of the relationship between religious law and secular law. On the one hand, those who perceive religious law as a form of oppression toward women envision the secular law as capable of ensuring gender equality and propose to emphasize a more meaningful accessibility to civil courts for minority women.[3] On the other hand, those who advocate the legitimacy of religious law claim that men and women use the religious narrative as a form of identity and that this private and parallel sphere of normative expression should be respected as such in a multicultural state.[4] Unfortunately, these positions fail to consider how religious men and women in Canada *actually* put forth religious claims inside and outside the courtroom and participate or resist in subversive ways to conventional disciplinary mechanisms.

In this chapter, based on my socio-legal fieldwork in Toronto, Ottawa and Montreal, I argue that the religious and secular spheres are *not* experienced by Jewish/Muslim women as two mutually exclusive domains but rather as one highly complex battlefield that distributes differentiated costs and benefits. In fact, the family is often conceived and understood as a *market* in which husbands and wives negotiate, in different aspects of their individual and collective life, their poverty or wealth, their national affiliations, their sexual freedom or submission, their marital conditions and their relation to God. Borrowing from the language of law and economics, this chapter attempts to shed light on the following questions: Are the interests of the different stakeholders in Canadian religious communities, such as rabbis/imams, Jewish/Muslim men, judges, family/community members and Jewish/Muslim women, overlapping, and if so, in what regulatory ways? How do differentially situated Jewish and Muslim women engage, within institutions and as individuals, in day-to-day bargains with their husband to obtain a religious divorce that is at first refused to them? Are men and women strategically 'flirting with God'[5] in such a way as to get the optimal economic outcome from both the secular and religious courts? How is this informal and fluid process operating?

I explore this intellectual endeavour in three main sections. The first section presents the methodology and theoretical framework employed in this chapter. The second describes the concepts of marriage and divorce within the Jewish and Islamic traditions, portraying husbands and wives as agents whose relationship is shaped by contractual rights and duties. The third section paints a juxtaposition of the 'law in books' and the 'law in action' by offering a series of narrative descriptions based on interviews conducted with ten Jewish and Muslim women in Canada. It outlines the unexpected and complicated ways in which Jewish and Muslim women who live on the religious margins perform their agency, identity and gender according to distributive motives that are often ignored by institutional authorities. Finally, the third also identifies the costs and benefits of both the religious and secular spheres as experienced by religious women and highlights the background legal rules and social norms that help produce, formally and informally, different bargaining endowments.

Methodology and theoretical background

This socio-legal study is based on my fieldwork within religious communities in Canada over the summer and autumn of 2009. It included visits to mosques and synagogues, discussions with practising and non-practising men and women, rabbis, *imams* and other religious experts, as well as ten formal interviews with Jewish and Muslim women, which were conducted in Toronto, Montreal and Ottawa.[6] The women were chosen from a variety of denominations (e.g. traditionalist and liberal Islam; Orthodox and Conservative Judaism) and socio-economic backgrounds. They had all been married[7] and were civilly divorced, religiously divorced, or both. The interviews lasted about two hours and incorporated demographic, religious, secular and community profiles.[8] They were held in women's homes, at their work places, in closed offices or at a café. Recruitment was done indirectly, as per the advice of the ethics committee, through community groups, women's organizations and religious leaders.[9]

The chapter applies a 'left law and economics' methodology[10] to approach religious subjects through a 'storytelling'[11] narrative. Religious law has long remained the ultimate outsider of market considerations and, as a result, is rarely accounted for in economic analysis literature.[12] In neoclassical welfare economics, consumers are portrayed as rational actors whose aim is to maximize 'utility' when they make choices.[13] The law and economics methodology,[14] which has been applied mostly to public issues,[15] predicts individual behavioural responses to current or proposed legislation and policies based on the assumption that human beings are motivated by rational self-interest. Law and economics scholars have also included in their scientific gaze private domains such as contract law[16] and tort law,[17] but less so family law,[18] which is perceived as emotional and situated *outside* the market. This sharp distinction between the family and the market has been challenged by several scholars[19] for its refusal to see the first as a pivotal productive entity, one that is an 'important economic actor in the national and global economy' (Halley 2011: 83). Reconnecting the family *within* the market allows us not only to view its role as 'a crucial site of social-welfare provision' (Halley 2011: 84), but also to perform a distributive analysis of how husbands and wives negotiate economic resources, desires and day-to-day decisions in all kinds of fair and unfair ways.

Despite its flaws,[20] the left law and economics methodology remains a powerful tool to understand how family members behave upon the dissolution of marriage.[21] In the context of this chapter, it helps develop a useful framework to appreciate how religious women act in a self-interested manner upon divorce and to identify the kind of power they deploy in utility-maximizing ways when navigating the religious/secular divide. Admittedly, my hope is to be attentive, through the stories of women, to the multiplicity of mechanisms through which religious divorce is filtered as a *distributive* practice. Reconstructing the field in this way makes it possible to conceive individuals – men and women, husbands and wives, fathers and mothers – as making choices based on preferences and the likelihood that benefits will be more profitable than the costs incurred at any given moment of their marital relationship. This is not to suggest, of course, that agency is 'free'; it is always already constrained by external and internal forces pulling in diverse directions. Rather, in an implicit and subversive way, my goal is to show that the family/market binary should be criticized and perhaps abandoned, especially in the religious context where other misleading binaries permeate public discourse (private/public; religious/secular; spiritual/civil).

Jewish and Muslim marriage/divorce in contractual terms

This section presents the institutions of Jewish/Muslim marriage and divorce as articulated in contractual terms, emphasizing the elements of agency, bindingness and legitimacy of the adjudicator. By employing terms traditionally reserved for a contractual framework to illustrate the convergences and divergences between Jewish and Muslim traditions, I envision and present religious family as a *distributive* legal space.

Marriage in Judaism and Islam: a set of contractual rights

Under Islamic family law, marriage establishes a reciprocity system in which each party is assigned a set of contractual rights and duties toward the other party.[22] An Islamic marriage contract can only be concluded through the principles of offer (*ijab*) and acceptance (*qabul*) by the two principals or their proxies (Nasir 2002: 45). Upon marriage, the husband acquires the right to his wife's obedience (Wani 1995: 49; Maghniyyah 1995: 359) and the right to restrict her movements outside the matrimonial home (Nasir 2002: 80). The wife acquires the right to her *mahr*[23] and the right to maintenance (Esposito and DeLong-Bas 2001: 25; Wani 1995: 195).

Like Muslim marriage, Jewish marriage is finalized according to contractual principles. The parties execute a marriage contract (a *ketubah*, pl. *ketubot*), often written in Aramaic,[24] which lists the duties of each spouse. Unlike the Muslim marriage contract, which is negotiated between the parties and is therefore unique to them and their relationship, the *ketubah* is fairly standard. Based on the Torah's articulation of a husband's duties toward his wife, this contract includes requirements for adequate food, clothing, shelter and regular intercourse, as well as the sum of a payment for the wife in the event of death or divorce (traditionally, the sum necessary for the woman to support herself for one year) (Epstein 2005: 163).

Divorce in Judaism and Islam: agency, bindingness and legitimacy of the adjudicator

In this section, I articulate divorce claims in terms of agency, bindingness and legitimacy of the adjudicator, so as to later conceive the interaction between religious and secular law in an overlapping and intersectional space. I borrow a contractual language to grasp women's agency and give centrality to the consent they give and the bindingness of the agreements they conclude when they are 'bargaining with patriarchy'.[25] In so doing, my aim is to move away from religious 'gendered images' or 'symbolic roles' (Shachar 2008: 591) and closer to an image of women entering conflicting and multiple worlds of negotiation.

Agency in Muslim and Jewish divorce

Agency, as determined by the governing legal structure at the time of divorce, points to which party can initiate the divorce proceeding and under what circumstances. Islamic legal institutions, such as *talaq*, *khul'* and *faskh* divorce, determine which party may or may not initiate divorce and the different costs associated with such transaction. According to classical Islamic family law, women have the agency to use the *khul'* or *faskh* divorce, but may not use the *talaq* divorce. The *khul'* divorce is introduced judicially by the woman with the understanding, however, that such route will dissolve the husband's duty to pay the deferred *mahr* (El Alami and Hinchcliffe, 1996: 27–28; Abdal-Rahim, 1996: 105). The *faskh* divorce is a fault-based divorce initiated by the wife before the Islamic tribunal, and it is by nature limited to specific grounds. Grounds to issue a decree of *faskh* include impotence on the part of the husband, insufficient material support and companionship ('the loneliness of the marriage bed'), non-fulfilment of the marriage contract, mental or physical abuse or a husband's lack of piety.[26] In the case of termination of marriage by *faskh* divorce, unlike in the case of *khul'* divorce, the wife is entitled to *mahr* (El Alami and Hinchcliffe 1996: 29). Finally, the *talaq* divorce (repudiation) is a unilateral act that dissolves the marriage contract by the husband's declaration only. The law recognizes the power of the husband to divorce his wife by saying *talaq* three times, and without any need for him to ask for the enforcement of his declaration by the court (El Alami and Hinchcliffe 1996: 22). However, what comes with this unlimited 'freedom' of the husband to divorce at will in the private sphere is the (costly) obligation to pay *mahr* in full as soon as the third *talaq* has been pronounced (Fyzee, 1974: 133).

Unlike Muslim women who may initiate divorce through *khul'* or *faskh*, Jewish women are not in a position to religiously divorce their husbands. In order to be 'halachically'[27] correct, a Jewish marriage may only end with the death of a spouse or the voluntary granting of a divorce (*get*) by the husband (Haut 1983:18) and its simultaneous acceptance by the wife (Blecher-Prigat and Shmueli 2009: 281; Carmit Yefet 2009: 443–44). The husband thus has the exclusive power to deliver the *get*, which comes in the form of a surprisingly brief written document written mostly in Aramaic. The most important passage of this document essentially states that the woman is now free to marry any man and, in so doing, she will not be guilty of committing adultery. If a Jewish woman is entitled to a *get* and has not received one due to her husband's refusal, she is referred to as an *agunah* (pl. *agunot*); literally, a 'chained' or 'anchored' woman. Several limitations are placed on a divorced Jewish woman who wishes to religiously remarry without a *get*. First, if she marries a man civilly, the relationship is considered adulterous under Jewish law. Therefore, the woman is *never* permitted to marry that man religiously (Cohn 2004: 66). Second, any children born to a woman who has not received a *get* are labelled *mamzer* (pl. *mamzerin*). Such children are sometimes 'effectively excluded from organized Judaism' (Nichols 2007: 155) as they are illegitimate and may never marry anyone but another *mamzer*. Although a wife can in theory refuse a *get* issued by her husband, in practice the consequences for the man are neither as serious nor as far-reaching as they are for an *agunah*.

Bindingness in Muslim and Jewish divorce

Bindingness highlights the conditions under which a contractual agreement becomes compulsory. In the case of Muslim and Jewish divorce, bindingness depends on the unilateral will of the husband and thus highlights the potential for gendered power imbalances. That being said, the bargaining parties complicate this narrative of unilateral bindingness in many ways, some of which this section outlines.

If a Muslim man repudiates his wife by issuing three *talaq*, the divorce is binding despite lack of consent on the part of the wife. The apparent potential for extortion through the *talaq* divorce has long been recognized in the literature on Islamic divorce.[28] However, the formally unequal rule of *talaq* plays out differently in practice depending on the amount of *mahr* in the marriage contract. Islamic jurists conceive *mahr* as a powerful limitation on the possibly capricious exercise of the *talaq* as well as a form of compensation to the wife once the marriage has been dissolved (Schacht 1982: 167; Coulson 1964: 207–8; Tucker 1985: 54). Indeed, if *mahr* is very high, chances are the husband will hesitate before repudiating his wife. As said by Hoodfar, 'the larger the sum of the m*ahr*, the more effective the wife's leverage' (1996: 131). In most cases, this constitutes a source of security for wives who do not want to divorce. However, for those who do want a divorce,[29] high *mahr* can be disconcerting: it may only be at the price of behaving in a disgraceful manner that the woman can obtain a *talaq* from her husband.[30] Thus, a closer look reveals the bindingness of the *talaq* divorce as highly contingent upon other religious institutions, such as *mahr*, that interlock with the *talaq* in complex, contradictory ways and can be manipulated by bargaining spouses to affect the outcome of the divorce proceedings in such a way as to maximize benefits and minimize costs.

If a Jewish man refuses to grant the *get*, the wife is left with very little religious recourse.[31] Hence, the opportunity for 'strategic behaviour' (Estin 2009: 464) in civil divorce proceedings is remarkable, making the *get* an ideal tool for blackmail. Lisa Fishbayn writes that 'the power men enjoy under Jewish law to withhold a *get* is of concern to civil law because this power becomes an effective bargaining endowment in the resolution of civil family law disputes' (2008: 85). In its seminal *Bruker v. Marcovitz* decision,[32] the Supreme Court of Canada similarly suggested: 'For example, the spouse could say, "Give up your claim for support or custody of the children and I will offer the get".'[33] The *get* thus appears as a formidable unilateral blackmailing tool (Syrtash 1992: 121).

That being said, the Jewish *agunah* has been provided with *some* countervailing bargaining instruments. If Jewish women cannot grant the *get* of their own initiative (Mielziner 1987: 117);[34] they may refuse their husbands' *get*, which will prevent rabbinical authorities from dissolving the marriage contract. Jewish women may refuse consent to the *get* for reasons related to the best interests of their children, to extract further concessions from the husband or for pecuniary incentives. In practice, however, this bargaining chip is severely limited by the fact that the Jewish husband can marry a second wife in the absence of a *get*. Much more potent is the bargaining power provided by section 21.1 of the Divorce Act.[35] With the introduction of Bill C-61 in 1990, the Divorce Act was specifically modified to address the problem of the *agunah* and provide courts with a discretionary power to prevent a husband from obtaining civil relief under the Act if he refuses 'to remove a barrier to religious remarriage'.[36]

Thus, the law surrounding Jewish divorce is revealed as replete with strategic avenues for spouses to explore. Its bindingness, just like that of Islamic law, is permeated and conditioned by the plural bargaining options with which parties are differentially endowed.

Legitimacy of the adjudicator: the Islamic qadi *and the Jewish* Beth Din

In Jewish and Islamic law, elements of both agency and bindingness may be played out in the presence of an adjudicator. This section illustrates how the voluntary will of the parties and the backdrop for the negotiation of divorce proceedings are legitimized by the structural nature of religious law. It outlines the ways in which sites of adjudication fuel and complicate husbands and wives' bargaining power.

Under classical Islamic law, the Islamic court (*qadi*) usually does not arbitrate *talaq* divorces but often adjudicates *khul'* divorces[37] and *faskh* divorces. In the latter instance, 'a wife who is unhappy in her marriage and who wishes to obtain a dissolution must petition the court but only in so far as she can demonstrate to the court that the limited grounds under which divorce can be granted have been met' (El Alami and Hinchcliffe 1996: 29). However, in the absence of Islamic courts in Canada, *imams* act as judicial authorities in religious family law matters (Boyd 2004). Julie Macfarlane, one of the few scholars conducting actual empirical research on Muslim practices in North America, has found that *imams* often assume roles that go beyond those assigned by classical Islamic law to *qadis*. Some act as informal mediators, while others align with the civil sphere and hold that an Islamic divorce is automatically granted upon civil divorce (Macfarlane 2012). Thus, the informal practices of Islamic adjudication in Canada produce myriad bargains and outcomes, shaping agency and bindingness in ways that require empirical assessment, diverging as they do from the classical Islamic law model.

Unlike the heterogeneous venues and audiences of Islamic religious divorce, one party systematically oversees the act of Jewish religious divorce: a *Beth Din* (pl. *Battei Din*). This tribunal of three Jewish judges (*dayanim*) functions according to formalities born of centuries of religious tradition. Although the *Beth Din* oversees the process, it does not execute the divorce. This is undertaken by the parties themselves, and more specifically by the man: '[n]o one – not the government, not the courts, not even a rabbi – is authorized to divorce a couple except for the husband' (Carmit Yefet 2009: 442–43). Therefore, the power of the *Beth Din* lies in its persuasive authority rather than its ability to mandate results, especially in diaspora countries where an order of the *Beth Din* will not necessarily be respected or enforced. Indeed, civil courts will bow out of enforcing the *Beth Din*'s order for lack of jurisdiction. As Greenberg-Kobrin bluntly puts it, 'Today the Beth Din's power exists only to the extent that it is recognized' (1999: 368).[38]

A cost-benefit analysis of religious and civil divorce

This section describes the interaction between religion and economics, focusing on the distributive conflict between husbands and wives as they move back and forth between the religious and the secular realms upon divorce. For the female participants interviewed, the outcome of divorce is often perceived and played out as a conflict over economic *distribution*. In this process, the background rules act as forces that shape the individual's capacity to bargain and influence distributive outcomes. Sometimes the religious sphere distributes benefits to the man and corresponding costs to the woman; at other times, it creates costs for the man and benefits for the woman. The secular sphere similarly distributes uneven costs and benefits. Drawing on the testimonies of ten religious women in Canada, I present in this section an economic analysis of religious identity and family law arrangements, inside and outside the courtroom.

This section presents the conflicts of interest between husband and wife as they penetrate the religious sphere upon divorce. Female participants have suggested to me that Jewish and Muslim husbands behave strategically before the religious authorities and use God to their own benefits. In each case illustrated here, the husband purposefully employed one narrow religious methodology in order to ensure that his priorities (monetary or not) prevailed:

> Participant 5
>
> He said '*talaq, talaq, talaq*' three times and I said 'What's that?' He said 'Well, I divorce you; that's all it takes you know, I'm divorcing you.' I said 'No it's not; you know in Islam there are conditions, there are reasons and there should be attempts of reconciliation.' I said 'How can we be divorced?' you know, so he said 'No, that's it, Islamicly we're divorced.' Then we suddenly found ourselves, you know, um, having to sell the house and basically going to a separation. I found out two months later, in June, … that he wanted me to be his second wife and I said 'Well, forget it.' I just laughed out loud and said 'You got to be joking; I cannot be a second wife, I'm still married to you, we're not legally divorced!' So anyway he did marry. He was married religiously to this second woman.

In this case, the husband not only completely ignored civil law norms but also twisted his understanding of Islamic law to yield the outcome he desired, that of marrying someone new. Paralleling this Muslim woman's experience, Jewish participants noted that their husbands purposefully ignored the fact that it is the man's religious duty to pay for the *get*. The rabbis, complicit with the men, did not rectify the situation. Quite the contrary, the women had to financially assume the costs in order to obtain a religious divorce before the *Beth Din*:

> Participant 3
>
> Now remember, it's the man's duty to give the women the divorce, but the *Vaad* [council of rabbis] does not give a shit as to who pays! Excuse my language. So when I paid, when he's technically supposed to pay for it, they didn't even ask him 'Why aren't you paying for it?' Nothing! They asked him for nothing! I had to run [get the money] the day before to bring them eight hundred dollars. Otherwise, I would never get a *get*!'

> Participant 8
>
> I did not want to go there but I felt the husband should pay for some things. He should be obligated! But I did not push it because I did not want to risk not getting the *get*. In a way, it is a type of blackmail.

When religious authorities fail to enforce existing religious rules that are in favour of women, a benefit in the religious sphere turns into a cost. These examples illustrate that religious divorce is far from being a static, unitary legal institution. Rather, it often functions as a disciplinary mechanism whereby husband and wife employ diverse strategies to lift some aspects of religion to the fore while downplaying other aspects when 'performing' agency.

Religious sphere as a benefit to the woman and a cost to the man

Acting alongside the negative aspects of the religious sphere are the transformative significance and direct benefits that religious divorce brings to the lives of observant religious women, to which I now turn. In all of the scenarios presented in this section, women used the religious script because they claimed it was in their interest to do so. This avenue either gave them emotional freedom, cooperative respect from well-known religious leaders and community members, or both. Distributive considerations play a central role in assessing what path women choose to adopt, often under considerable constraints.

Several Jewish and Muslim participants explained how they sought to identity benefits while avoiding identity costs. This bargaining strategy often involved reference to family and community members as a way to use threats and other emotional penalties against the husband during the divorce process. Power can thus be deployed in concrete ways to provoke shame and displeasure:

> Participant 4
>
> After thinking about how I could convince him [to give the *get*], I came to the conclusion that it would be impossible to persuade him on my own and enlisted the help of those I thought would be most embarrassed by his behaviour. I called an aunt of his with whom he was quite close and has a great deal of respect for. … She was quite disappointed to hear this, as her daughter had had a similar experience. She is an observant Jew and understood the importance this held for me, and after having gone through the same thing she said she would absolutely speak to him and encourage him to do the right thing. … To this day, I don't know for sure what led to his finally agreeing to a *get*, but I think the pressure and embarrassment of my exposing his behaviour in front of others led to success. I think he simply didn't want to look bad to those he respected.

In a sense, this participant used one aspect of her religious foundation (community assistance) against the negative influence of another aspect (the right of a husband to grant or refuse a *get*). When negotiating within the process of religious divorce, this participant was able to mitigate a religious cost by drawing on a positive aspect of the same rubric. Many Jewish women whose husbands refused to give them a *get* enlisted the help of rabbis, in the hope that they would put pressure on the husbands through emails and phone calls, a strategy that often proved successful. Community members, including lawyers belonging to the same religious faith, can also play an influential role on the husband: 'The attorney that he retained is also Jewish. From what I understand, but I am not a hundred percent sure, I think he was told that his attorney would not represent him, unless he promised to give me the *get*.' (Participant 6). Here, the lawyer's actions (presumably motivated by his own religious ethics) yielded a direct benefit to the woman.

The participants indicated that not only do community resources have the potential to pressure and influence religious outcomes, but they also reach out into the civil sphere and compensate costs incurred in civil courts. For instance, a participant calculated that it was more advantageous to waive spousal support in order to gain the custody of her children because community resources and networks compensated for the economic loss of renouncing support:

> Participant 6
>
> He decided that he would take me to court and take the kids away from me and I won! … But I don't get spousal support anymore since we signed this custody agreement a couple of months ago. The spousal support thing was all part of the negotiations [for custody]. So I was lucky that I was getting it up until the end of July. I mean now it's hard, but we'll manage, you know. In the beginning when he left, I didn't have money for two or three months. My community sent me food, they sent me money. I found envelopes of money on my doormat! People knew that I needed it and there's no, like, 'please pay back'. The community organizations brought us milk and eggs and bread and cheese and all that kind of stuff. There are wonderful organizations there, and it is not [conditional on whether] you are religious or you are not religious. It is for the community, you know?

Thus, the autonomy and clean break that some participants needed was not attained solely through the equitable treatment promised under the civil law route.[39] Instead, many women used the religious/cultural resources available to them to yield the desired result.

Civil sphere as a benefit to the man and a cost to the woman

Stories shared by participants in this project systematically suggest that, upon divorce, husbands adopt highly distributive strategies: they pursue the path leading to the maximization of (often economic) outcomes. They manipulate the civil side of the law to their own advantage in order to either pay less or get more assets out of the divorce, even if such strategies are in direct violation of the espoused beliefs of their religious communities. One might assume that parties who adhere more closely to religious marriage and divorce would adopt a pro forma approach to the civil law. However, from my discussions with participants, this does not seem to be the case. Instead, the secular courts were used as an additional bargaining venue, which provided weighty strategic interaction. In fact, religious advantages were leveraged against civil disadvantages and vice versa:

> Participant 5
>
> The most ironic thing about this is that in Islam, you know, whatever the woman brings into the marriage, … the woman keeps. Well, here he used the civil side, provisions for a division of property, you know, fifty-fifty division of property, to take from the marriage furniture we acquired together, the proceeds from the sale of the house, the 50 per cent in lieu of child support payments. So when it was convenient for him, he invoked the civil system, when it was convenient for him he invoked, you know, the religious system.

> Participant 7
>
> It really bothered me when he tried to get my pension and I wrote a letter to him. I didn't talk to him but I wrote a letter to him. I said 'You know this family patrimony became law because of the feminist movement, because then women did not have pension, women did not have a job. So when a marriage broke women were left with nothing. … And you who is anti-feminism, against all this women's movement, now you are taking advantage of the law that was brought up by women.' So I said 'you should be ashamed of yourself'.

Many of the other participants similarly reported that their husbands consciously made a calculation of which venue, religious or civil law, would yield them the greatest benefits, and acted accordingly. This tactic is commonly referred to in economics literature as the 'threat point' (Pollak 2003). This 'point' is the maximal level of utility attainable outside the marriage. Often, the civil sphere becomes a cost to the woman because of its failure to sufficiently verify reported assets. In fact, several Jewish and Muslim women mentioned that their husbands had been running a business and declared close to nothing on their income statements, despite the fact that they were financially comfortable. In the opinion of the women, the secular system is complicit in such dishonest behaviour:

> Participant 3
>
> He gave me a lump sum of money, he kept the house and whatever. Today I kinda regret it because he's a multimillionaire and I helped him

start the business, but that goes way back when! The sad part is I find men know how to hide money. And the law allows them to hide things from their wives; they make it easy for them. So he gave them papers [stating that] he's making, I don't know, maybe thirty thousand a year. And I'm thinking 'What kind of legal system do we have here?' Here is a man: two cars, a house, making thirty thousand dollars a year, whatever!

Participant 4

That's what he wanted and he really wasn't interested in financial contributions. He felt that it was my idea and, he, you know, painted a picture of himself as being rather destitute, though we had lived a fairly comfortable life. So he got away with a lot of that!

Participant 8

My husband had a judgment in 1996 for child support. I never sued for alimony. My lawyer told me to only go after child support. We went to court many times. He would claim poverty. 'Severe poverty'?! He got himself into a government property with two vehicles!

Much like many of those who only go through a civil law divorce, many spouses who go through both the religious and civil law divorce processes fail to disclose to the court information that puts them at a disadvantage. It is normally the responsibility of the civil court to verify that all assets have been reported. Is there a connection between a court's failure to adequately verify the husbands' assets and the religious context surrounding the divorce proceedings? There is irony in the fact that religious authorities, precisely because know their members well, are more likely to notice when a husband lies about his income. Civil courts, by comparison, can be disempowering for those from whom assets are concealed.

Civil sphere as a benefit to the woman and a cost to the man

Religious women in this study reported making choices in a utility-maximizing fashion, using the civil law either as a means to get an equitable outcome or as a way to punish and discipline, even if such strategies often meant bearing corresponding personal and social costs in the religious sphere. It was often the case that notwithstanding women's families actively promoting the husbands' interests, participants persisted in obtaining the equitable results they sought before the civil court. Some participants defied their husband's efforts by making a distinction between their loyalty to their family and their right to a fair settlement upon divorce:

Participant 9

The uncles came to see me and they tried to get me settle and to abandon the court, and I said 'No, I made my deposit, I have my lawyer, and I will continue. I want my rights! I respect the family; I respect the

> elders; I respect the religion, but it doesn't work for me.' And that's what I explained to my uncles. Even if my father, the most important man in my life, rises from his tomb, I would refuse to proceed in this manner. (Translated from French.)[40]

Jewish and Muslim participants also indicated that they were willing to lose economically if it allowed them to gain something else of value in exchange, such as a religious divorce that would otherwise be refused to them or simply some peace of mind for themselves and their children. Though some Jewish and Muslim participants could be seen as having suffered economic losses, they described themselves as what we, in the economic lexicon, would call rational maximizers of their own self-interest. They discussed how husbands used the promise of financial security as a way to maintain control over their wives after separation. To undermine this strategy, some women affirmatively refused an obvious economic benefit in an active repudiation of this assertion of male power. For participants, this often translated into not wanting to obscure the religious process by including alimony and other payments and leaving everything in the house for their husbands as a way of showing their freedom and independence:

> Participant 1
>
> I didn't talk to him directly. It was my father and I asked him 'Dad, please tell him that it is me who is asking for the divorce; I want to exempt my ex from all alimony, I want nothing to do with him. Even the alimony which I have a right to I don't want, and I want nothing to do with my dower.' (Translated from French.)[41]

> Participant 7
>
> So I took the two kids, rented an apartment and left. I didn't even take furniture, nothing. I just packed; we just packed our clothes, left home and started buying our own furniture.

The decision to walk away from a clear civil law monetary benefit is often perceived as worth the immediate freedom and clean break it provides. Many women see this outcome as a benefit and act accordingly. For instance, a Muslim participant valued the well-being of her child more than the benefit of some additional dollars. Speaking in purely economic terms to her lawyer, she assessed the risks at stake and reasoned from this premise.

> Participant 5
>
> He [the lawyer] said 'It's going to be costly if you do it [negotiate a civil settlement] because obviously you'll have to fight for it; he doesn't sound like he'll give it to you, you know.' So I said 'You know what? I don't want to do all of these things. It will drag my child out. It will be tough on my child because he's probably going to keep on fighting. I don't have the time or the energy to fight him so let's just walk away from it', and I did.

Interestingly, this distribution scenario is far from peculiar to Muslim women's strategies. The comments of one Jewish woman reflect the pride involved in *not* begging for money. She explained how her ex-husband used money as a form of power over her. If she had to beg and plead for more financial assistance for her children, he perceived this as a form of control. Eventually, the woman felt that it was not worth fighting with him anymore and settled for the minimal child support payments. Oftentimes, choosing to withdraw from the 'battleground' of divorce negotiation does not mean the caving in of a position, but can rather constitute an active breaking of the grasp of male power.

> Participant 3
>
> To him, it was all about control. You see, to him money is control. And if I asked and begged and this and that, it gave him more power over me. And it came to a point where it wasn't even worth fighting with him over that. So we went a long time like that. … With [him] there is nothing else to accept! [He] is not the kind of person you want to start with. I've had him arrested; I had a restraining order; I've done all of those things. To get to the point where I want to beg him for more money? Absolutely not! And the lawyer looked at me, like, 'You're crazy.'

Some religious women valued and benefited from the equitable division of property granted in the civil sphere; others traded money for freedom or for their children's well-being, neither of which were perceived as antithetical to their own interests. In all instances where the religious participants mobilized civil resources to achieve their aims, the civil sphere revealed itself as a plural, composite entity that, far from translating into systematic 'gender equality' or clean break, distributes highly differentiated endowments. The women I interviewed reached from one civil recourse to another and from the civil to the religious spheres, intertwining custody, property, spousal support, community standing, dispute settlement and tranquillity for their children in one multifaceted, fascinatingly complex bargaining terrain.

Conclusion

Upon divorce, a Canadian Jewish or Muslim woman is faced with a puzzling dilemma that highlights the complex relationship between the civil and religious spheres: under the civil family law regime, she may divorce her husband without his consent, whereas under Jewish or Islamic law, she may involuntarily remain married to him. A Muslim woman cannot repudiate her husband (*talaq*). She can use either the *faskh* or *khul'* divorce, but these forms of divorce are either difficult to obtain or financially costly. A Jewish wife can never religiously divorce her husband. Moreover, her husband's decision to give her the *get* must be 'freely' made, which means that rabbinical courts will not intervene easily to force a man to grant such a divorce. Thus, some religious women, though divorced by civil courts, might remain religiously married to a husband who refuses to religiously divorce them. Through a series of interviews, I explored the distributive consequences of the secular/religious divide on differentially situated religious women in Canada. By understanding their *agency*, i.e. how different women use the law as 'it lives' out in the real world, I attempted to examine the ways in which Jewish and Muslim women navigate the interplay of legal systems and religious norms in various multidimensional contexts.

The insights of the 'left law and economics' approach I proposed were used to identify the background formal and informal legal rules, social norms and distributional practices that help produce asymmetric bargaining locations for Jewish and Muslim women, both between and among themselves. In this chapter I employed the economic language of cost/benefits to argue that religious parties bargain strategically upon divorce. The interviews I conducted with religious women strongly refute the market/family distinction by bringing these under-recognized market claims to the fore. As women, wives and mothers, participants have described their bargaining strategies in the religious *and* the secular domains as sometimes beneficial and sometimes detrimental to them, depending on various factors. In approaching the relational dynamics of religious subjects moving inside and outside the secular realm, I noticed that the participants' invocation of religious law was often strategic, serving distributional purposes. For instance, if the woman could get benefits from the religious sphere that she would not be able to secure under the secular legal system, she would follow this advantageous path. Such empirical knowledge helps undermine the idea that religious law is systematically used as a *punishing* force that makes women worse off economically or morally inferior. Indeed, in today's increasingly globalized world, religious families are walking into the courtroom and across the gender line in unanticipated and contradictory ways. Is there anything left once we dismantle law's secular impulse and religion's sacred aspiration? Is the family just another market consideration? Are religious claims really about God, ever?

Appendix: Questionnaire used for the interviews

Dimension 1 – Religious normative framework

What are your religious practices?

At the time of your wedding, what was your understanding of religious marriage and divorce?

(For a Jewish person: did you sign a *ketubah* at the time of your wedding, and if so, what was its content?)

(For a Jewish person: before or during your marriage, did you discuss the *get* and its unilateral nature with your husband?)

(For a Muslim person: did you sign a *nikah* (Islamic marriage contract) at the time of your wedding, and if so, what was its content?)

(For a Muslim person: before or during your marriage, did you or have you discussed the *talaq* and its unilateral nature with your husband?)

Dimension 2 – Secular normative framework

How was your married life, and for what reasons did you opt for a civil divorce?
How were the divorce procedures in the civil court?
What were the key elements discussed before the court and the arguments of both parties?
What people were involved in the civil law process and how would you describe their role?
Is your civil divorce recognized by the religious authorities of your community?

Dimension 3 – Personal, family and community normative framework

How would you describe your present situation?
During the divorce procedure, did you benefit from the approval of your family and your community?
Which events made strongest impression on you?
What were your expectations and to what extent have they been satisfied?
Are there any aspects of the divorce process that you would like to see changed, on the secular level as well as on the religious level?
Would you like to add anything to what was previously discussed? Would you like to clarify anything that was said earlier?

Notes

* I am grateful for funding received to support this project from the Québec Bar Foundation, the Foundation for Legal Research, Borden Ladner Gervais, the Law Foundation of Ontario and the Social Sciences and Humanities Research Council of Canada. I thank Pascal McDougall and Viviane Bartlett for their able research assistance. I also wish to acknowledge the generosity and spontaneity of the Jewish and Muslim women who kindly accepted to share their stories with us. This article is dedicated to them.

1 See in general Manji (2004). See also specific submissions by the Canadian Council of Muslim Women, 'Review of the Ontario *Arbitration Act* and Arbitration Processes' and the Muslim Canadian Congress, 'Review of Arbitration Process', on file with the author. For similar positions adopted by other individuals or NGOs, see Boyd (2004: 29–34).

2 See Gaudreault-DesBiens (2005: 23), Farrow (2006: 81), Shachar (2005), Korteweg (2008), Bakht (2006) and Emon (2009: 31–32).

3 See Stopler (2003: 27). In the specific context of Canada, see Rahnema (2006: 21) and Alia Hogben, 'The laws of the land must protect all of us, irrespective of gender or religion', *Toronto Star*, 1 June 2004. For a critique of civil law's pretence of 'protecting' minority religious women by setting aside religious law, see Fournier (2011).

4 See Razack (2007, 2008), Bakht (2007) and Abu-Lughod (2002).
5 I borrow this expression from my previous work on the adjudication of *mahr*. See Fournier (2010a). A translation of the article has appeared as Fournier (2010c).
6 It is important to acknowledge that this qualitative research cannot cover every Jewish and Muslim community. The women with whom I conducted interviews are not necessarily representative of all Jewish/Muslim communities in Canada. Therefore, this data must be treated with caution as a method to reflect the subjective and individual experiences of religious women who go through divorce.
7 Given the topic of this article and the religious laws governing Muslim and Jewish marriage, only heterosexual marriage is considered in this context.
8 See Appendix for the questionnaire used during the interviews. The format of the interviews was reviewed by the University of Ottawa's ethics committee, which ensured that safeguards were in place for the safety and well-being of the participants.
9 I selected the interview participants through many different channels. None of the women were approached directly; rather, a third party identified and contacted them on my behalf. I also benefitted from the assistance of community organizations and personal contacts in religious communities. Although signs were placed in Jewish and Muslim community centres and religious places soliciting for the participation of women, this method proved unsuccessful. Rabbis and *imams* were also approached. Few of them responded, and those who did made contact with women who later declined to participate.
10 I borrow specifically from the methodology of 'left law and economics' scholars such as Kennedy (1982, 1992), Olsen (1983) and Mnookin and Kornhauser (1979).
11 See, for instance, Van Praagh (1996, 1999a, 1999b), Campbell (2009, 2010), Sarat and Kearns (1993).
12 For scholarship addressing specifically the impact of religious identity on economic patterns, see Cogel and Minkler (2004). For general analyses of the impact of identity on economic behaviour, see Akerlof and Kranton (2002, 2005), Darity, Mason and Stewart (2006) and Fang and Loury (2005).
13 See Gilboa and Schmeidler (1997), Encarnación (1990), Chipman (1960), Hartman, Doane and Woo (1991) and Michael and Becker (1973).
14 For an introduction to law and economics literature, see Trebilcock (2007), Shavell (2004), Kaplow (1986) and Posner (2004).
15 Law and economics scholars have long been attached to the analysis of commercial law (Gomez 2006), international trade law (Trachtman 2008), criminal law (Garupa 2009), securities law (Duggan 2005) and constitutional law (Lee 2008).
16 Ayres and Gertner (1989: 87), Kaplow and Shavell (2004), Shavell (2006), Jolls (1997), Schwartz (2004).
17 Donohue (1989), Landes and Posner (1987).
18 Key articles on the topic include Cohen (1987), Trebilcock and Keshvani (1991), Trebilcock and Elliot (2001), Kaplow (1996). For recent work on law and economics in family law matters, see Dnes and Rowthorn (2010).
19 See Olsen (1983) and Halley and Rittich (2010).
20 The law and economics approach has been strongly criticized in the context of family relations. For instance, Nobel Prize for economics winner Gary Becker (1993) argued that sex differences justify the sexual division of labour observed in contemporary societies because such division is efficient. For an analysis of the tension between economic methodology and feminist thought, see Tsoukala (2007) and Kotiswaran (2011: 185ff).
21 It is worth noting, for instance, that Canadian courts specifically and convincingly used the law and economics approach to view unmarried cohabitation as generating claims in unjust enrichment. See the Supreme Court of Canada decision *Sorochan v. Sorochan* (1986) 2 S.C.R. 38.
22 See Abu-Odeh (2004).

23 *Mahr*, meaning 'reward' (*ajr*) or 'nuptial gift' (*sadaqa* or *faridah*), is the expression used in Islamic family law to describe the 'payment that the wife is entitled to receive from the husband in consideration of the marriage' (Esposito 1982: 23). See generally Fournier (2010b).

24 Nowadays, Hebrew *ketubot* are also available. However, this is still seen by American courts as a linguistic obstacle to the enforcement of the financial provisions of the *ketubah* (Reiss and Broyde 2005: 202). In Canada, despite judicial sympathy toward the enforceability of this type of agreement, the *ketubah* is still considered unenforceable before civil courts. See Fournier (2012).

25 I borrow this expression from Kandiyoti, who examines the coping strategies and lifestyle choices that women make under patriarchal constraints. She writes that 'these patriarchal bargains exert a powerful influence on the shaping of women's gendered subjectivity and determine the nature of gender ideology in different contexts [and that they] influence both the potential for and specific forms of women's active or passive resistance' (1988: 275).

26 Grounds to issue a decree of *faskh* include impotence on the part of the husband, insufficient material support and companionship ('the loneliness of the marriage bed'), non-fulfilment of the marriage contract, mental or physical abuse or a husband's lack of piety. See Abdal-Rahim (1996: 105), Tucker (1985: 54) and Esposito and DeLong-Bas (2001: 25).

27 *Halacha* is the entire corpus of Jewish law, which draws on the Torah, rabbinical laws and customs. See Jacobs and De Vries (2007: 251).

28 See Romney (1982: 17) and Anisah (2003: 41).

29 It can often be the case that women do not wish to divorce. For instance, Judith Tucker, in analysing peasant women in nineteenth-century Egypt, affirms that 'many women who wanted a divorce preferred that their husbands repudiate them [because of] the material advantages of *talaq*' (1985: 55).

30 The forms of disobedience used by Muslim women to *push* men in the direction of repudiation are manifold. In her study, Judith Tucker noticed the following: 'Having enlisted the cooperation of the local shaykh al-Bald, one woman managed to bully her husband into pronouncing a divorce. Another used blackmail: she threatened to take her husband to court and claim that he had stolen her jewelry unless he divorced her; so she 'frightened him' and he indeed complied with a repudiation' (1985: 55).

31 The situation may be worse in Israel, where civil divorce is non-existent (Halperin-Kaddari, 2000–2001: 350). For a critical appraisal of the Israeli context, see Fournier, McDougall and Lichtsztral (2012).

32 (2007) 3 S.C.R. 607.

33 *Bruker v. Marcovitz*, ibid., at para. 8.

34 It is regarded as against the spirit of Jewish law for a wife to be able to dismiss her husband by granting him the *Get* (Mielziner 1987: 117).

35 R.S.C. 1985, c. 3 (2nd Supp.).

36 Divorce Act, ibid., s. 21.1. For a comparative analysis of this legal mechanism, see Fournier (2012).

37 In cases of mutual consent where the wife waives the deferred portion of *mahr*, divorce can be finalized outside the court system. However, in most cases, the parties will disagree as to the amount and file their respective claims with the *qadi*.

38 Civil courts will bow out of enforcing the *Beth Din*'s order for lack of jurisdiction. As Greenberg-Kobrin bluntly puts it, 'Today the Beth Din's power exists only to the extent that it is recognized' (1999: 368).

39 Canadian civil divorce law presents itself as a channel to ensure the operation of free bargaining on the part of equal rational individuals. This was at the core of the clean break approach to post-divorce alimony: see McLachlin (1990: 136) and Leckey (2008: 105).

40 Translated from French.
41 Translated from French.

Bibliography

Abdal-Rahim, A.R. (1996) 'The family and gender laws in Egypt during the Ottoman Period', in A.E.A. Sonbol (ed.), *Women, the Family, and Divorce Laws in Islamic History*, Syracuse, NY: Syracuse University Press.

Abu-Lughod, L. (2002) 'Do Muslim women really need saving? Anthropological reflections on cultural relativism and its others', *American Anthropologist*, 104(3): 783–90.

Abu-Odeh, L. (2004) 'Modernizing Muslim family law: the case of Egypt', *Vanderbilt Journal Transnational Law*, 37(4): 1043–146.

Akerlof, G.A. and Kranton, R. (2002) 'Identity and schooling: some lessons for the economics of education', *Journal of Economic Literature*, 40(4): 1167–201.

——(2005) 'Identity and the economics of organizations', *The Journal of Economic Perspectives*, 19(1): 9–32.

Anisah, H. (2003) 'Divorce', in N. Noriani and N. Badlishah (eds), *Islamic Family Law and Justice for Muslim Women*, Kuala Lumpur: Sisters in Islam.

Ayres, I. and Gertner, R. (1989) 'Filling gaps in incomplete contracts: an economic theory of default rule', *Yale Law Journal*, 99(1): 87–130.

Bakht, N. (2006) 'Were Muslim barbarians really knocking on the gates of Ontario? The religious arbitration controversy – another perspective', *Ottawa Law Review*, 40th anniversary issue: 67–82.

——(2007) 'Religious arbitration in Canada: protecting women by protecting them from religion', *Canadian Journal of Women and the Law*, 19(1): 119–44.

Becker, G.S. (1993). *A Treatise on the Family*, Cambridge, MA: Harvard University Press.

Blecher-Prigat, A. and Shmueli, B. (2009) 'The interplay between tort law and religious family law: the Israeli case', *Arizona Journal of International and Comparative Law*, 26(2): 279–302.

Boyd, M. (2004) *Dispute Resolution in Family Law: Protecting Choice, Promoting Inclusion*, Toronto: Government of Ontario. Available online at www.attorneygeneral.jus.gov.on.ca/english/about/pubs/boyd (accessed on 9 August 2011).

Campbell, A. (2009) 'Bountiful voices', *Osgoode Hall Law Journal*, 47(2): 183–234.

——(2010) 'Bountiful's plural marriages', *International Journal of Law in Context*, 6(4): 343–61.

Carmit Yefet, K. (2009) 'Unchaining the *Agunot*: enlisting the Israeli constitution in the service of women's marital freedom', *Yale Journal of Law and Feminism*, 20(2): 441–504.

Chipman, J.S. (1960) 'The Foundations of utility', *Econometrica*, 28(2): 193–224.

Cobin, D.M. (1986) 'Jewish divorce and the recalcitrant husband. Refusal to give a "get" as intentional infliction of emotional distress', *Journal of Law and Religion*, 4(2): 405–30.

Cogel, M.M. and Minkler, L. (2004) 'Religious identity and consumption', *Review of Social Economy*, 62(3): 339–50.

Cohen, L. (1987) 'Marriage, divorce, and quasi rents; or, "I gave him the best years of my life"', *The Journal of Legal Studies*, 16(2): 267–304.

Cohn, M. (2004) 'Women, religious law and religious courts in Israel. The Jewish case', *Retfaerd, Scandinavian Journal of Social Sciences*, 27: 57–76.

Coulson, N.J. (1964) *A History of Islamic Law*, Edinburgh: Edinburgh University Press.

Darity, W.A. Jr., Mason, P.L. and Stewart, J.B. (2006) 'The economics of identity: The origin and persistence of racial identity norms', *Journal of Economic Behavior and Organization*, 60(3): 283–305.

Dnes, A.W. and Rowthorn, R. (2010) *The Law and Economics of Marriage and Divorce*, Cambridge: Cambridge University Press.

Donohue, J. (1989) 'The law & economics of tort law: the profound revolution', *Harvard Law Review*, 102(5): 1047–73.

Duggan, A. (2005) 'Constructive trusts from a law and economics perspective', *University of Toronto Law Journal*, 55(2): 217–52.

El Alami, D.S. and Hinchcliffe, D. (1996) *Islamic Marriage and Divorce Laws of the Arab World*, London: Kluwer Law International.

Emon, A. (2009) 'Islamic law and the Canadian mosaic: politics, jurisprudence, and multicultural accommodation', *The Canadian Bar Review*, 87(2): 391–425.

Encarnación, J. Jr. (1990) 'Consumer choice of qualities', *Economica*, 57(225): 63–72.

Epstein, L.M. (2005) *The Jewish Marriage Contract: a study of the status of the woman in Jewish law*, Clark, NJ: Lawbook Exchange.

Esposito, J.L. (1982) *Women in Muslim Family Law*, Syracuse, NY: Syracuse University Press.

Esposito, J.L. and Delong-Bas, N. (2001) *Women in Muslim Family Law*, Syracuse, NY: Syracuse University Press.

Estin, A.L. (2009) 'Unofficial family law', *Iowa Law Review*, 94(2): 449–80.

Fang, H. and Loury, G.C. (2005) 'Toward an economic theory of dysfunctional identity', in C.B. Barrett (ed.), *The Social Economics of Poverty*, New York: Routledge.

Farrow, T.C.W. (2006) 'Re-framing the sharia arbitration debate', *Constitutional Forum*, 15(2): 79–86.

Fishbayn, L. (2008) 'Gender, multiculturalism and dialogue: the case of Jewish divorce', *Canadian Journal of Law and Jurisprudence*, 21(1): 71–96.

Fournier, P. (2010a) 'Flirting with God in Western secular courts: *Mahr* in the West', *The International Journal of Law, Policy and the Family*, 24(1): 1–28.

——(2010b) *Muslim Marriage in Western Courts: lost in transplantation*, Farnham: Ashgate.

——(2010c) 'Courtiser Dieu devant les tribunaux occidentaux', *Canadian Journal of Law and Society/Revue canadienne droit et société*, 25(2): 167–93.

——(2011) 'Borders and crossroads: comparative perspectives on minorities and conflicts of laws', *Emory International Law Review*, 25(2): 987–1006.

——(2012) '*Halacha* the "Jewish State" and the Canadian *agunah*: comparative law at the intersection of religious and secular orders', *Journal of Legal Pluralism*, 65: 165–204.

Fournier, P., McDougall, P. and Lichtsztral, M. (2012) 'Secular rights and religious wrongs? Family law, religion and women in Israel', *William and Mary Journal of Women and the Law*, 18(2): 333–62.

Fyzee, A.A.A. (1974) *Outlines of Muhammadan Law*, 4th edn, Delhi: Oxford University Press.

Garupa, N. (2009) *Criminal Law and Economics*, Northampton, MA: Edward Elgar Publishers.

Gaudreault-Desbiens, J.-F. (2005) 'The limits of private justice? The problems of the state recognition of arbitral awards in family and personal status disputes in Ontario', *World Arbitration and Mediation Report*, 16(1): 18–31.

Gilboa, I. and Schmeidler, D. (1997) 'Cumulative utility consumer theory', *International Economic Review*, 38(4): 737–61.

Gomez, F. (2006) 'The unfair commercial practices directive: a law and economics perspective', *European Review of Contract Law*, 2(1): 4–34.

Greengerg-Kobrin, M. (1999) 'Civil enforceability of religious prenuptial agreements', *Columbia Journal of Law and Social Problems*, 32(4): 359–99.

Halley, J. (2011) 'What is family law: a genealogy. Part I', *Yale Journal of Law & Humanities*, 23(1): 1–109.

Halley, J. and Rittich, K. (2010) 'Critical directions in comparative family law: genealogies and contemporary studies of family law exceptionalism', *The American Journal of Comparative Law*, 58(4): 753–76.

Halperin-Kaddari, R. (2000–2001) 'Women, religion and multiculturalism in Israel', *UCLA Journal of International Law and Foreign Affairs*, 5(2): 367–402.

Hartman, R.S., Doane, M.J. and Woo, C.-K. (1991) 'Consumer rationality and the status quo', *The Quarterly Journal of Economics*, 106(1): 141–62.

Hogben, A. (2004) 'The laws of the land must protect all of us, irrespective of gender or religion', *Toronto Star*, 1 June, p. A19.

Hoodfar, H. (1996) 'Circumventing legal limitation: *mahr* and marriage negotiation in Egyptian low-income communities', in H. Hoodfar (ed.), *Shifting Boundaries in Marriage and Divorce in Muslim Communities*, Montpellier: Women Living Under Muslim Laws.

Haut, I.H. (1983) *Divorce in Jewish Law and Life*, New York: Sepher-Hermon Press.

Jacobs, L. and De Vries, B. (2007) 'Halakhah', in M. Berenbaum and F. Skolnik (eds), *Encyclopaedia Judaica*, 2nd edn, Detroit: Macmillan.

Jolls, C. (1997) 'Contracts as bilateral commitments: a new perspective on contract modification', *Journal of Legal Studies*, 26(1): 203–38.

Kandiyoti, D. (1988) 'Bargaining with patriarchy', *Gender and Society*, 2(3): 274–90.

Kaplow, L. (1986) 'An economic analysis of legal transitions', *Harvard Law Review*, 99(3): 509–617.

——(1996) 'Optimal distribution and the family', *Scandinavian Journal of Economics*, 98(1): 75–92.

Kaplow, L. and Shavell, S.M. (2004) *Contracting*, New York: Foundation Press.

Kennedy, D. (1982) 'Distributive and paternalist motives in contract and tort law, with special reference to compulsory terms and unequal bargaining power', *Maryland Law Review*, 41(4): 563–658.

——(1992) 'Sexual abuse, sexy dressing, and the eroticization of domination', *New England Law Review*, 26(4): 1309–94.

Korteweg, A.C. (2008) 'The sharia debate in Ontario: gender, Islam and representation of Muslim women's agency', *Gender and Society*, 22(4): 434–54.

Kotiswaran, P. (2011) *Dangerous Sex, Invisible Labor: sex work and the law in India*. Princeton, NJ: Princeton University Press.

Landes, W.M. and Posner, R. (1987) *The Economic Structure of Tort Law*, Cambridge, MA: Harvard University Press.

Leckey, R. (2008) 'What is left of Pelech?', in J. Cameron (ed.), *Reflections on the Legacy of Justice Bertha Wilson*, Markham: LexisNexis Canada.

Lee, I.B. (2008) 'Can economics justify the constitutional guarantee of freedom of expression?', *Canadian Journal of Law and Jurisprudence*, 21(2): 355–98.

Macfarlane, J. (2012) 'Practicing an "Islamic imagination": Islamic divorce in North America', in A. Korteweg and J. Selby (eds), *Debating Sharia: Islam, gender politics and family law arbitration*, Toronto: University of Toronto Press.

Maghniyyah, M.J. (1995) *The Five Schools of Islamic Law*, Qum: Anssariyan.

Manji, I. (2004) *The Trouble with Islam Today: a Muslim's call for reform in her faith*, New York: St. Martin's Press.

McLachlin, B. (1990) 'Spousal support: is it fair to apply new-style rules to old-style marriages?' *Canadian Journal of Family Law*, 9: 131–42.

Mielziner, M. (1987) *The Jewish Law of Marriage and Divorce and its Relation to the Law of the State*, Littletown, CO: Fred B. Rothman.

Michael, R.T. and Becker, G.S. (1973) 'On the new theory of consumer behavior', *The Swedish Journal of Economics*, 75(4): 378–96.

Mnookin, R.H. and Kornhauser, L. (1979) 'Bargaining in the shadow of the law: the case of divorce', *Yale Law Journal*, 88(5), 950–97.

Nasir, J.J. (2002) *The Islamic Law of Personal Status*, New York: Kluwer Law International.

Nichols, J.A. (2007), 'Multi-tiered marriage: ideas and influences from New York and Louisiana to the international community', *Vanderbilt Journal of Transnational Law*, 40(1): 135–96.

Olsen, F. (1983) 'The family and the market: a study of ideology and legal reform' *Harvard Law Review*, 96(7): 1497–578.

Pollak, R.A. (2003) 'Gary Becker's contributions to family and household economics' *Review of Economics of the Household*, 1(1–2): 111–41.

Posner, R. (2004) 'Law and economics in common-law, civil-law, and developing nations', *Ratio Juris*, 17(1): 66–79.

Rahnema, S. (2006) The perils of faith-based multiculturalism: the case of shari'a in Canada', *Canadian Dimension*, 40(1): 21–23.

Razack, S.H. (2007) 'The sharia law debate in Ontario: the modernity/postmodernity distinction in legal efforts to protect women from culture', *Feminist Legal Studies*, 15(1): 3–32.

——(2008) *Casting Out: the eviction of Muslims from western law and politics*, Toronto: Toronto University Press.

Reiss, J. and Broyde, M.J. (2005) Prenuptial agreements in Talmudic, medieval, and modern Jewish thought', in M.J. Broyde and M. Ausubel (eds), *Marriage, Sex, and Family*, Oxford: Rowman & Littlefield Publishers.

Romney, J. (1982) 'The status of women in Jewish and Islamic marriage and divorce law', *Harvard Women's Law Journal*, 5: 1–34.

Sarat, A. and Kearns, T.R. (1993) *Law in Everyday Life*, Ann Arbor, MI: University of Michigan Press.

Schacht, J. (1982), *An Introduction to Islamic Law*, Oxford: Clarendon Press.

Schwartz, A. (2004) 'The law and economics approach to contract theory', in D.A. Wittman (ed.), *Economic Analysis of the Law: selected readings,* Boston, MA: Blackwell Publishing.

Shachar, A. (2005) 'Religion, state and the problem of gender: new modes of citizenship and governance in diverse societies', *McGill Law Journal*, 50(1): 49–88.

——(2008) 'Privatizing diversity: a cautionary tale from religious arbitration in family law', *Theoretical Inquiries in Law*, 9(2): 573–608.

Shavell, S.M. (2004) *Foundations of Economic Analysis of Law*, Belknap, MA: Harvard University Press.

——(2006) 'Specific performance versus damages for breach of contract: an economic analysis', *Texas Law Review*, 84(4): 831–76.

Stopler, G. (2003) 'Countenancing the oppression of women: how liberals tolerate religious and cultural practices that discriminate against women', *Columbia Journal of Gender and Law*, 12(1): 154–221.

Syrtash, J. (1992) *Religion and Culture in Canadian Family Law*, Toronto: Butterworths.

Trachtman, J.P. (2008) *The Economic Structure of International Law*, Cambridge, MA: Harvard University Press.

Trebilcock, M.J. (2007) 'The lessons and limits of law and economics', in P. Noreau (ed.), *In the Eye of the Beholder*, Montreal: Thémis.

Trebilcock, M.J. and Elliot, S. (2001) 'The scope and limits of legal paternalism: altruism and coercion in family financial arrangements', in P. Benson (ed.), *The Theory of Contract Law*, New York: Cambridge University Press.

Trebilcock, M.J. and Keshvani, R. (1991) 'The role of private ordering in family law: a law and economics perspective', *The University of Toronto Law Journal*, 41(4): 533–90.

Tsoukala, P. (2007) 'Gary Becker, legal feminism, and the costs of moralizing care', *Columbia Journal of Gender and Law*, 16(2): 357–429.

Tucker, J.E. (1985) *Women in Nineteenth-Century Egypt*, Cambridge: Cambridge University Press.

Van Praagh, S. (1996) 'The Chutzpah of chasidism', *Canadian Journal of Law and Society*, 11(2): 193–216.

——(1999a) 'Faith, belonging, and the protection of "our" children', *Windsor Yearbook of Access of Justice*, 17: 154–203.

——(1999b) The education of religious children: families, communities and constitutions, *Buffalo Law Review*, 47 (3): 1343–96.

Wani, A.M. (1995) *The Islamic Law on Maintenance of Women, Children, Parents and Other Relatives: classical perspectives and modern legislations from India and Muslim countries*, New Delhi: Qazi Publishers.

4 Judicial encounters with Islamic and Middle Eastern family law in Switzerland from a private international law perspective – marriage and divorce

Andrea Büchler and Amira Latif

Introduction

Around 50 per cent of all marriages and divorces in Switzerland involve at least one foreign national.[1] Because of the principle of domicile that obtains in Switzerland, they are generally subject to Swiss procedural and substantive law. However, when Swiss state authorities are asked to assess the domestic effects of changes in civil status undertaken abroad, they frequently need to take foreign marriage and divorce statutes into account. Whenever there is a foreign connection (*Auslandsbezug*), private international law rules specify which law is to be applied and whether a foreign decision or a foreign status document respectively, is to be recognised.

Family law has always been strongly intertwined with religio-cultural traditions. Affecting most personal spheres of the individual citizen, it has been subjected to constant renegotiation by changing moral values, economic needs and political demands. From a comparative point of view, Islamic-influenced family law codes and the Swiss Civil Code have shown converging and diverging tendencies as well as parallel developments in the wake of law reforms on both sides during recent decades.

The private international law principle of equality of all legal orders requires the acceptance of foreign provisions and the results of their application, as long as the requirements set by international law are fulfilled. Inter alia, the interests of *ordre public*, which include the basic principles and values of the national legal order, deserve uncompromising protection.

This chapter examines, from a perspective of private international law, how Swiss judicial and administrative authorities deal with Islamic and Middle Eastern marriage and divorce law.

Switzerland's Federal Act on Private International Law (PILA)

A historical perspective

Switzerland's Federal Act on Private International Law (PILA) entered into force in 1987. The PILA is an overall codification, its 13 chapters reflecting the whole body of Swiss private law and, to a great extent, is structured similarly to Swiss private law.

Prior to the enactment of the PILA, in family, inheritance and personal status law, the Federal Act on the Private Law Conditions of Domiciliaries and Sojouners of 1891 was applied in addition to the Swiss-ratified international treaties. This Act was originally drafted to regulate conflict-of-laws issues involving different Swiss cantons. In 1912 the Swiss Civil Code (CC) transformed the Act of 1891 to provide rules on conflicts of laws at an international level (Message of the Swiss Federal Council 1983: 266). Nevertheless, the 1891 Act's regulations remained incomplete, not least because of changing social values throughout the twentieth century. Therefore, the Swiss Federal Supreme Court's jurisdiction (*Rechtsprechung*) had pivotal importance (Message of the Swiss Federal Council 1983: 267; Schnyder and Liatowitsch 2011: 18). It set the grounds for the shift from the principle of nationality to the principle of domicile for determining applicable law in various family law issues (Courvoisier 2007: 302–03). On the whole, the PILA introduced a very modern private international law codification in Switzerland, particularly in respect to its connection with the state of domicile, which has for a long time been exceptional compared with other European legal orders.

Applicable law

The PILA is committed to identifying the legal order that is most closely connected to each case in order to determine the applicable law. It principally considers the individual's domicile as the most relevant indicator to locate the facts of a case within a particular context. A person has his or her domicile in the country in which he or she intends to live permanently, according to Article 20, para. 1 (a), PILA.[2] In compliance with the Swiss Federal Supreme Court's case law, the person's intention is manifested by where they have created their centre of vital life interests. In contrast to what is suggested by the wording of the Article, these interests must be reflected in facts that can be seen from an objective perspective.[3] Thus, it must be obvious to a third party where an individual is most anchored in terms of family and professional relationships (Keller and Kren Kostkiewicz 2004: 306). There is no minimum period of time in which one's centre of life must be established, despite what 'permanently' may suggest. Instead, it is the intensity of relations between a person and a particular place or country that matters (Bucher 2004: 22).

In the absence of a domicile, the individual's habitual residence serves as a connecting factor (Article 20, para. 2, PILA).[4] Article 20, para. 1(b), PILA provides that a natural person's ordinary residence is in the country where he or she has been living for some time, even if from the outside the person only intended to stay for a limited period of time. The emphasis is on the physical presence. In legal practice however, the term habitual residence has been interpreted, as in case of the domicile, as the centre of life (Bucher 2004: 24; Keller and Kren Kostkiewicz 2004: 311). Such a interpretation supports rejecting minimal physical presence as the deciding factor and focuses on the relational intensity of the individual's presence instead (Bucher 2004: 24).

The principle of domicile is best suited to take into account the specific social and economic conditions of the parties (Schnyder and Liatowitsch 2011: 19). It furthermore lays the foundation for equal treatment of foreign and Swiss nationals before the law (ibid.). This latter aspect is of concern inasmuch as Switzerland has stuck to the principle of *ius sanguinis.*[5] The application of the law of national origin may not meet the demands of such residents who are born in Switzerland, and even if it does, it reveals tendencies of social fragmentation threatening the coherence of society. The principle of domicile, however, is a means to foster the integration of immigrants to Switzerland.[6]

Under specific circumstances, deviations from the regular rules are permissible at different stages of identifying applicable law. The so-called exceptional clause provides that if it is obvious in view of all the circumstances that the case has only a remote connection to the law designated by the PILA, and a much closer connection to a different law, the latter shall be applied (Article 15, para. 1, PILA). Although it may be considered as the most all-encompassing exceptional clause when compared to the legal orders of other European countries, it has not jeopardised legal certainty. This is not at all a result of its restrictive wording and the equally restrictive application by the Federal Supreme Court. The exceptional clause aims to prevent connections that would be in contradiction with conflict-of-laws rules, but it must not be applied for the sake of the better law or to provide justice for individual cases (Mächler-Erne and Wolf-Mettier 2004: 127).

Another mechanism to exert corrective influence on the application of foreign law is located towards the end of the procedure when identifying applicable law. It may be considered a final quality control (Schnyder and Liatowitsch 2011: 94). Article 17, PILA, states that provisions of a foreign law are not to be applied if the outcome would be incompatible with Swiss *ordre public*. While the PILA does not limit the application of foreign law that deviates from mandatory Swiss law, it does not tolerate the application of foreign law that violates the basic values of society and that contradicts the fundaments of the Swiss legal order (Vischer 2004: 256). As these principles are subject to perpetual renegotiation against the backdrop of changing social conditions and political demands, the notion *ordre public* is open to change (Bucher 2004: 18; Schnyder and Liatowitsch 2011: 92).

Article 17, PILA, must be applied cautiously in any event, but especially when the facts' or the parties' links with Switzerland (*Binnenbeziehung*) are loose (Vischer 2004: 258).[7] Conversely, the closer the ties with the domestic legal and cultural values, the more important become *ordre public* considerations and the corrections of results stemming from the application of foreign law appear more justified (Schnyder and Liatowitsch 2011: 94–95).

Cases involving Iranian citizens require special consideration because of a bilateral agreement between Switzerland and Iran, which provides in Article 8, para. 3 that nationals of each member state shall be subjected to the legislation of their native country in matters of family law (*Convention d'établissement entre la Confédération suisse et l'Empire de Perse du 25 avril 1934*). As an international treaty, the agreement takes precedence over the PILA (Article 1, para. 2, PILA). Courts are therefore required to apply Iranian family law to nationals of Iran who are domiciled in Switzerland. However, certain general provisions of the PILA, such as the *ordre public* reservation of Article 17, remain applicable. Because of this agreement, a significant number of family law cases brought to Swiss courts in relation to the application of foreign law are connected with Iran. Apart from that, Swiss courts' and administrative authorities' main preoccupation has been with the recognition of foreign decisions and civil status documents.

Recognition of foreign decisions

Recognition of foreign decisions implies that sovereign decisions of foreign countries are given effects beyond their borders. When implementing the PILA, the Swiss Federal Council reasoned that valid legal decisions taken abroad create social facts (Message of the Swiss Federal Council 1983: 327). Their non-recognition would be in conflict with these social realities and lead to undesirable legal relationships and uncertainties. In addition, it is a matter of fairness to respect citizens' legal positions obtained by a lawful decision abroad (Volken 2004a: 357). Furthermore, giving credit to such decisions may encourage the foreign country to grant reciprocal rights in reverse cases.[8] For these reasons, valid foreign legal decisions should in principle be recognised. The foreign decision may be issued by either judicial or administrative authorities, irrespective of its formal designation as a judgment, decision or resolution (Berti and Däppen 2007: 218). Particularly in personal status and family law, questions of recognition usually involve foreign documents regarding civil status, rather than foreign decisions in the strict sense. The procedure to obtain an entry in the Swiss civil registry is specified in Article 32, PILA, which at para. 1 states that foreign civil status documents are recorded by order of the cantonal supervisory authority. This authority is responsible for assessing whether the conditions for recognition according to the PILA are fulfilled. Article 32, para. 2, PILA, explicitly states that the conditions of Articles 25–27, PILA, need to be met. Recognition of a foreign civil status document is frequently a preliminary question in proceedings dealing principally with another question. For example, when a court has to decide about the effects of divorce, the existence of a valid marriage must be assessed as a preliminary question. In this case, the authority, which is in charge of the divorce case, is competent to decide on recognition itself, as Article 29, para. 3, PILA, provides.

Article 25, PILA, specifies three prerequisites that must all be fulfilled for recognition. According to Article 25(a), PILA, the first prerequisite concerns jurisdiction (*Zuständigkeit*) of the foreign authority. It is Swiss law that decides on the criteria that need to be met for jurisdiction, regardless of whether the concerned foreign authority considers itself competent or not. The criteria are set in article 26, PILA. For family law issues, Article 26 (a), PILA, is most relevant, giving the foreign authorities jurisdiction if provided for by a provision of the PILA. If such a provision does not exist, foreign authorities have jurisdiction if the defendant was domiciled in the country where the judgment was given. The recognition of foreign jurisdiction by domestic law is called indirect jurisdiction, whereas direct jurisdiction describes the conditions under which Swiss authorities consider themselves competent to decide upon an international civil law dispute (Berti and Däppen 2007: 222; Volken 2004a: 371). There is some interrelation between direct and indirect jurisdiction because generally Swiss jurisdiction is claimed under the same prerequisites as are granted to foreign authorities by the PILA, based on the general idea that the authority with the closest or at least the most significant link to the case should have jurisdiction (Volken 2004a: 365). However, particularly in family law, direct and indirect jurisdiction often do not coincide. For provisions dealing with substantive effects of family relations, there is an overlap in favour of Switzerland's jurisdiction at the expense of recognition of foreign jurisdiction. The Swiss legislator thereby aims to grant protection to both Swiss expatriates and the Swiss residential population (Message of the Swiss Federal Council 1983: 328). In contrast, particularly in relation to issues of personal status law, recognition of foreign jurisdiction exceeds the PILA's claim for Swiss jurisdiction to prevent limping legal relationships *in favor recognitionis* and to foster international accord in jurisdiction (*Rechtsprechung*) (Volken 2004a: 373). In light of this lack in congruence between direct and indirect jurisdiction, the Swiss PILA necessarily contains complex rules.

The second prerequisite for recognition requires that the foreigh decision have a certain degree of finality: it is recognised if there are no further legal remedies available to challenge the decision or if the decision is final according to Article 25 (b), PILA. The term 'legal remedies' is defined by Swiss law, whereas the question of whether there is no further legal remedy is subject to the law of the deciding state (Berti and Däppen 2007: 222; Volken 2004a: 360).

Article 25 (c), PILA, refers to the *ordre public* clause in Article 27, PILA, as a third prerequisite for recognition. Article 27, para. 1, PILA, provides the so-called substantive *ordre public* reservation, stating that a decision rendered abroad is not recognised in Switzerland if such recognition is clearly incompatible with Swiss *ordre public*. Whereas the *ordre public* clause of Article 17, PILA, exerts influence on upcoming decisions, Article 27, PILA, is confronted with firm results from applying law in a foreign country and with corresponding social facts (Volken 2004a: 388). These facts remain legally effective abroad, i.e. in third-party countries or at least in the deciding country, independent from their assessment by Swiss authorities (Volken 2004a: 393). Thus, limping legal relationships may be created. To prevent such problems, the Swiss legislator called for a very restrictive use of this exception clause (Message of the Swiss Federal Council 1983: 329). It shall only be applied in case of complete incompatibility with the domestic sense of justice. With this in mind, the difference in wording between Articles 17 and 27, PILA, should be noted: whereas Article 17, PILA, requires the outcome of application of the foreign legal provisions to be incompatible with Swiss *ordre public*, Article 27, PILA states non-recognition of a foreign jurisdiction decision in cases of clear incompatibility.[9] Some uncertainties remain regarding where to draw the line between affirmed incompatibility and the additional requirement of affirmed clear incompatibility (Berti and Däppen 2007: 232). Finally, it must be noted that Article 27, PILA, does not bear the same legal consequences as Article 17, PILA. When applying Article 27, PILA, the competent Swiss authority cannot substitute its own decision for that of another country, whereas in case of Article 17, PILA, it is possible to make a decision with recourse to an alternative connecting factor (Berti and Däppen 2007: 237; Volken 2004a: 392–93).

The foreign legal provisions and their correct application must not be considered when assessing incompatibility with Swiss *ordre public*. Instead, as pointed out above, under Article 17, PILA, the focus must be entirely on the outcome, i.e. on the compatibility with the Swiss legal order of the effects derived from the recognition. In this respect, Article 27, para. 3, PILA, states that except as provided therein, the foreign decision may not be reviewed its the merits.[10] According to the prevailing opinion, the intensity of domestic connections needs equally to be taken into account.[11] At any rate, it is remarkable that the *ordre public* reservation is much more often pronounced in personal and family law matters, compared for example to the international law of obligations which is also part of the PILA (Volken 2004a: 389). Article 27, para. 2, PILA, deals with the so-called procedural *ordre public*. It states five procedural principles the violation of which can be brought to court. In contrast to Article 27, para. 1, PILA, the procedural *ordre public* is not observed *ex officio*, but only at the request of the concerned party.

Finally, specific provisions in the family law part of the PILA also contain *ordre public* considerations. Current amendments of legislation reveal a trend towards further implementation of unilateral conflict of law norms, whereby the *ordre public* rationale is used as a justification for their implementation. Simultaneously, Swiss courts have adopted an increasingly liberal stance towards the recognition of foreign decisions.

Marriage

Jurisdiction and applicable law on marriages celebrated in Switzerland

Recent legal reforms

Both the substantive as well as the formal conditions for marriage in Switzerland are solely subject to the provisions of Swiss matrimonial law (Article 44, PILA), irrespective of the spouses' nationality. In cases involving foreign nationals, Swiss authorities, in general, only have jurisdiction if at least one of the spouses is domiciled in Switzerland.[12] Thus, it is the law of the Swiss domicile which governs marriage in Switzerland (*lex fori in foro proprio*).

Previously, marriages between foreign nationals could be concluded under the law of the country of citizenship if the substantive conditions for marriage under Swiss law, notably regarding marriage age, had not been fulfilled. The exception clause, as provided by the former version of Article 44, para. 2, Swiss CC, allowed taking into account the *favor matrimonii*. For marriages under Swiss law (Article 94, Swiss CC), it is compulsory, without any exceptions, that parties to a marriage must have attained their majority, which was reduced from 20 to 18 years in 1996. Having said that, civil registration offices accepted the minority of either one or both foreign nationals provided that, first, each spouse was at least 16 years old, in conformity with the age of sexual consent in accordance with Article 187, Swiss Criminal Code, and that, second, the conditions of marriage under a foreign law were fulfilled. However, in the wake of recent legal reforms adopted by the Swiss Parliament in June 2012, the aforementioned exception clause was deleted. By way of justifying the amendment, the Federal Council referred to an altered *ordre public* ratio that no longer accepts marriages between foreigners below the age of 18 (Message of the Swiss Federal Council 2011: 2186, 2202, 2208).

Potential problems and consequences

The reference to domestic law as the unique law applicable to marriages in Switzerland was implemented within the framework of the Federal Act on Measures against Forced Marriages, which was adopted by the Swiss Parliament on 15 June 2012. The Act entered into force on 1 July 2013.[13] Several parliamentary motions that asked the Swiss Federal Council to take action against forced marriages in Switzerland preceded these legal reforms.

Forced marriages have attracted increasing attention in public debate all over Europe in recent years. The public discourse has undoubtedly been fuelled by particular cases where there was physical violence and coercion within families, and which were dragged into the media spotlight. Furthermore, studies reported on numerous cases of forced marriage in Switzerland (Büchler 2007: 731–40). For a variety of reasons, however, it has been impossible to get reliable data about the quantitative proliferation of such cases. The Swiss Federal Council pointed out in a report in 2007 that it was mainly immigrants to Switzerland who entered into forced marriages. It maintained however that this phenomenon cannot be linked to any particular religion or culture, but rather with patriarchal values (Report of the Swiss Federal Council 2007: 6, 7). Contrary to this fact, public debate often manifests generalisations and inappropriate assumptions; forced marriages are wrongly claimed to be rooted in Islam. In addition, they are lumped together with arranged marriages (Büchler 2011a: 42–43). Indeed, some of the parliamentary motions called for measures against forced and arranged marriages alike. In this regard, the Swiss Federal Council correctly argued that arranged marriages are not necessarily accompanied by coercion (Message of the Swiss Federal Council 2011: 2192). Instead, as long as the spouses' free will is guaranteed, the practice of involving family members in the organisation of a marriage is unproblematic. Thus, the delicate question has remained: where to draw the boundaries between exertion of influence or even psychological manipulation on the one hand and proper coercion on the other (Message of the Swiss Federal Council 2011: 2215–16). This difficulty certainly supports the recourse to distinct objective criteria, such as maintaining a strict marriage age limit by annulment of the exception clause for marriages between foreigners. The Federal Act against Forced Marriages introduces two additional reasons for the unlimited invalidity of marriage. First, Article 105(5), Swiss CC, states that a marriage should be annulled if a spouse has not contracted the marriage at his or her own free will. Second, Article 105(6) provides that a marriage is annulled if one of the spouses is a minor, unless continuation of the marriage corresponds with the minor spouse's prevailing interests.[14]

Recognition of marriages concluded abroad

General remarks

Article 45, para. 1, PILA reflects Switzerland's longstanding tradition of taking a most favourable position towards the recognition of foreign marriages by simply stating that a marriage validly concluded abroad is recognised in Switzerland. This provision is committed to protecting a status acquired abroad and to preventing limping legal relationships, and is based on the conviction that non-recognition increases rather than lessens problems, particularly for the more vulnerable parties (Courvoisier 2007: 326). Article 45, PILA, does not particularly deal with foreign decisions, but refers to foreign civil status documents issued extra-judicially by foreign state authorities.[15] Recognition is preceded by a threefold process that starts by asking whether a marriage abroad has been concluded, then proceeding to evaluate its validity and ending by assessing if recognition would violate Swiss *ordre public* according to Article 27, PILA. The answer to the first question is fairly obvious in general, apart from cases of so-called consular marriages in Switzerland

(Bucher 2004: 57). As far as indirect jurisdiction is concerned, legal experts predominantly argue in favour of recognition of a marriage if its validity is secured either according to the law of the place where the marriage was celebrated (*Eheschliessungsort*) or, subsidiarily, to the law of the domicile or the home country of either of the spouses (Siehr 2002: 23). Article 45, para. 2, PILA, provides an additional *ordre public* clause, which should, like the general clause, be applied restrictively.[16] It selectively tightens requirements for the recognition of marriage if spouses have close links with Switzerland (Courvoisier 2007: 332). It has been claimed that this provision overshoots the mark because it privileges Swiss expatriates over foreign spouses who are domiciled in Switzerland. Whereas the former are unconditionally allowed to marry in Switzerland under Swiss law, the latter are subject to Article 45, para. 2, PILA, when they would like to marry in their home country (Siehr 2002: 27). On the whole, Article 45, para. 2, PILA, advances the principle of applying different standards in *ordre public* considerations depending on the closeness of parties' links to Switzerland (*Intensität der Binnenbeziehung*).

Marriage by proxy

Swiss civil law requires both spouses to be present at the marriage ceremony. If at least one of them is represented by a proxy, the marriage is considered to be non-existing.[17] Judicial and administrative authorities have had to take decisions on the recognition of marriage by proxy on several occasions. In 2011 a Swiss Regional Court had to assess the validity of a marriage between a female Muslim Sudanese and a male, formerly Christian German, who had been domiciled in Switzerland during their marriage, where both parties had mandated a representative to conclude their marriage in Sudan in 2005.[18] After separation, the wife submitted the marriage certificate to the Swiss authorities for registration and requested preliminary measures, including maintenance payments. The husband challenged the legitimacy of recognition. Therefore, the issue – if the marriage was valid – was dealt with in a preliminary fashion by the Court according to Article 29, para. 3, PILA. After stating that the marriage had taken place in Sudan, the Court meticulously examined its validity according to the relevant Sudanese law, which was *in casu* the Family Law for Muslims of the Year 1991.[19] Whereas the presence of both spouses is generally required according to Article 14(c) of the Sudanese Family Law, Article 14(f) provides that a marriage may be concluded in written form if one of the spouses is absent or cannot express him or herself. Being aware that the absence of both spouses is not explicitly mentioned in the law, the Regional Court assumed that the option for deviating from the obligation to attend the ceremony must apply to both spouses. The Court, thus, did not hesitate to interpret foreign law, supposing that the omission constituted a genuine legal loophole that it needed to fill in. The Court confirmed that both spouses were validly represented: the Sudanese bride by an uncle and marriage guardian, and the German groom by a properly authorised representative. The marriage was concluded by the competent Sudanese Islamic marriage registrar in the presence of the already mentioned representatives and two witnesses. The Swiss Regional Court also assessed and confirmed the further conditions that needed to be fulfilled for a valid marriage, e.g. the requirement of the groom's conversion to Islam and his payment of a dower. It negated any impediments to marriage according to Articles 15 ff. of the Sudanese Family Law.[20] The Court therefore concluded that the marriage certificate issued by the Islamic marriage registrar had full legal effectiveness and that a valid marriage had been concluded between the parties under Sudanese law. Subsequently, the marriage was registered with the Sudanese judicial authorities. Finally, the Court went on to decide if there were any *ordre public* reservations. The latest decisions by Swiss authorities reveal that the mere fact of concluding a marriage by proxy abroad is not considered as a violation of *ordre public* as long as the following two criteria are fulfilled: first, the proxy must not lack validity. This would be the case, for example, if it was *carte blanche* or if it was falsified.[21] Second, both spouses have to consider themselves to be married according to the foreign statute's understanding of marriage. Above all, it must be confirmed that the parties consented to marriage by their own free will, i.e. in the absence of any coercion, error or deception (Büchler 2011b: 951). In contrast, how the consent to marriage was delivered on a formal level cannot be decisive. In this regard, it is appropriate to differentiate between the proxy for declaration (*Stellvertretung in der Erklärung*) and the proxy for decision-making (*Stellvertretung im Wille*) (Büchler 2011b: 950). The former is in line with the contractual nature of Islamic marriage. In case of the discussed marriage, the validity of the representation was affirmed. In addition, the Court, when assessing the groom's intention to conclude the marriage, reached the conclusion that his will corresponded to the definition of marriage in Sudanese law. On the whole, the recognition of the validly concluded marriage abroad implied safeguarding the wife's claim to legal protection in Switzerland.

The argumentative strategy adopted in the case discussed above was most likely inspired by a decision taken by the former Swiss Asylum Appeals Commission five years earlier.[22] The recognition of a marriage concluded in Egypt in absence of the groom was also subject to preliminary assessment according to Article 29, para. 3, PILA, in view of his request for family reunification. Before elaborating on the conditions of the marriage under scrutiny, the Appeals Commission outlined the requirements and impediments for Muslim marriage according to Egyptian law, which is strongly influenced by precepts of classical Islamic law and allows for marriage by proxy. In the case considered by the Swiss Asylum Appeals Commission, the groom, an Egyptian national with refugee status in Switzerland, had appointed his father as a proxy for the marriage concluded by a religious marriage official in Egypt in the presence of the Egyptian bride, who was also represented by a marriage guardian. After assessing the circumstances of the case, the Appeals Commission concluded that the marriage was valid under

Egyptian law and proceeded to examine if there were *ordre public* reservations. The Appeals Commission argued that *ordre public* considerations were only to be taken into account if the case had sufficient links to Switzerland (*Binnenbeziehung*). It stated that in the case of family reunification requests by refugees in Switzerland, sufficient links were regularly found. Regarding the proxy's validity, the Appeals Commission stated that there were no minimum formal standards required by the Swiss *ordre public*, e.g. that official legalisation of the proxy was not mandatory. However, on the substantive level, it was required that the principal clearly indicate the person that he or she wanted to enter into marriage with and that this indication had been put on record. Regarding the spouses' desire to be married according the statute under which the marriage was concluded, the Appeals Commission emphasised the necessity to accept deviating functions and ideas of marriage given 'culturally and socially different conditions'. The spouses' free-will decision to enter a marriage abroad, implying their consent to the concept of marriage in the corresponding state must, consequently, be respected. In the present case, the marriage was recognised because the stated requirements were fulfilled and because each spouses' will was sufficiently proven. Finally, the Appeals Commission indicated that only by recognition could legal protection be granted to the party in need if the marriage should be dissolved later on.

In contrast, in 1988 a Cantonal Supervisory Authority refused to recognise a marriage by proxy between a male Lebanese national and a female Swiss national.[23] The couple had mandated a lawyer to conclude their marriage by proxy in 1997 after failing to get married on the occasion of their stay in Lebanon in the same year. The Supervisory Authority made its decision on *ordre public* grounds. For this reason, the question whether the marriage had been validly concluded under the Lebanese marriage statute for Muslims could be ignored. In its reasoning, the Supervisory Authority focused on the spouses' centre of vital life interests, which it identified as being in Switzerland. *In casu*, the Supervisory Authority considered that because of the close link to Switzerland (*Binnenbeziehung*) the proxy marriage violated *ordre public*. It argued that because the marriage's legal effects would mainly unfold in Switzerland, the Swiss concept of marriage as a far-reaching contractual obligation had to be taken into account. The Supervisory Authority went on to explain that the Swiss formal conditions for marriage, which require personal presence at the ceremony, had been implemented to guarantee freedom of marriage and to guarantee that the parties are not overhasty in their actions or under undue influence. The question of whether it would have been possible to safeguard the spirit and the purpose of the *ordre public* objection by means other than the solution provided by Swiss law remained unconsidered in this decision.[24]

Temporary marriage

According to Shi'ite jurisprudence, it is possible to get married for a limited period of time that is defined, or at least definable, in advance. Besides the temporary aspect, such a marriage also differs from indefinite marriage regarding its consequences. By law, the groom is not committed to any financial support during the marriage or after its expiry, with the exception of the obligation to pay a dower to the bride upon celebration of the marriage. In addition, there are no inheritance rights between the spouses. However, the provisions guiding temporary marriage are principally dispositive, i.e. the spouses are free to agree upon deviating provisions in their marriage contract (Jourabchi 2011: 822). For example, the groom may be required to support the wife financially during marriage or to grant inheritance rights within the freely available quota. In other words, generally, upon mutual agreement, it is possible to give the union effects similar to those of a permanent marriage.

The vast majority of the population of Iran is Shi'ite. Thus, the Iranian Civil Code (CC) provides several provisions regarding temporary marriages.[25] Between 2005 and 2009, several Swiss administrative and judicial authorities assessed the recognition of a temporary marriage (for the duration of 50 years) celebrated between a male Swiss national and a female Swiss-Iranian national in Iran.[26] The various authorities unanimously ruled in favour of recognition in compliance with Article 45, para. 1, PILA, arguing that temporary marriage as a legal institute is officially acknowledged in Iran and that the marriage was validly concluded in Iran. However, the authorities also agreed on declaring the marriage to be permanent on *ordre public* grounds. The competent Regional Court reasoned that the dissolution of a marriage uniquely falls within the competence of the judge. Against this, it may be argued that according to the Iranian CC, a temporary marriage can be dissolved ahead of time either by renunciation or by court decision (Jourabchi 2011: 834). Thus, the reference to the judiciary's field of competence cannot be the only reason for the stated *ordre public* violation. Rather, it may be assumed that the authorities' consideration is implicitly anchored in the traditional idea of Christian marriage, in which spouses enter into marriage as long as they shall live, despite the gap between this concept and domestic social reality where currently nearly 50 per cent of marriages are dissolved by divorce (Büchler 2011a: 48).[27] In addition, contractual elements have gained increasing importance, not only in contexts of unilaterally motivated divorce, but also for non-marital cohabitation in Switzerland (Jourabchi 2011: 837).[28]

In the case discussed immediately above, the duration of 50 years is *de facto* a lifetime marriage. Therefore, its registration as an unlimited marriage is mainly of normative importance. Nevertheless, the marriage was thereby granted a temporary extension that deviates from the effect awarded in the state where the marriage was concluded. Such a discrepancy may result from applying the principle of controlled extension or takeover of effects of a foreign decision or a civil status document.[29] However, it is at odds with the *ratio legis* of Article 45, para. 1, PILA, the basic purpose of which is to recognise a foreign marriage with those effects provided by the marriage statute (Siehr 2002: 24).

Recognition provided by Article 45, PILA, covers the civil status of the person. Correspondingly, Article 48, para. 1, PILA, states that marital rights and obligations are governed by the law of the country of domicile of the spouses. With regard to the case of the recognised temporary marriage described above, this means that the effects of marriage are governed by Swiss law. Nevertheless, it may be argued that effects of the temporary marriage according to the foreign marital statute should also be taken into account.[30] By choosing the form of temporary marriage, the parties agreed on its contractual nature, thus implying, *inter alia,* the absence of financial commitments of the groom during marriage unless explicitly agreed on in the marriage contract. *In casu*, the couple broke up about two and a half months after their marriage was concluded in Iran, whereupon the wife required registration of the marriage and, subsequently, filed for maintenance. It might be argued that when assessing her claims, the limited effects of marriage accorded by the foreign statute should be taken into account. However, such an approach is tantamount to stripping marriage as a legal institute from its basic contents, which includes conjugal solidarity, and therefore would most likely be considered an impediment to *ordre public*.[31]

A final remark regarding the seemingly uncontested validity of the temporary marriage case: the Regional Court, which was in charge of assessing the legitimacy of recognition at first instance and which had full cognition, did not substantively assess the marriage's validity according to the Iranian CC. It mainly based its conclusion on the validity of the certified documents, stating that they were an expression of a marital status acquired abroad. The groom's claim that he had not converted to Islam and that, therefore, the marriage was not validly concluded according to Iranian law had not been considered. Article 1059, Iranian CC, provides that a non-Muslim groom needs to present a formal attestation of conversion to Islam to the registration office upon conclusion and registration of the marriage. *In casu,* it was stated that the marriage was validly registered in Iran, but there was no explicit evidence that the attestation had been effectively produced and submitted. If the Swiss authorities had concluded that the marriage had not been validly concluded in Iran, they would have had to assess its validity under Swiss law.[32]

Polygamous marriage

Article 105 (1), Swiss CC, states that for domestic cases (*Binnensachverhalte*) a marriage must be annulled if one of the spouses was already married at the time of the wedding and the previous marriage had not been dissolved by divorce or by the death of the previous spouse. According to Article 106, Swiss CC, a bigamous marriage must be brought to court *ex officio* during the ongoing marriage.[33] Any interested party can seek annulment any time, even after dissolution of the marriage. The procedurally unlimited time period to claim invalidity of a bigamous marriage reaches its limits upon discontinuation of the first marriage. Indeed, it is broadly agreed by scholars and judges that as soon as the first marriage is validly dissolved, the second marriage must not be considered invalid anymore. Having said that, a Cantonal Tax Appeals Commission affirmed the validity of a marriage that had been temporarily bigamous.[34] The plaintiff, a Swiss resident of Tunisian origin had entered a marriage in Switzerland and, a year later, one in Tunis. The Swiss marriage was validly ended three years later, whereas the Tunisian marriage persisted at the time of the proceedings. The Tax Appeals Commission based its decision on Article 45, para. 1, PILA, stating that a foreign marriage is recognised if it was validly concluded (a) according to the law at the place where the marriage was concluded, or (b) the law of the domicile or (c) the law of one of the country of origin of one of the spouses. An expert assessment by the Swiss Institute of Comparative Law revealed that the marriage was null and void under Tunisian law.[35] The Tax Appeals Commission also examined the marriage's validity under Swiss law, i.e. the law of the plaintiff's domicile. The Commission reached the conclusion that the Tunisian marriage had become valid under Swiss law at the time in question, which was after the dissolution of the first marriage. Similarly, a cantonal court ruled in favour of recognition of a marriage between a female Moroccan and a male Algerian national, which was validly celebrated abroad, although the groom's previous marriage had not at the time been dissolved.[36] The wife filed for divorce in Switzerland. Therefore the validity of the marriage needed to be assessed once again as a preliminary question (Article 29, para. 3, PILA). Because the first marriage had lawfully been dissolved four years before the divorce case was brought to court in Switzerland, the Court denied the existence of any *ordre public* reservation, which would have prevented the marriage's recognition.[37]

Conversely, as long as a previous marriage has not been validly dissolved, recognition of a new marriage abroad must be refused. For this reason, the Federal Supreme Court refused to recognise a marriage between a male Moroccan national and a female Swiss national who got married in London after the Moroccan's divorce at the Moroccan Consulate in Switzerland.[38] The Federal Supreme Court argued that a consulate was not entitled to pronounce a divorce, adding that the decision for non-recognition of the divorce was furthermore motivated by the impression that the divorce seemed to be a repudiation.

The prohibition on entering into a polygamous marriage in Switzerland, according to Article 96, Swiss CC,[39] is complemented by the unlimited invalidity clause of Article 105 (1), Swiss CC. It is acknowledged that the invalidity clauses of Article 105, Swiss CC, sanction violations of *ordre public*. Therefore, it is not possible to use the conflict of law provisions to conclude a polygamous marriage in Switzerland because the *ordre public* clause of Article 17, PILA, would intervene. However, this does not necessarily imply that recognition of bigamous and polygamous marriages equally violates *ordre public* according to Article 27, PILA, taking its attenuated effect into account. Thus, the recognition of polygamous marriages has remained a contested matter (Courvoisier 2007: 330 with further references). The Federal Supreme Court has not been called upon to decide on the recognition of polygamous marriages concluded abroad. Meanwhile, several cantonal courts ruled both in favour as well as against recognition of polygamous marriages (Othenin-Girard 1999: 418–21). The prevailing legal opinion goes towards accepting polygamy as a marital status in very exceptional cases only, but to concede certain consequences arising from polygamous marriages to all involved spouses (Büchler and Fink 2008: 59). It is acknowledged that enduring family relationships that have been established abroad with the agreement of the concerned parties deserve protection and that, for the sake of equality, a second wife should be granted the same legal protection as the first wife. Nevertheless, while second wives have been granted financial rights in the field of maintenance, social security and inheritance, the authorities have been restrictive when it comes to granting residence rights to protect family rights. Having said that, the Federal Administrative Court ruled in 2007 in favour of granting provisory admission to the Romanian cohabitant of a recognised Turkish refugee and their three common children, while rejecting his request for further family reunification, which would have included two spouses and 11 children from Turkey.[40] The practice of granting family reunification to one wife only is widespread in Europe, although it is not only unjustifiable on equality grounds, but also with regard to the principle of the unity and protection of the family, a principle that has international *ordre public* standard, and which is recognised in Switzerland as a cornerstone of society.[41] In the present case, the Court quotes the Federal Office for Migration which argued that it would be a violation of *ordre public* to recognise several partners indirectly as spouses and consequently as refugees according to Article 51, para. 1, Federal Asylum Act. Furthermore, the Office for Migration claimed that the refugee's behaviour must be interpreted as a clear position in favour of his Romanian cohabitant, while abandoning his Turkish wives and children. Therefore, according to the Office for Migration the family relationships no longer existed in real terms. It furthermore claimed that the conditions of Article 51, para. 2, Federal Asylum Act, according to which other close relatives may be admitted where there are special reasons in favour of family reunification, were also not fulfilled. This provision could only be applied in case of an existential emergency situation affecting the concerned family members that could not be solved other than with the help of the recognised refugee. The Office for Migration concluded that the family members in Turkey were not affected by such a situation. The refugee, in contrast, claimed that he had spent about a year with the three wives and the children in Turkey and that they had apparently all agreed to share family life. The Federal Administrative Court, however, maintained with regard to consistent case law that family reunification could be granted to one spouse only and that a long-term separation was an impediment to family reunification. It equally rejected the request concerning admission of the children on the grounds that the refugee did not have a priority relationship to them. In contrast to the other cases outlined above, the authorities in this case did not take into account the legal situation in Turkey where polygamy is prohibited by law, which could most probably have been invoked in favour of granting family reunification to one spouse only. On the whole, even if the decision in this particular case could be considered as adequate in its result, it reveals the authorities' assumption of self-entitlement to define the shape and intensity of family life that deserves protection.[42]

The Federal Administrative Court further restricted the principle of generally granting family reunification to one spouse within a polygamous family situation in a 2012 decision. Briefly, the facts of this case are as follows:[43] an Iraqi, with the status of a recognised refugee in Switzerland since 2005, had married two compatriots in Iraqi Kurdistan, the first in 1978 and the second most probably before 1998. He lived together with the latter, who was apparently recognised as his wife in Switzerland, till middle of July 2007, when they separated, and in June 2011 finally divorced under Swiss law. He validly married his third wife, a Syrian national, in Syria under Syrian law in November 2006. The marriage was registered with a Shari'a Court in Damascus in February 2007. The Syrian national joined him in Switzerland in October 2007, shared domicile with him since then and gave birth to two children in 2009 and 2011. If one focuses on the actual family relationships, as in the last discussed case, the Iraqi's behaviour could have been interpreted as an obvious orientation towards his Syrian wife and their common children, which would have meant their inclusion in the family asylum application. This is also suggested by the fact that the Iraqi refugee had been married and, later on in Switzerland, validly divorced from his second spouse,[44] that his first marriage dates back three decades and that the facts as presented in the judgment do not reveal that he had ever requested family reunification in favour of his first wife. Furthermore, he claimed to have divorced her by repudiation in Iraq in 1995.[45] Nevertheless, his Syrian wife's request to be included in her husband's refugee status was denied, irrespective of the social facts and the civil status obtained abroad. In its reasoning, the Federal Administrative Court stated that inclusion in a family asylum application was generally possible for one spouse according to prevailing court practice. However, if granting a family asylum required that a decision be made on the recognition of a foreign decision on marriage before any decision on asylum is made, the following further conditions shall apply: a refugee's marriage validly concluded abroad after his being granted asylum in Switzerland must not be recognised and consequently does not have any effect regarding family asylum (Article 51, Federal Asylum Act), as long as his previously entered marriage(s) has/have not validly been dissolved (Article 27, para. 1, PILA, or Article 45, para. 2, PILA, in combination with Article 105 (1), Swiss CC). In its reasoning, the Court repeatedly invoked the principle of monogamy as the basis of the institution of marriage in Switzerland, concluding that any deviating institution would violate Swiss *ordre public*. In addition, polygynous marriages are opposed to gender equality, which, according to the Court, is also a part of Swiss *ordre public*. The Court's motivation for explicitly setting additional conditions for refugees is set out as following in the judgment: first, refugees, unlike other foreigners, are equated to Swiss citizens in the PILA (cf. Article 24, para. 3, PILA) because they are expected to have close domestic connections (*enge Binnenbeziehungen*) due to their permanent Swiss domicile and their establishment of their centre of vital life interests in Switzerland. Therefore, the Court concluded that particular attention should be paid not to recognise a foreign decision, obtained abroad because of foreign citizenship, which refugees would not have been able to get in Switzerland and by which they would be able to undermine fundamental principles of Swiss *ordre public*.[46] Second, the Court gave financial reasons: recognition of a polygamous marriage would allow refugees to considerably extend their family circle while not being able to pay their living expenses. Instead, they would be dependent on public assistance, provided by Swiss taxpayers, for whom polygamy is prohibited. Third, referring to the contested matter regarding the effects that a valid foreign decision on marriage may lead to despite its non-recognition in Switzerland, the Court differentiated between granting simple property rights on the one hand, and awarding protection as well as a status that is privileged in comparison to the residence rights granted to other foreigners on the other hand. According to the Court, because the latter has long-lasting and sensitive consequences in Switzerland, and because it would be tantamount to recognition of the polygamous marriage, the non-recognised foreign decision on marriage must not produce any effect regarding residence rights. For the same reason, the Syrian wife was not considered to have entered into cohabitation with the Iraqi refugee and, subsequently, the two children's request for family asylum was also denied. On the whole, the Court's decision seeks to differentiate between decisions obtained abroad before and after establishing domestic connections in Switzerland, which may be understood in accordance with the legislative goal of Article 45, para. 2, PILA. However, the result of this differentiation in the present case appears to be disproportionate because the concerned family members were refused protection of their individual rights granted by Article 8, European Convention on Human Rights, although their *de facto* family situation is far from being polygamous.

Divorce

Jurisdiction and applicable law on divorce in Switzerland

All divorce matters involving persons who are domiciled in Switzerland strictly fall into the Swiss courts' sphere of competence (Article 59, PILA), which implies that divorces by private bodies such as religious institutions and foreign consulates in Switzerland or unilaterally pronounced private divorces, such as *talaq* and other forms of unilateral repudiation, do not have any legal consequences (Bopp 2007: 401; Bucher 2004: 111–12; Volken 2004c: 592). Similar to the marriage statute, the divorce statute first invokes Swiss law as applicable law (Article 61, para. 1, PILA). The Swiss legislator thereby envisaged the principle of the closest connection of a case with regard to both spouses, based on the assumption that filing for divorce in Switzerland is preceded by the couple's establishment of a Swiss domicile (Message of the Swiss Federal Council 1983: 358). In the absence of a common domicile, common foreign citizenship is considered as a connecting factor, and the foreign law of the country of citizenship becomes binding as applicable law for Swiss courts (Article 61, para. 2, PILA). Subsubsidiarily, the law of the Swiss domicile of one of the spouses must be applied. Thus, the PILA has structured applicable law on divorce in a cascade style, favouring, first, common domicile and, second, common nationality (Volken 2004c: 605). If the thereby designated law exceptionally fails to identify the law of the closest connection of a case, Article 15, PILA, may interfere for the sake of realising equality at the level of private international law (Bopp 2007: 416; Bucher 2004: 117–18). Article 61, para. 3, PILA, provides a specification of the general *ordre public* clause laid down in Article 17, PILA, regarding application of foreign law based on Article 61, para. 2, PILA. It asserts the application of Swiss law if divorce is impossible or only possible under extremely restrictive conditions under the law of the foreign country if one of the spouses is also Swiss citizen or has been living in Switzerland for two years. Thus, in contrast to Article 17, PILA, this provision determines the intensity of the required domestic connections (*Binnenbeziehung*), as well determining as the alternatively applicable law. The existence of extremely restrictive conditions must be assessed if marriages can only be dissolved in cases of absolute reasons for divorce or if the divorce options are gender-biased.[47] It has been claimed that Article 61, para. 3, PILA, does not preclude application of Article 17, PILA. If a foreign legal order does not grant divorce at all or refuses it for discriminating reasons, Swiss law should be applied even if the required domestic connections are insufficient or do not exist (Schwander 1997: 63). In addition, Article 17, PILA, should apply to legal orders that grant divorce too easily, i.e. without observing any minimum duration of *de facto* separation, or that allow divorce based on unilateral declaration (ibid.).

Recognition of foreign divorces

General remarks

The three general criteria for recognition of foreign decisions that must be fulfilled cumulatively also govern the recognition of divorces obtained outside Switzerland. Regarding the first criterion, which is indirect jurisdiction, Article 65, para. 1, PILA, specifies Article 25 (a), PILA, in connection with Article 26 (a), PILA.[48] Accordingly, foreign decisions concerning divorce are recognised in Switzerland if they were rendered in the country of domicile, habitual residence or in the country of citizenship of one of the spouses or if they are recognised in one of these countries. It is broadly agreed that possible interpretations of the term 'decision' reach far beyond its domestic understanding in the Swiss CC (Bopp 2007: 442; Bucher 2004: 147–49; Volken 2004c: 650). Thus, it is not confined to judgments within civil court proceedings, but includes extra-judicially obtained divorces, such as divorces obtained through administrative or religious bodies, as well as private divorces based on unilateral declaration or bilateral agreement. In order to be recognisable, such a divorce must be valid according to the law of the country where it was obtained. In addition, the decision must not be taken on Swiss territory, i.e. divorces granted by foreign consular authorities in Switzerland do not meet this requirement.[49] However, residents of Switzerland may seek divorce abroad and subsequently ask for recognition in Switzerland, i.e. there is no additional *ordre public* barrier as in the case of marriage (Article 45, para. 2, PILA) apart from Article 27, PILA. Indeed, a spouse who is willing to divorce may obtain a decision abroad sooner than in Switzerland (Schwander 2009: 832). If there is no joint request for divorce, however, Article 65, para. 2, PILA, must be observed, protecting the party that does not want to divorce from being subject to a foreign forum.

The second criterion for recognition, which concerns the firmness of the foreign decision according Article 25 (b), PILA, is usually not contested, while the third one, i.e. non-violation of the Swiss *ordre public*, Article 25 (c), PILA, in connection with Article 27, PILA, deserves some closer consideration. In general, as stated above, the outcome of the recognition must not contradict Switzerland's basic legal principles (Bopp 2007: 445). Equally, the connection to Switzerland (*Binnenbeziehung*) is advanced as a significant factor influencing the weight awarded to Swiss *ordre public* (ibid.; Bucher 2004: 152). When assessing the result of recognition, divorces based on mutual consent on the dissolution of marriage and its consequences, and divorces in which one spouse disagrees with the change in civil status or with its consequences must be differentiated.[50] In the first case, court evidence is required that both spouses wanted a divorce. If affirmed, a foreign divorce concept or divorce procedure that deviates from basic principles of the Swiss legal order should not be an impediment to recognition. Thus, results from unilateral forms of divorce, known as *talaq* in Islamic legal orders, whereby the right to divorce is reserved to the husband, in violation of principles of gender equality, must not be excluded from recognition at the outset. If the spouses' mutual consent is clear, the procedural *ordre public* according to Article 27, para. 2, PILA (e.g. the right to be duly summoned and heard in court) does not matter because it requires, according to case law of the Federal Supreme Court during recent decades, evidence provided by the concerned party. In contrast, if there is no verification of the spouses' agreement on divorce, for example because dissolution of marriage was obtained by representatives of the spouses' families without the knowledge or against the will of one or both spouses, recognition of a divorce obtained abroad is refused (Bopp 2007: 446). Furthermore, as long as one spouse opposes the divorce, Swiss *ordre public* is violated if the breakdown of the marriage was not assessed by the court. Apart from exceptional cases of irretrievable breakdown for compelling reasons (Article 115, Swiss CC), Swiss civil law uniquely takes the duration of separation as an indication of the breakdown. Article 114, Swiss CC, stipulates separation of at least two years in cases of unilateral petitions for divorce. Thus, it has been claimed that a separation of six months would violate Swiss *ordre public*, while a duration of at least one year could be accepted (Bucher 2004: 151). In addition, Swiss *ordre public* is violated if a divorce against one or both spouses' will is not founded on the marriage's breakdown, but on discriminating grounds such as infertility or the spouses' religious beliefs (ibid.).

Court practice

The key issue which Swiss courts have been struggling with in their assessment of recognisability of foreign divorces is the *ordre public* reservation (Article 27, PILA). One of the earliest landmark decisions by the Swiss Federal Supreme Court, which has been repeatedly quoted since, dates back to 1962 when the Federal Act on the Private Law Conditions of Domiciliaries and Sojouners of 1891 was still in force and thus applicable to international cases.[51] In this decision, the Federal Supreme Court refused recognition of a divorce between a Swiss national and her Egyptian husband who had been domiciled in Egypt. The couple had agreed to get divorced prior to the husband's pronunciation of the repudiation with the Egyptian consular authorities in Moscow, while his wife took residence in Switzerland. The Federal Supreme Court argued that according to case law the responsible foreign authority did not necessarily have to be a court, but that a divorce could not be effective without the authority's active assessment of the substantive conditions and reasons for divorce, and the authority's pronouncement of a judgment. The Court concluded that the Egyptian consulate's mere hearing of the husband's declaration was incompatible with the basic principles of the Swiss legal order and, therefore, the foreign divorce could not be recognised, irrespective of the wife's consent to the divorce and her request for recognition in Switzerland. The Court's decision must be seen in the light of the principles of Swiss family law at that time, when obtainment of divorce was compulsorily preceded by an examination of fault by the competent authorities, and when there was no option for divorce by joint request.[52] While Swiss divorce law has had numerous modifications in the last two decades, the corresponding provisions on divorce in the PILA have remained unchanged since the enactment of the PILA in 1987. However, Swiss court practice in divorce cases with international connections developed in line with developments in domestic civil law. Thus, by 1991, a Cantonal Appeals Court explicitly refrained from not recognising unilateral forms of divorce between foreign spouses as a principle, but advocated considering the circumstances instead.[53] *In casu*, an Egyptian national who lived with his Egyptian wife and their children in Switzerland for many years divorced his wife by proxy in Egypt. The wife was not summoned to appear at the responsible notary's office in

Egypt, but was only informed by the Egyptian consular authorities in Switzerland upon completion of the procedure. A few years later, the wife filed for divorce in Switzerland, referring to the foreign deicsion's violation of Swiss *ordre public*. The Court initially affirmed that the document issued by the notary in Egypt was a valid judgment on divorce according to Egyptian law. Because Switzerland and Egypt are both member states of the Hague Convention on the Recognition of Divorces and Legal Separations, which has been in force since 1975, the Cantonal Appeals Court correctly stated the Convention's precedence over the PILA, by virtue of Article 1, para. 2, PILA. The Court then argued that the Egyptian judgment contradicted Articles 8 and 10 of the Hague Convention, which may be compared to the procedural and substantive *ordre public* reservation of Article 27, para. 1 and 2, PILA. On a procedural level, the wife's plea for non-recognition was well founded due to her complete absence and her lack of knowledge of the divorce procedure (Article 8, Hague Convention). In addition, the Court asserted violation of substantive *ordre public*, as laid down in Article 10 of the Hague Convention, mainly with reference to the close domestic connection, as indicated by the wife's residence in Switzerland for 20 years, her stable employment, the naturalisation of two of her children's and the steps she had taken towards acquiring citizenship for herself and her third child. The Court emphasised that the stronger the domestic connections, the more strictly the Swiss *ordre public* must apply, which was the reason why, when considering of the circumstances, the foreign judgment on divorce could not be recognised.

In a decision in 1995, another cantonal court confirmed that a *talaq* can be recognised in Switzerland provided that three conditions are fulfilled.[54] The first condition concerns the responsible foreign authority's participation. In contrast to the above mentioned decision from 1962, the authority is no longer required to participate actively but its minor assistance, e.g. by undertaking registering and certificating functions, is deemed to be sufficient. According to the second condition, which addresses the domestic connection of a case, recognition is possible if a *talaq* is pronounced between two foreign Muslims abroad. It corresponds to the recommendation of the Swiss Federal Council (Message of the Swiss Federal Council 1983: 361). Remarkably, the connecting factors of nationality and *locus actus*, and not the domicile, are considered as significant indicators for a weak or even no domestic connection. The third condition requires the wife's consent, particularly if recognition in Switzerland is at stake. Her implicit consent by not invoking Article 27, para. 2, PILA, is sufficient. In its conclusion, the Court concedes that a *talaq* per se seems to be unreconcilable with the Swiss notions governing the legal institutes of marriage and divorce. However, it advocates attending to the result of a *talaq* with the wife's consent, drawing a parallel with the already widespread court practice of allowing divorce by mutual consent (*Konventionalscheidung*), which was, at that time, contrary to the wording in the former Swiss CC.

The discussion in a cantonal court decision of 1996 involving a Moroccan and an Algerian national, both domiciled in Switzerland, largely revolved around the same issues.[55] The Algerian husband had divorced his wife by repudiation in Morocco in 1994. One year later, the wife filed for divorce in Switzerland. The husband opposed the Swiss divorce procedure, invoking *res iudicata* or *lis pendens.* According to the Court's appraisal *in casu*, the parties' Swiss domicile implied their close domestic connection, notwithstanding their foreign nationalities and the foreign *locus actus.* Consequently, recognisability needed to be assessed in view of the substantive *ordre public*, while the question of whether a divorce procedure, in which the competent foreign authorities had mere registering functions, could be recognised could remain open according to the Court. The Court also emphasised that the evaluation of whether the recognition violates the substantive *ordre public* must be carried out in respect of the concrete result for the Swiss sense of justice. It concluded that the decision was issued by a system that privileges one of the spouses because of their gender, in strong violation of the foundations of Swiss divorce law and gender equality, and stated this as the reason why recognition of the foreign decision must be refused. Remarkably, the fact that both husband and wife intended to be divorced, at least as far as the change in civil status was concerned, remained unconsidered. Presumably, the wife's action for divorce in Switzerland and her husband's opposition may have been due to the discrepancy between the ancillary matters of divorce according to the Swiss CC on the one hand and the foreign civil code on the other. Indeed, in numerous divorce cases involving a divorce obtained abroad, it is not the judgment on civil status as such, but issues such as custody, matrimonial property rights and maintenance that are the reasons for the spouses' contrary views about the foreign decision. Thus, it has been claimed that the Swiss authorities' generous practice of recognising foreign judgments should be restricted to the judgment on civil status. In addition, they should be willing to amend the ancillary matters of foreign decisions upon the request of the spouses concerned (Schwander 2009: 838–39).[56]

The Swiss Federal Supreme Court commented on the definition of a 'recognisable foreign decision' on divorce under the PILA for the first time in 1996.[57] It unequivocally declared itself in favour of placing private divorces by joint request on an equal footing with divorces by judicial and administrative authorities. The Federal Supreme Court explained that private divorces were recognised in numerous states, and that they often represented the only way to dissolve a marriage. Thus, maintaining the formerly required decisive or at least active participation by state authorities would contravene the liberal practice of recognition. The Court furthermore stressed that recognition of private divorce by joint request must fulfil reinforced conditions for recognition because there is no official document as a basis for recognition, but a private agreement, which is more susceptible to error. If the spouses' will to divorce can be affirmed without doubt, there is usually no reason to refuse recognition in Switzerland. According to the Court, this even applies to divorces obtained abroad by proxy. If either or both spouses did not know of or opposed the divorce procedure, or if their consent is unverifiable, recognition must be refused. In this regard, a cantonal court ruled in favour of non-recognition of a divorce by proxy, referring to violation of the procedural *ordre public* (Article 27, para. 2(b), PILA).[58] The divorce was granted in Jordan in 1998 and the wife's father, to whom she had given a general authorisation, participated. The Court initially stated the absolutely personal nature of divorce. For this reason the right to divorce could not be transferred to a proxy. According to Article 111, para. 1, Swiss CC, the parties have to appear in court personally to obtain a divorce by joint request. However, with reference to established cantonal court practice, the minimum requirement for recognition of a foreign divorce by proxy was a specific authorisation, stating consent to divorce. Such a declaration was not available *in casu*. The proxy himself even confirmed that he had executed the divorce of his own volition, without the knowledge of his principal, i.e. his daughter. Thus, as in case of marriage by proxy, Swiss courts seem to apply the same distinction between the proxy for declaration (*Stellvertretung in der Erklärung*) and the proxy for decision-making (*Stellvertretung im Wille*), when assessing recognition of foreign divorces. According to a decision by the Federal Supreme Court in 2005, Swiss *ordre public* requires that the court be sufficiently assured that a divorce by joint request corresponds to the spouses' will and that they declared their will themselves.[59] In contrast, it does not matter how the divorce is achieved (whether personally or through a proxy) and does not concern the *ordre public*. While the Swiss legislator considered the rules of Article 111, Swiss CC, as most suitable to establish the will to divorce, Swiss courts also accept the spouses' written declaration to the attention of the responsible authority as evidence.

Another landmark decision on unilateral divorce was issued by the Swiss Federal Supreme Court in 2000.[60] It is in line with the jurisdiction (*Rechtsprechung*) developed by cantonal courts in the 1990s. The facts of the case, which was initiated in 1998, are as follows: the wife, a Lebanese national, domiciled in Lebanon, filed for divorce in Switzerland, the forum of her Swiss husband, who was domiciled in Jordan at the time. She emphasised her intention to take domicile in Switzerland and requested custody of their two children, who had Swiss nationality. Thereupon, the husband submitted a decision on dissolution of marriage issued by a shari'a tribunal of Beirut to the Swiss Court of First Instance in the same month as the wife's request for divorce, and claimed custody of the children. Both Swiss cantonal courts, which were entrusted with the case prior to the Federal Supreme Court, affirmed jurisdiction (*Zuständigkeit*) because of non-recognisability of the Lebanese decision on *ordre public* grounds. The Federal Supreme Court's assessment revealed that the Lebanese decision resulted from a procedure of de facto unilateral repudiation by the husband, in which the judge had merely a registering function. In its reasoning, the Court confirmed that recognition of unilateral repudiation must not be refused from the outset, but needs careful examination that focuses on the compatibility of its concrete results and the *ordre public* in its actual interpretation. Nevertheless, the Court justified non-recognition of the foreign decision in an objective and rather general fashion, claiming that 'such a repudiation' must be refused recognition because it is an expression of gender inequality in divorce matters. In this case again, the couple's conflict was most probably due to the ancillary matters of divorce (*in casu*, attribution of child custody), and again, the wife's equal will to divorce was not considered. Thus, the question arises of whether this court practice, in the guise of advancing gender equality, disadvantages women by refusing recognition of dissolution of marriage by repudiation in a categorical fashion. Women may be subjected to another divorce procedure in Switzerland, while men may enter a new marriage because of the recognition of the repudiation abroad (Bucher 2004: 153–54). A case- and result-oriented perspective was adopted by a cantonal court in 2005 regarding violation of *ordre public*.[61] On a procedural level, the Court concluded that the *ordre public* reserve could not be invoked if one had consented to divorce. Concerning the substantive reserve, the Court argued that the result of recognising the foreign decision must be compared with the result of a decision reached by a Swiss judge. This comparison does not necessarily lead to a positive result, but it must be an acceptable result at least. Thus, in this decision, the Court rejected categorical refusal of foreign divorces by repudiation because of foreign provisions that do not award women equal options to defend their personal rights.

On the whole, domestic connection (*Binnenbeziehung*) appears as the crucial point to balance (non-)interference of *ordre public*. Somewhat as a remnant of the principle of nationality, the foreign *locus actus* and the spouses' foreign nationality were deemed indicators of the lack of or weak domestic connection when the PILA was implemented (Message of the Swiss Federal Council 1983: 361). These indicators seem to have been gradually replaced by jurisdiction in favour of the domicile. Thus, in the case discussed above,[62] the Federal Supreme Court affirmed sufficient domestic connection despite the wife's Lebanese nationality and the fact that the divorce by repudiation was carried out in Lebanon. Instead, the Court decided that establishment of her domicile in Switzerland, her prospective stay and her children's nationality were decisive. The focus on the effective centre of life as a benchmark for *ordre public* considerations as an alternative to the *locus actus* is justified. It better meets the requirements in the current era of easy mobility, where legal situations are no longer necessarily anchored in the place of their establishment.

Conclusion

There has been a growing awareness in the past decade that recognition of foreign decisions concerning civil status must not be refused without good reasons because the recognition regularly constitutes an essential requirement to grant legal protection to the party in need. Simultaneously, however, the courts' practice also seems to cling to traditional ideals of marriage as a life-long, heterosexual, monogamous institution, which are underpinned by Christian morality, when advancing interests of *ordre public*. Undoubtedly, the traditional ideals of marriage universal validity is challenged by multiple forms of deviating social realities (Dethloff 2011: 409). Nevertheless, an *ordre public* rationale has served to justify non-tolerance of marriages below the age of 18 and the recent amendments of the PILA and the Swiss CC. It is undisputed that child marriages must be rejected. In contrast, it may be disputed whether setting a strict age limit is an effective strategy to prevent forced marriages. In Swiss court practice on divorce, abstract notions of *ordre public* have been the prevailing arguments for non-recognition of foreign divorces obtained by *talaq*, instead of the court focusing on the involved parties' interests and needs for legal protection. When substantiated justification is lacking, the *ordre public* reservation becomes an empty shell or a cover for processes of self-affirmation that are catalysed by the confrontation with other forms of law (cf. Büchler 2011a: 40–55).

Islamic law, wrongly perceived as a uniform entity, seems to have particularly provocative effects. Traditional interpretations of Islamic law, which have, to varying degrees, been incorporated in family law codes in the Muslim world, challenge recent and yet fragile attainments of European modernity (Büchler 2011a: 12; Büchler 2012: 197). Indeed, the majority of families in Switzerland still practise a traditional model where the wife has the main responsibility for household and children and this model was enshrined in the Swiss Civil Code till 1988. Furthermore, gender equality regarding family surname and citizenship has only sanctioned in Switzerland in 2013. Remarkably, in political debates, conservative actors are among the most willing to use gender equality as an argument to advance their xenophobic, and particularly, Islamophobic agendas. Instead of engaging in a binary discourse, whereby one's own legal precepts are essentialised and shielded against what is perceived as 'other', it is worth having a closer look at what is really at stake and to reflect on the core of private international law. Above all, the *ordre public* rationale should focus on ensuring internationally recognised personal rights and it should not be instrumentalised for any construct of public morality (Büchler 2011a: 54–55). The contractual concept on which marriage in Islamic law is based, offers fruitful inputs for reforms in matrimonial law. While marriage as an institution is losing ground, law will remain the cornerstone of family life, allowing for multifaceted structures and lifestyles, safeguarding the parties' autonomy upon conclusion and dissolution of family agreements, balancing unequal distribution of power and resources and, last but not least, protecting the interests of the children involved.

Notes

1 On average, according to the provisional 2012 figures published by the Swiss Federal Statistical Office, 45% of the marriages concluded in Switzerland between

January and November 2012 and 55% of the divorces obtained between July and November 2012 involved at least one foreign national (Federal Statistical Office FSO, Eheschliessungen und eingetragene Partnerschaften nach Kanton, Scheidungen nach Kanton 2012, Neuchâtel, of 23 January 2013).

2 Because English is not an official language of the Swiss Confederation, there is no officially acknowledged translation of laws and other legal materials. To the extent that they are available, suggested translations by the Swiss federal authorities have been used.

3 The wording of the current Article 20, para. 1(a), PILA, corresponds exactly to the definition of domicile in Article 23, para. 1, Swiss CC. Notwithstanding this fact, the concept of domicile in the PILA must be considered independently from the Swiss CC, as stated in Article 20 para. 2, PILA: '[T]he provisions of the Civil Code on domicile and usual place of residence do not apply.' Therefore, Article 20, PILA was designed as a substantive provision itself, instead of simply introducing a unilateral conflict-of-laws rule referring to Swiss substantive law (Schnyder and Liatowitsch 2011: 191–92).

4 Article 20, para. 2, PILA provides that if someone has no domicile, the usual place of residence is deemed to be the domicile.

5 Over the last decade, the requirements for Swiss citizenship have become less rigorous, particularly for the second generation. While the Swiss Federal Council proposed take a further step towards *ius soli* for the third generation of foreign nationals in Switzerland, the current parliamentary debates reveal an opposite trend towards general reinforcement of the conditions for naturalisation. The matter is currently pending in Swiss Parliament (as at April 2013).

6 For a more detailed analysis of nationality and domicile as connecting factors, as well as the complex intertwining of legal aspects and cultural impacts, see Büchler 2011a: 27–40.

7 Domestic connection is not required when the interests of international *ordre public* are affected. They enjoy absolute priority over possibly deviating norms of Swiss legal principles. International *ordre public* comprises those legal standards that are considered as indispensable by the international community, such as the bona fide principle, the prohibition of abuse of law, and the safeguarding of dignity (Vischer 2004: 260, 265–66; Bucher 2004: 18).

8 This reason deserves particular attention against the backdrop that the Swiss legislator waived the requirement of reciprocity which has been widely spread in traditional law of recognition and which is still practiced in various European countries and overseas. The Swiss legislator's waiver was intended, *inter alia*, to foster the recognition of personal status and to reinforce legal certainty in the fields of protection of the family and minors (Volken 2004a: 363–4).

9 The French doctrine therefore developed the expression attenuated *ordre public* of recognition (*ordre public atténué de la reconnaissance*).

10 In the French doctrine, it is called *interdiction de révision au fond.*

11 The opinions of legal scholars are strongly divided on whether the strength of domestic connections need to be taken into account. Affirmative: Volken 2004a: 392; negative: Berti and Däppen 2007: 232–33, with references to the deviating (i.e. affirmative) opinion of the Swiss Federal Supreme Court. For a detailed discussion in favour of the domestic connection's relevance, cf. Othenin-Girard 2001.

12 Article 43, para. 2, PILA, also grants couples, both of whom have a foreign domicile, the ability to marry in Switzerland on condition that the marriage is recognised in the countries of domicile or citizenship of both future spouses.

13 The Act entered into force on 1 July 2013.

14 According to the Swiss Federal Council, a marriage declared invalid, based on Article 105(6), Swiss CC, would be remedied as soon as the concerned spouse reaches the age of 18, cf. Message of the Swiss Federal Council 2011: 2216.

15 The issuance of a certificate or at least the registration by a state authority of a marriage concluded by a non-state (e.g. a religious or private) authority is compulsory for recognition under Swiss law.

16 Article 45, para. 2, PILA, states that if the bride or the bridegroom is a Swiss citizen or both future spouses are domiciled in Switzerland, a marriage concluded abroad is recognised unless the marriage ceremony was conducted abroad with the manifest purpose of circumventing the Swiss legal provisions on the invalidity of a marriage. Article 45, para. 2, PILA, must be only applied to the reasons of invalidity set out in Article 105, Swiss CC, cf. Courvoisier 2007: 331. Accordingly, a marriage is invalid, (1) if one of the spouses is already married, (2) if one of the spouses lacks capacity to consent, (3) if the marriage is prohibited due to kinship, or (4) if one of the spouses has no intent of living with the other but wishes to circumvent the provisions on the admission and residence of foreign nationals.

17 Cases of non-existing marriages are not codified by law, but judges and scholars agree that a marriage is to be considered as non-existing in three circumstances: first, when both spouses of the same sex at the time of the celebration of the marriage; second, if there is no civil servant present at the ceremony; and third, if the spouses have not expressed their will to marry at all or not unconditionally, or if they were married by proxy, cf. Büchler and Vetterli 2011: 33.

18 Regional Court Bern-Mittelland, decision of 8 July 2011 – CIV091986LUF, *Die Praxis des Familienrechts* 2011, 4: 944–51.

19 In classical Islamic law, marriage is concluded without the involvement of the state. For the sake of clarity, numerous countries where family law has been influenced by Islamic law introduced reform laws requiring that marriage contracts be concluded in written form and at a public authority that is also responsible for registration. Only in these cases are marriages recognised in public law, which then allows for marriage issues to be brought before courts, cf. Büchler 2003: 26–27.

20 Marriage between a female Muslim and a male non-Muslim is generally not tolerated in legal orders influenced by Islam (Büchler 2003: 33–34).

21 The Federal Supreme Court refused to recognise a foreign marriage on the grounds that its celebration was based on a falsified proxy (Federal Supreme Court decision of 19 April 1996, Pra 86, 1997, 11). *In casu*, the bride had herself signed the proxy on behalf of the groom. The Court argued that because the way the marriage was concluded was incompatible with Swiss *ordre public*, it was irrelevant whether the groom agreed to the marriage or not. Thus, the Court based its decision on a formal, objective perspective without assessing the will of the spouses. Furthermore, the validity of the marriage under the relevant foreign law was not an issue.

22 Excerpt from the judgment by Swiss Asylum Appeals Commission of 7 March 2006, VPB 2006, 70/IV, 71.

23 Appeals decision of the Building Department of 24 April 1998, GER 1998, 3.

24 Likewise, Article 45, para 2, PILA, which sanctions 'the spouses' manifest purpose of circumventing the Swiss legal provisions on the invalidity of Swiss law', was not considered in this decision because this provision only entered into force in 2000. It should be noted however that marriage by proxy is a non-existing marriage according to principles of Swiss civil law, i.e. such a marriage has an even more serious deficiency than a merely invalid marriage according to Article 105, Swiss CC.

25 In Persian: *nekaheh monghateh* or *sigheh* marriage; in Arabic: *mut'a* marriage.

26 Judgment of the Administrative Court of 28 April 2009, ATA/203/2009; Federal Supreme Court decision 5A_404/2009.

27 The divorce rate in Switzerland, which, according to the Swiss Federal Statistical Office, 'describes the proportion of marriages which will end in divorce for each length of marriage, should the divorce patterns of the reference year persist',

climaxed at 54.4% in 2010 and declined in 2011 to 43.2%. Available online at www.bfs.admin.ch/bfs/portal/en/index/themen/01/06/blank/key/06/03.html (accessed 18 April 2013).

28 Non-marital cohabitation does not enjoy legal protection under Swiss law.

29 Accordingly, a foreign judgment should not produce effects that are different or considerably further reaching than a corresponding domestic judgment would have produced (Volken 2004a: 359).

30 This idea has already been considered with regard to foreign marriages of same sex couples, which are recognised in Switzerland as registered partnerships only (Courvoisier 2007: 333).

31 *In casu*, the Federal Supreme Court rejected the request for maintenance. The Court mainly relied on the wife's apparently good financial situation (decision 5A_528 2011).

32 Assumedly, the authorities might have concluded differently, i.e. not recognising the marriage. Whereas the spouses' different religions are not an impediment to marriage under Swiss law, the marriage concluded in Iran by a mullah who is also a notary, violates the principle of compulsory civil marriage prevalent in Swiss law. Such a conclusion would be unsatisfactory because it would be religion that sent the marriage in the direction of non-recognition. This would be at odds with the human right to freedom of religion and marriage, and thus contrary to *ordre public* (cf. Büchler 2011a: 45; Schwander 1997: 54).

33 Bigamy is also prosecuted under Swiss Criminal Law (Article 215, Swiss Criminal Code).

34 Judgment of the Cantonal Tax Appeals Commission of the Canton Basel-Stadt No. 22/2000 of 24 February 2000, 22 2000, BStPra 2002, 4: 262–68.

35 Polygamy has been prohibited under Tunisian law since 1956.

36 Appeals Court VD, decision of 21 October 1996, JdT 1997 III, 87–94.

37 In contrast, an invalid divorce due to violation of Swiss *ordre public* cannot be remedied by a subsequently concluded valid marriage (Swiss Federal Supreme Court decision 122 III 344, 352).

38 Swiss Federal Supreme Court decision 110 II 5.

39 Article 96, Swiss CC, provides that a person wishing to remarry must prove that any previous marriage has been annulled or dissolved.

40 Judgment of the Federal Administrative Court, Division IV of 28 September 2007, D-4189/2006.

41 Indeed, safeguarding the rights of the family is a basic principle of international law, cf. inter alia, Article 14, Federal Constitution of the Swiss Confederation, Article 8, European Convention on Human Rights and Article 16, Universal Declaration of Human Rights.

42 It is worth noting that, for the purpose of this chapter, the cited examples are connected to the legal orders of countries with Muslim majorities in order to take account of how the legislation of these countries deal with polygamy and, with this in mind, to consider if and to which extent their approaches matter for Swiss courts. However, a significant number of international cases that the Swiss courts deal with regarding polygamy do not have any connection with the Muslim world.

43 Decision of the Federal Administrative Court of 23 March 2012, E-1022/2008.

44 The judgment does not reveal though, how the Iraqi's second marriage could have been recognised in Switzerland, given the same conditions, i.e. the not yet validly dissolved marriage to his first wife in Iraq, nor does it include any hint that it was annulled later.

45 This claim was not further assessed within this judgment as the authorities considered it to be implausible when compared with the refugee's former claims and his previously filed documents.

46 As far as bigamy or polygamy is concerned, however, the Court contends that recognition must be refused in any event, i.e. even in absence of any domestic connection.
47 Women's rights to obtain a divorce have, in recent decades, improved in countries with legal orders influenced by Islam. However, those rights are not equal to those of men, with the exception of the provisions in the Tunisian code of personal status. Therefore, Article 61, para. 3, PILA, could apply for couples who have a common citizenship of such a country. However, as no case law in application of Article 61, para. 3, PILA, has yet been published, the number of such cases brought to Swiss courts is unknown.
48 Article 25(a), PILA, states that a foreign decision is recognised in Switzerland if the court or public authorities of the country where the decision was rendered had jurisdiction. Additionally, the first part of Article 26(a), PILA, assigns jurisdiction to foreign authorities if provided for by a provision within the PILA.
49 Embassy buildings belong to the territory of the receiving country under modern international law (Bopp 2007: 443).
50 PILA provisions regarding divorce do not explicitly address divorce by joint request according to Articles 111–12, Swiss CC, because they date from before the revision of Swiss divorce law when divorce by joint request was introduced into the Swiss CC for the first time. The Swiss legislator has not considered it necessary to adapt the wording of the PILA Articles on divorce since then.
51 Swiss Federal Supreme Court decision 88 I 48.
52 The option for divorce by joint request was only introduced into the Swiss CC on the occasion of a revision of Swiss divorce law in the 1990s. One of its main aims was to abolish the principle of fault in favour of implementing provisions for divorce by joint request and unilateral divorce after a four-year separation. The revised provisions in the Swiss CC entered into force in 2000. In 2004, the four-year period for unilateral divorce after separation was reduced to two years.
53 Judgment of 14 November 1991, A.Z. c. Dame F.A. (GE), SJ 1992: 219–24.
54 Cantonal Court, Civil Division II, 14 September 1995, GVP 1995, 44: 117–19.
55 Appeals Court VD, decision of 21 October 1996, JdT 1997 III, 87–94.
56 Whether the scope of Article 65, PILA, is restricted to recognition of divorce on the level of civil status or if it also applies to the side effects is highly contested, cf. Volken 2004c: 651; decision of 25 October 2010 by the Cantonal Appeals Court of Thurgau, RBOG 2010, No. 23.
57 Swiss Federal Supreme Court decision 122 III 344.
58 Cantonal Appeals Court of Luzern decision of 31 August 2001, Division II, LGVE 2002 I, No. 31.
59 Swiss Federal Supreme Court decision 131 III 182.
60 Swiss Federal Supreme Court decision 126 III 327.
61 Cantonal Appeals Court of Berne decision of 30 May 2005, Division II, APH 05 89 (BE), in *Die Praxis des Familienrechts*, 2006, 2: 410–14.
62 Swiss Federal Supreme Court decision 126 III 327.

Bibliography

Berti, S.V. and Däppen, R.K. (2007) 'Art. 25'–'Art. 27', in H. Honsell, N.P. Vogt, A.K. Schnyder and S.V. Berti (eds), *Basler Kommentar. Internationales Privatrecht*, 2nd edn, Basel: Helbing Lichtenhahn, 216–39.

Bopp, L. (2007) 'Art. 59'–'Art. 65', in H. Honsell, N.P. Vogt, A.K. Schnyder and S.V. Berti (eds), *Basler Kommentar. Internationales Privatrecht*, 2nd edn, Basel: Helbing Lichtenhahn.

Bucher, A. (2004) *Le couple en droit international privé*, Basel, Geneva and Munich: Helbing Lichtenhahn; Paris: L.G.D.J.
——(2008) 'Internationales Scheidungsrecht in der Praxis', in I. Schwenzer and A. Büchler (eds), *Vierte Schweizer Familienrechtstage*, Bern: Stämpfli.
Büchler, A. (2003) *Das islamische Familienrecht. Eine Annäherung unter Berücksichtigung des Verhältnisses des klassischen islamischen Rechts zum geltenden ägyptischen Familienrecht*, Bern: Stämpfli.
——(2007) 'Zwangsehen in zivilrechtlicher und internationalprivatrechtlicher Sicht. Rechtstatsachen – Rechtsvergleich – Rechtsanalyse', *Die Praxis des Familienrechts*, 4: 725–51.
——(2011a) *Islamic Law in Europe? Legal pluralism and its limits in European family laws*, Farnham and Burlington, VT: Ashgate.
——(2011b) 'Bemerkungen zu Regionalgericht Bern-Mittelland Entscheid vom 8. Juli 2011 – CIV091986LUF', *Die Praxis des Familienrechts*, 4: 944–51.
——(2012) 'Islamic family law in Europe? From dichotomies to discourse – or: beyond cultural and religious identity in family law', *International Journal of Law in Context*, 8(2): 196–210.
Büchler, A. and Fink, S. (2008) 'Eheschliessungen im Ausland. Die Grenzen ihrer Anerkennung in der Schweiz am Beispiel von Ehen islamischer Prägung', *Die Praxis des Familienrechts*, 1: 48–68.
Büchler, A. and Vetterli, R. (2011) *Ehe Partnerschaft Kinder. Eine Einführung in das Familienrecht der Schweiz*, 2nd edn, Basel: Helbing Lichtenhahn.
Courvoisier, M. (2007) 'Vor Art. 43–65d'; 'Art. 43–45', in H. Honsell, N.P. Vogt, A.K. Schnyder and S.V. Berti (eds), *Basler Kommentar. Internationales Privatrecht*, 2nd edn, Basel: Helbing Lichtenhahn.
Dethloff, N. (2011) 'Polygamie – Wer definiert Ehe und Familie in Europa?', in A. Büchler and M. Müller-Chen (eds), *Festschrift für Ingeborg Schwenzer zum 60. Geburtstag; Private Law (Band I) – national global comparative (Band II)*, Bern: Stämpfli.
Federal Statistical Office FSO (2013) *Eheschliessungen und eingetragene Partnerschaften nach Kanton, Scheidungen nach Kanton 2012, Neuchâtel*, of 23 January 2013.
Furrer, A., Girsberger, D. and Müller-Chen, M. (eds) (2012) *Internationales Privatrecht (Art. 1–200 IPRG), Handkommentar zum Schweizer Privatrecht*, 2nd edn, Zurich: Schulthess.
Geiser, T. (2008) 'Scheinehe, Zwangsehe und Zwangsscheidung aus zivilrechtlicher Sicht', *Zeitschrift des Bernischen Juristenvereins*, 144: 817–49.
Guillaume, F. (2008) '"O tempora! O mores!": l'effet du temps sur l'ordre public en droit international privé', in P. Zen-Ruffinen (ed.), *Le temps et le droit, Recueil des travaux offerts à la Journée de la Société suisse des juristes*, Basel: Helbing Lichtenhahn.
Jourabchi, T.E.Z. (2011) 'Le mariage temporaire en droit iranien', *Die Praxis des Familienrechts*, 4: 807–38.
Keller, M. and Girsberger, D. (2004) 'Art. 15', in D. Girsberger, A. Heini, M. Keller, J. Kren Kostkiewicz, K. Siehr, F. Vischer and P. Volken (eds), *Zürcher Kommentar zum IPRG*, 2nd edn, Zurich: Schulthess.
Keller, M. and Kren Kostkiewicz, J. (2004) 'Art. 20', in D. Girsberger, A. Heini, M. Keller, J. Kren Kostkiewicz, K. Siehr, F. Vischer and P. Volken (eds), *Zürcher Kommentar zum IPRG*, 2nd edn, Zurich: Schulthess.
Mächler-Erne, M. and Wolf-Mettier, S. (2004) 'Art. 15', in H. Honsell, N.P. Vogt, A.K. Schnyder and S.V. Berti (eds), *Basler Kommentar. Internationales Privatrecht*, 2nd edn, Basel: Helbing Lichtenhahn.

Müller-Chen, M. (2001) 'Auswirkungen des revidierten Scheidungsrechts auf das internationale Zivilverfahrensrecht', *Die Praxis des Familienrechts*, 2: 187–99.

Neubauer, A. and Dahinden, J. (2012) *'Zwangsheiraten' in der Schweiz: Ursachen, Formen, Ausmass*, Bern-Wabern: Bundesamt für Migration (BFM).

Othenin-Girard, S. (1999) *La réserve d'ordre public en droit international privé suisse. Personnes – Famille – Sucessions*, Zürich: Schulthess.

——(2001) 'Reconnaissance des répudiations en Suisse et ordre public. Quelques réflexions à la lumière d'un récent arrêt du Tribunal fédéral (ATF 126 III 327)', *Revue suisse de jurisprudence*, 97: 21–30.

Schnyder, A.K. and Liatowitsch, M. (2011) *Internationales Privat-und Zivilverfahrensrecht*, 3rd edn, Zurich Basel Geneva: Schulthess.

Schwander, I. (1997) *Einführung in das internationale Privatrecht. Zweiter Band: Besonderer Teil*, St. Gallen Lachen: Dike.

——(2002) 'Die Anwendung und Anerkennung islamischen Rechts im Internationalen Privat-und Zivilprozessrecht der Schweiz', in R. Pahud de Mortanges and E. Tanner (eds), *Muslime und die schweizerische Rechtsordnung*, Freiburg: Universitätsverlag Freiburg Schweiz.

——(2009) 'Anerkennung und Vollstreckbarerklärung ausländischer Scheidungsurteile', *Die Praxis des Familienrechts*, 4: 832–66.

Schwander, M. (2012) 'Schweizerische Antworten auf Zwangsheiraten als Menschenrechtsverletzung', *Neue Kriminalpolitik*, 4: 126–33.

Schwander, I. and Füllemann, D. (2010) 'Bundesgerichtliche Rechtsprechung zum Internationalen Privat-und Zivilverfahrensrecht 1', *Aktuelle Juristische Praxis*, 1037–45.

Siehr, K. (2002) *Das Internationale Privatrecht der Schweiz*, Zürich: Schulthess.

Vischer, F. (2004) 'Art. 17', in D. Girsberger, A. Heini, M. Keller, J. Kren Kostkiewicz, K. Siehr, F. Vischer and P. Volken (eds), *Zürcher Kommentar zum IPRG*, 2nd edn, Zurich: Schulthess.

Volken, P. (2004a) 'Vor Art. 25–32'; 'Art. 25'–'Art. 27', in D. Girsberger, A. Heini, M. Keller, J. Kren Kostkiewicz, K. Siehr, F. Vischer and P. Volken (eds), *Zürcher Kommentar zum IPRG*, 2nd edn, Zurich: Schulthess.

——(2004b) 'Vor Art. 43–65'; 'Art. 43'–'Art. 45', in D. Girsberger, A. Heini, M. Keller, J. Kren Kostkiewicz, K. Siehr, F. Vischer and P. Volken (eds), *Zürcher Kommentar zum IPRG*, 2nd edn, Zurich: Schulthess.

——(2004c) 'Art. 59'–'Art. 65', in D. Girsberger, A. Heini, M. Keller, J. Kren Kostkiewicz, K. Siehr, F. Vischer and P. Volken (eds), *Zürcher Kommentar zum IPRG*, 2nd edn, Zurich: Schulthess.

Widmer Lüchinger, C. (2011) 'Migration und Zwangsehe im internationalen Privatrecht', *Die Praxis des Familienrechts*, 4: 787–806.

Legislation and related legal materials (in chronological order)

Federal Act on the Private Law Conditions of Domiciliaries and Sojouners of 25 June 1891, repealed.

Swiss Civil Code of 10 December 1907, as amended.

Civil Code of the Islamic Republic of Iran of 23 May 1928, as amended.

Convention d'établissement entre la Confédération suisse et l'Empire de Perse du 25 avril 1934.

Swiss Criminal Code of 21 December 1937, as amended.

Message of the Swiss Federal Council regarding the Federal Act on Private International Law of 10 November 1982, Federal Paper 1983 I, 263–519.
Federal Act on Private International Law of 18 December 1987, as amended.
Federal Asylum Act of 26 June 1998, as amended.
Council of Europe, Parliamentary Assembly, Resolution 1468, Forced marriages and child marriages, 2005.
Report of the Swiss Federal Council, Forced and Arranged Marriage as a Criminal Offence, 2007.
Message of the Swiss Federal Council regarding the Federal Act on Measures Against Forced Marriages of 23 February 2011, Federal Paper 2011, 11, 2185–228.
Federal Act on Measures against Forced Marriages of 15 June 2012.

5 The recognition of transnational Muslim marriages and divorces by Norwegian courts and other competent authorities

Dynamics between legislation and legal practice

Katja Jansen Fredriksen

The Muslim population in Norway

Norway has in a relatively short time developed from a fairly homogeneous society with deep roots in Lutheran-Protestant norms and traditions into a multicultural and pluralistic society (Naguib 2003: 112).[1] The increasing presence of Muslim migrants and their descendants in Norway has had an impact on domestic legislation, case law, legal doctrine and administrative practice in recent years.

In comparison with other European countries, migration from Muslim countries started rather late in Norway. During the late 1960s, the first groups of Muslim migrants began coming from countries such as Pakistan, Morocco and Turkey to perform low-skilled and low-paid labour to financially support their families at home and to make investments in their country of origin. Initially, these migrants only intended to stay in Norway for a limited period, but at the beginning of the 1970s many started to realize that their stay in Norway would have a more permanent character, resulting in the establishment of the first Muslim religious institutions (mosques) in Norway (Vogt 2008: 35–38).

In 1975, Norway halted immigration for foreign labour, specifically aiming to restrict labour migration from non-European Economic Area (EEA) countries. These immigration restrictions led to a new phase of 'family immigration' from Muslim countries (Naguib 2003: 112). Family immigration comprises both 'family reunification', i.e. immigration with the purpose of reunifying with a close family member resident in Norway, and 'family establishment', i.e. immigration in order to establish a family with a spouse resident in Norway, e.g. marriage migration.

During the 1990s, refugees from countries such as Bosnia-Herzegovina, Iran, Iraq, Kosovo, Somalia sought protection in Norway, as have refugees from Afghanistan and Syria in more recent years.[2] In the period from

1990–2008, the Muslim population in Norway increased mainly as the result of 'transnational marriages' and family reunification (Daugstad 2006, 2008a: 3, 2008b: 162–72; Henriksen 2010: 13–19).

It is not possible to determine the exact size of the Muslim population in Norway as Statistics Norway censuses do not register the religious denomination of Norwegian residents.[3] Statistics are available about the nationality of Norwegian residents and the membership rates of registered Muslim faith communities with state funding, but it should be emphasized that the numbers provided in this section are by no means accurate and should be understood as approximations.

As at 1 January 2011, there were 106,735 members of registered Muslim faith communities with state funding (Statistics Norway 2011a). This number, which constituted the group with 22 per cent of all the funding that the Norwegian state granted to religious and non-religious ethnic communities outside the Church of Norway that year, is the minimum number of Muslim residents in Norway as at 1 January 2011.

Also as at 1 January 2011, there were 201,233 nationals from 30 predominantly Muslim countries who had residence in Norway.[4] Using the percentage of Muslims living in these countries as the calcuation basis, the number of Muslim immigrants in Norway can be estimated at 178,204 persons at the time.[5]

However, these statistics do not include Muslim immigrants with Norwegian passports. Again as at 1 January 2011, there were 121,129 applicants from countries with Muslim majorities[6] who had been granted Norwegian citizenship; the total Norwegian population at the time was 4,920,305 (Statistics Norway 2011b). However, this does not necessarily mean that these applicants have either renounced their original citizenship or had it removed from them. Despite the fact that Norway – in principle – does not allow dual citizenship, exemption can be granted if the applicant cannot be released from his original nationality, or if the release takes a disproportionate amount of time or the charges for release from one's original nationality are high.[7] Applicants from Muslim countries are often granted exemption and maintain their original citizenship. As a consequence, they are still subject to the personal status law of their country of origin, even when they live abroad.

In addition, there is a small group of approximately 500 converts in Norway, most of the them women married to Muslim men (Vogt 2008: 24).[8] This implies that the Muslim population currently constitutes about 2.5 to 4 per cent of the total Norwegian population (Østby 2011). This figure is low relative to that of other European countries.

Transnational marriages among Muslim migrants and their descendants

As mentioned in the previous section, because of tighter immigration controls that came into effect in the mid-1970s, transnational marriages now account for most of the increase in the number of Muslim immigrants resident in

Norway. Statistics Norway defines 'transnational marriages' as marriages between a person with residence in Norway and a person with residence abroad (Daugstad 2006: 19). The increase in transnational marriages among Muslim migrants and their descendants in Norway can not, however, be solely explained by an interest in immigration.

First, the definition does not take into consideration that it is a tradition in Muslim cultures to arrange marriages between spouses with a similar (family) background in terms of nationality, ethnicity, language, culture, religion, class, kin, etc. Because the Muslim population in Norway is so small and diverse, chances of finding a spouse with a similar background are, as a rule, greater in the parental region of origin. Second, family relations usually remain strong despite migration and extend across national borders in Muslim family structures. Third, migration from Muslim countries not only takes place to Europe, Australia and North America, but also to other Muslim countries. Marriages between persons who live in Norway but who have an immigration background from different Muslim countries can, therefore, also be seen as transnational marriages.

It is, nonetheless, important to emphasize that there are broad variations in transnational marriage patterns among Muslim migrants and their descendants in Norway. First- and second-generation immigrants[9] from Asian and African countries usually marry a foreign spouse from their parents' country of origin, who after marriage moves to Norway. Refugees from Bosnia-Herzegovina and Iran, on the other hand, more often choose a partner from their own local migrant community in Norway. Also, second-generation Turks find their spouse in the Turkish migrant community in Norway, and in recent years an increasing number of Turkish citizens (i.e. foreigners) have entered into marriage with a spouse with residence in Norway, who either is an ethnic Norwegian or a foreign national (Daugstad 2008a: 70, 2008b: 166–67, 170; Henriksen 2010: 6, 13, 15–16, 18–19).

In this chapter, transnational marriages are thus seen as marriages with a cross-cultural and cross-national dimension, and in which the spouses are connected to more than one country as the result of immigration.

Marriages of convenience

As new regulations aim to lessen the possibility for non-EEA citizens to acquire a Norwegian residence permit on the basis of labour, family reunification or humanitarian grounds, marriage with a Norwegian resident may be a way to circumvent strict Norwegian immigration rules.[10] In practice, however, it is not always clear where to draw the line between 'arranged', 'transnational' and 'sham or bogus' marriages, which are also called 'marriages of convenience'.[11]

Marriage of convenience is defined in section 40 para. 4 of the Norwegian Immigration Act of 2008[12] as a marriage in which it is most likely that the main objective of the marriage is to establish a basis for residence in Norway for the applicant. Marriages of convenience legally constitute grave breaches of the Norwegian Immigration Act, and may lead to criminal prosecution of both the applicant and the reference person (e.g. 'supporter' or 'supporting person' or 'the person whom they have married'). The applicant may also have his or her residence permit revoked, and be expelled from Norway and the Schengen Area.

Foreign nationals may be tempted to enter into a marriage of convenience in situations where their application for a work permit or refugee protection has been rejected. Situations where a foreign national dissolves a marriage with a Norwegian resident as soon as the foreign spouse has acquired enough residence time in Norway to either petition for Norwegian citizenship[13] or to gain a permanent residence permit[14] may also indicate that the marriage was entered into mainly to provide the foreign spouse with a basis for residence in Norway.[15] However, no statistics are available that could provide insight into the scale of marriages of convenience among Muslims in Norway.[16]

Recent legal practice regarding marriages of convenience involving Muslim parties has led to variable results. In 2006, the Supreme Court had to consider whether a marriage between a Pakistani man, born in 1979, and a Norwegian woman, born in 1956, was real, mainly because of the age difference between the spouses.[17] At the time of marriage, the Norwegian woman already had five children from an earlier marriage and an earlier cohabitation with two other Pakistani men. As divorced women may have a rather low status in Muslim communities in Norway (Salimi 2001: 61), this could indicate that the man's main intention was to acquire a residence permit in Norway. On the other hand, as the Norwegian woman had good connections within the local Pakistani community and had converted to Islam and understood and spoke some Urdu, the spouses had a common religious and cultural basis for communication. Furthermore, the Supreme Court was not convinced that the couple did not have serious intentions as to the marriage at the time the Norwegian state decided to withdraw the man's Norwegian residence permit. The court also placed considerable weight on the testimonies of the woman's family and friends who stated that they – even though sceptical at beginning – gradually had been convinced that the man was serious about the relationship. Depite some dissent, the Supreme Court concluded that the legal effects of a deportation would be such a comprehensive intervention in the couple's private and family life that such an intervention had to weigh heavier than the potential risk of granting a foreigner a basis for residence in Norway on false premises, as argued for by the Norwegian state. Consequently, the Norwegian state lost. Three other recent cases, decided by the Norwegian Court of Appeal,[18] went, however, in favour of the Norwegian state.

The main principles of Norwegian private international law

Even though there appears to be a correlation between transnational marriages, immigration law and the legal challenges that these transnational marriages may pose,[19] this potential tension is not the main reason why transnational marriages and divorces between Muslim spouses seem to cause problems in European legal systems, including Norway. The problem is rather that the spouses, because of their (difference in) nationality, are connected to more than one country and therefore have to take into account more than one legal system simultaneously when entering into or dissolving transnational marriages. Norwegian private international law deals with such legal questions.

Norwegian private international law is a part of substantive Norwegian law, comprising a set of rules that determines the choice of law in cross-border cases. Cross-border disputes occur when there is a strong connection to a foreign country, for instance because one of the parties to the dispute is a foreign national or because the dispute concerns a conflict related to more than one country and consequently requires a decision concerning the applicable law. Even though a case is brought before a Norwegian court and the Norwegian court has jurisdiction, the legal question does not necessarily have to be decided on the basis of Norwegian law. Sometimes the interests of parties are better served by the application of foreign law. This particularly concerns private law cases, where judges as a rule are granted more discretion and where the possibilities for applying foreign law in order to do justice are greater. The main purpose of private international law is to coordinate justice in cross-border disputes on the basis of the principle of equality among legal systems.

The domicile principle and limitations with respect to the application of foreign law

In contrast to the private international law of many other European countries, Norwegian private international law follows the domicile principle.[20] According to Norwegian private international law, a foreign national acquires domicile in Norway as soon as that person actually moves to Norway with the intention of staying there for an indefinite period.[21] Once foreign nationals have achieved domicile in Norway according to Norwegian private international law principles, they automatically become subject to Norwegian law in their family law matters.[22]

Another important feature of Norwegian law is that the field of family law is subject to many internationally mandatory rules. Consequently, cross-border divorce disputes are subject to Norwegian law.[23] These limitations, together with the general *ordre public* reservation and a ban on applying a foreign rule of law when the result of the application of the foreign law would conflict with the prevailing sense of justice in Norway (e.g. the *ordre public*), leads to the fact that foreign law is seldom applied in Norwegian cross-border cases.

'Limping marriages' and 'limping divorces'

When a couple has a connection to more than one state, it may be of importance for both or at least one of the parties that the marriage or divorce is recognized in all of the states to which the parties have a relevant connection. A general principle in private international law is that a marriage or a divorce that has taken place in one country will also be recognized in another. Even so, there will be situations where provisions on marriage or divorce in one country so clearly contradict the provisions of another country that recognition will be denied.

When recognition is denied, there is a 'limping marriage' or 'limping divorce'. This means that a person may be considered married or divorced in one country, but not in another. This may cause problems for the parties, and these problems can be of a legal and/or a social nature, as will be seen below. Because of the differences between Norwegian and Muslim personal status law, which is based on *shari'a* principles, there is a significant risk of limping marriages and divorces when one or more Muslim parties are involved. Muslim migrants and their descendants in Norway already have problems with limping marriages and limping divorces (Ferrari de Carli 2008: 7–14).

The effects of decisions regarding the recognition of foreign marriages and divorces

Decisions regarding the recognition of foreign marriages and divorces may have considerable legal consequences for the parties involved and thus require careful consideration. Marriage to a Norwegian citizen or a person with residence in Norway may, for instance, entitle the foreign spouse to a residence and working permit in Norway and may also provide certain tax benefits during the marriage, and pension entitlements, succession rights and insurance payments upon the death of the other spouse. A legal divorce may also entitle the divorcee to certain social benefits. A Norwegian national or a Norwegian resident may not enter into a new marriage in Norway as long as a previous (foreign) marriage still exists. The right to marry is protected by international human rights instruments to which Norway is bound.

Decisions regarding the recognition of foreign marriages and foreign divorces may also have considerable social consequences for the parties involved because of the religious meaning that marriage and divorce has to Muslims in Norway and elsewhere in Europe. Young people may face strong social pressure by members of their family or local faith community to 'formalize' their relationship by entering into a 'religious marriage' in compliance with Islamic law (Liversage and Jensen 2011: 66).

The Norwegian approach to the recognition of Muslim marriages

Foreign marriages are, as a rule, recognized in Norway and given legal effect as long as the marriage is entered into in compliance with the formal rules of the country where the marriage was solemnized (based on the *lex loci celebrationis* principle). This rule has long historical roots in the customary law on which Norwegian private international law is, to a large extent, based, but since 1 June 2007 it has been codified in section 18a para 1 of the Norwegian Marriage Act, primarily for reasons of legal policy. The main intention behind this rule is to prevent limping marriages and 'forum shopping'. Decisions regarding the recognition of foreign marriages are mostly made administratively rather than judicially,[24] and are left to different competent authorities, such as the Norwegian immigration authorities and the National Registration Offices. As these authorities may operate with different standards of proof, a foreign marriage may be recognized by the National Registration Office, while the Norwegian immigration authorities may come to the conclusion that the foreign marriage is not valid in Norway and consequently cannot grant the foreign spouse a residence permit.

Muslim marriages that are entered into abroad may, however, under certain circumstances conflict with the Norwegian notion of the *ordre public* and may consequently be refused recognition. This implies that the foreign marriage is considered to be validly entered into in the country where it took place, but it is not given legal effect in Norway because certain aspects of the marriage conflict with the prevailing sense of justice in Norway. Muslim marriages are deemed to contradict the Norwegian notion of the *ordre public* if they are entered into under coercion (so-called forced marriages) or while (one of) the spouses were under age (so-called child marriages). Proxy and polygamous marriages are also deemed to contradict the Norwegian notion of the *ordre public*.

Norwegian law and arranged marriages

Arranged marriages are marriages in which the choice of suitable marriage candidates is left not to the prospective spouses, but to others, usually the parents or other close relatives. Factors that often are taken into account in this process are equality in religion, caste and culture, social status and reputation, wealth and education of the parties to the marriage (Nasir 2009b: 59–60). Arranged marriages are by no means exclusive to the Islamic faith (ibid.: 28) and should not be confused with marriages that are entered into under coercion.

Generally, arranged marriages are not prohibited by Norwegian law. This follows from the *travaux préparatoires* to the Norwegian Marriage Act and the Criminal Act.[25] However, there may also be circumstances where the line between arranged marriages and forced marriages may be thin (Mehdi 2007: 72). It follows from the *travaux préparatoires* to the Immigration Act of 2008[26] that 'in a broader perspective the tradition of arranged marriages under circumstances may contribute to create and maintain ethnic minority environments who exist outside the wider society' and that 'those groups in Norway who practice traditions of arranged marriages in general also are those groups who meet large problems in connection to their integration into the Norwegian society' (Daugstad 2008a: 10).

Norwegian law and forced marriages and child marriages

'Forced marriages' are marriages in which at least one of the parties was coerced to marry against his or her own free will and without his or her consent. In a 'child marriage', at least one of the parties is under the age of 18 (i.e. the age of majority and of marriage in Norway). Forced marriages and child marriages coincide if the compelled person was a minor at the time of marriage.[27] The use of coercion in marriage has long been prohibited by Norwegian law[28] and is also governed by the international human rights instruments to which Norway is bound.[29]

It is important to emphasize that most Muslim countries prohibit both forced marriages and child marriages (Nasir 2009a: 54–55, 2009b: 28–29, 50–52; Mehdi 2007: 73–75), but there also seem to be indications that, nonetheless, local clerks in, for instance, Egypt have developed ways to register such marriages in practice (Lindbekk 2013).

The Norwegian government dedicates considerable human and financial resources to prevent and combat the occurrence of forced marriages and child marriages among immigrant communities. The use of force in contracting marriages abroad is not only practised by Muslim communities, but also among Hindu and Sikh communities, as well as African Christian communities (*IMDi-rapport No. 6* 2008: 4, 30, 144). Yet, there may be circumstances in which Muslim marriage traditions, transnational family relations and loopholes in Muslim law may lead to the use of 'improper pressure' or 'unlawful behaviour'.

As explained above, it is not uncommon among Muslim migrants and their descendants in Norway to arrange marriages abroad, where the parties to the marriage are represented by a legal guardian, a *wali*. Marriage guardianship does not necessarily lead to coercion as long as both spouses approve of their legal guardian's decision and they can influence the choice of their marriage partner. There may, however, also be circumstances in which it may be arguable whether a young person actually had a choice, for instance when he or she is offered the choice between a set of pictures of potential marriage candidates, or when he or she is not given the option not to marry. The right not to marry is protected by the human right to marry.[30] The question of whether or not coercion has taken place should therefore be carefully considered in each case as the legal effects of such a decision may have a considerable impact on the private family life of the parties involved.

The case of Sima

The first government initiatives to combat forced marriages were the direct result of a tabloid newspaper article of 1992 concerning a Norwegian–Pakistani girl, known by the pseudonym 'Sima', who had been married off against her will to her cousin in Pakistan (Storhaug 1992). The girl managed to return to Norway with the assistance of the Norwegian Embassy in

Islamabad. Just before the new Norwegian Marriage Act came into force on 1 January 1993, the Norwegian court declared Sima's Pakistani marriage null and void and convicted her Pakistani husband (Ot.prp.nr. 44 (1993–94): 12; Wikan 2008a: 248–49, 2008b: 25–31).

Despite the fact that the Pakistani marriage was nullified, Sima's father refused to let her marry a British-Pakistani man, with whom she had fallen in love. However, in the face of all the difficulties, the couple entered in a so-called religious marriage in a mosque in Great Britain. The *imam* of the mosque had heard about Sima's case and was willing to solemnize the marriage without the consent of her father.[31] This religious marriage has no formal status in Great Britain and the couple was therefore not married under UK law. The couple currently lives in Norway as cohabitants and have two children together. When I asked Sima why they never got civilly married in Norway, Sima answered that to her, personally, only the religious marriage was of importance because this had helped her to obtain her local faith community's acceptance of the relationship. Sima meant that without the religious marriage '[she] and [her] children would not have been able to live their lives in dignity and respect and would not have been left in peace by the local faith community' (author's translation).[32]

Sima's narrative confirms that the religious marriage and its social effects may be at least as important to Muslim immigrants and their descendants as the formal marriage and the legal effects that can be derived from it.

The alleged need for a religious marriage

'Religious marriages' (also called 'informal', 'unregistered', 'customary', '*imam*' or *nikah* marriages) are marriage celebrations that are not valid under *lex fori*, but which enjoy the status of a marriage between the spouses and their local faith community. Among Muslim communities in Norway, as well as in other European countries, it is not however, always clear what in fact is meant by a religious marriage (Jänterä-Jareborg 2010: 215; Liversage and Jensen 2011: 37). Muslim migrants and their descendants in Norway seem to equate a religious marriage with a marriage that is contracted by an *imam*. Muslims in Norway have the possibility of entering into a marriage in a mosque that has solemnization rights.[33] Parties to the marriage may not always distinguish between the formal part of the marriage ceremony as delegated by the Norwegian state to an *imam* with solemnization rights, which constitutes the civil marriage according to Norwegian law, and the religious rites that follow afterwards. It may be particularly confusing when the parties to the marriage during the ceremony in the mosque enter into a Muslim marriage contract (*nikah*),[34] as this constitutes a marriage according to Islamic law. The *nikah*, together with the Norwegian marriage certificate, is later legalized at the diplomatic representation in Norway of the country of (family) origin of (one of) the spouses and sent that country for recognition and registration. The Muslim marriage contract is necessary to meet the conditions of the shari'a-inspired personal status laws (Muslim law) to which the spouses, because of their (multiple) nationality, are subject. Once the Norwegian civil marriage is recognized as a legally valid marriage and registered in the country of origin, certain legal rights, such as, for example, *mahr* (the Islamic dower), *nafaqa* (spousal maintenance), and the legitimacy of children born from the marriage, can be derived after registration in the country of origin.[35] Under such circumstances, the Norwegian marriage ceremony in the mosque by an *imam* with solemnization rights may easily be perceived to be a religious marriage.

Legislative measures to prevent and combat forced marriages and child marriages among migrant communities

In recent decades several amendments have been made to Norwegian law to reduce the occurrence of forced marriages among Norwegian migrant communities. In 1994, section 16 para. 3 was added to the Norwegian Marriage Act. According to this new provision, either of the spouses can have a (foreign) marriage contracted under coercion declared null and void by a Norwegian court, irrespective of who has exercised force. Furthermore, it follows from section 16 para. 4 that legal action to annul the marriage should be undertaken within a time limit of six months. Initially, Norwegian judges interpreted this provision broadly,[36] but in recent years legal practice seems to have developed towards a more strict interpretation of the law.[37] In addition, a Norwegian county governor may on his or her own initiative petition the court to have a marriage nullified, pursuant to section 16a of the Norwegian Marriage Act. In practice, however, Norwegian county governors appear reluctant to take such steps.

Spouses who have been forced into marriage also have the option to dissolve the marriage, pursuant to section 23 para. 3 of the Norwegian Marriage Act. This may be a better option in case children are born from the marriage and paternity needs to be established.

There are also relevant amendments to the Norwegian Penal Code, which primarily aim to have a general deterrent and pedagogical effect.[38] The use of violence, deprivation of liberty, improper pressure or any other unlawful conduct, or the making of threats involving such behaviour in order to force someone into marriage has, since 2003, been punishable by imprisonment for up to six years, pursuant to the section 222 para. 2 of the Norwegian Penal Coode. Aiding or contributing to marriage coercion can is also punishable under the same provision.

In addition, section 220 of the Norwegian Penal Code aims to protect minors from force by their parents, legal guardians or other relatives to enter into marriages, so-called child marriages. Pursuant to section 220, entering into marriage with a person under the age of 16 or actively participating in contracting the marriage is made punishable by up to four years of imprisonment. The use of physical or mental force or threats is thus not a formal requirement for legal action under this provision.

Another legal measure to prevent and combat the use of coercion in marriage among Norwegian migrant communities is that, pursuant to section 53 para. 3 of the Norwegian Immigration Act of 2008, the compelled party is entitled to a Norwegian resident permit and criminal injuries compensation if he/she can provide evidence in the from of a judgment that he/she has been forced into marriage.[39]

Legal practice regarding forced marriages and child marriages

Most case law regarding forced marriages has been initiated by the compelled party, be they male or female, and concerns the annulment of the marriage, pursuant to section 16 para. 3 of the Marriage Act.[40] There have been limited convictions under section 220 and section 222 of the Penal Code. There is one Supreme Court ruling from 2006[41] regarding section 222 para. 2 of the Penal Code, convicting a Kurdish father and his son for threatening violence to force the family's eldest daughter into a religious marriage in Iraq. Even though the local court in Iraq had declined to register the religious marriage,[42] as a consequence of which the marriage was not legally valid according to Iraqi law, the Supreme Court nonetheless sentenced the father and his son to imprisonment for a period of respectively two and a half years and two years.

The agreement between Norway and Pakistan

On 6 December 2005, Norway ratified an agreement with Pakistan, the country of origin of the largest non-EEA minority in Norway, to exchange information and advice in marital and family matters. The agreement, which came into force on 1 May 2006, establishes a consultation body (steering group) for issues relating to marriage, family and children as the result of migration between the two state parties. One of the primary reasons for entering into this agreement was to discuss the problems that Pakistani women in Norway experience with limping marriages and divorces and with forced marriages, a practice that is prohibited also by Pakistani law. The steering group has only met once.[43] Nevertheless, the agreement shows a willingness to discuss these issues on an intergovernmental level and a mutual intention to find solutions that are in compliance with each country's national legislation and international human rights obligations.

Norwegian law and proxy marriages

Proxy marriages are no longer recognized in Norway, as of 1 June 2007. This follows from section 18a para. 2(a) of the Norwegian Marriage Act. According to this provision a marriage that is contracted outside Norway shall not be recognized if at least one of the parties is a Norwegian national or permanent resident in Norway at the time of marriage, and the marriage was contracted without the presence of both parties at the marriage ceremony. In many Muslim countries either party, male or female, can be represented by a proxy (Nasir 2009a: 55–56), and prior to this amendment Norwegian residents could marry by proxy if they were not able – for various reasons – to be present in person during the marriage celebrations abroad. This amendment has been criticized in Norwegian legal theory for contradicting fundamental private international law principles.[44]

Nonetheless, the provision leaves scope for granting an exemption upon the request of both parties when there are strong reasons for doing so (Frantzen 2007: 223–24). However, it follows from the *travaux préparatoires* to the Marriage Act that the threshold for the recognition of proxy marriages is high.[45] In practice, the Norwegian Directorate for Children, Youth and Family Affairs (Bufetat), which is responsible for dealing with these requests, appears to be reluctant to grant exemption.[46]

Norwegian law and polygamous marriages

Polygamy is prohibited by section 4 of Norwegian Marriage Act and punishable by imprisonment for up to six years[47] or a fine, pursuant to section 220 of the Norwegian Penal Code.

It follows from section 18a para. 2(c) of the Norwegian Marriage Act that Norwegian nationals and residents may not enter into a new marriage abroad while their previous marriage still exists, even when the foreign polygamous marriage is entered into in compliance with the formal rules of a country that allows polygamy.[48] Under such circumstances the Norwegian county governor may on his or her own initiative take measures to have the second marriage dissolved, irrespective of the consent of the parties to the marriage.

It follows from section 40 para. 6 of the Norwegian Immigration Act of 2008 that if a person (the sponsor), who is granted residence in Norway, is married to two or more persons, only one of the spouses may be granted a residence permit, leaving the choice between them to the sponsor.

There are, however, some restrictions, which are mainly intended to combat marriages of convenience. It follows from section 40 para. 6 of the Norwegian Immigration Act 2008 that if the sponsor is already married to a Norwegian resident, no residence permit may be granted pursuant to this section. This applies, for instance, in situations where a person is already married in Norway and enters into a second marriage in his country of origin or in situations where a person was already married abroad and entered into marriage with a Norwegian national or resident in order to obtain a residence permit to Norway. Also, if the sponsor has previously been married to another person, and it appears most likely that the former spouses intend to continue their cohabitation (abroad) after divorce, a residence permit may be refused.

Even though polygamy is not allowed in Norwegian law and is deemed to contradict the Norwegian notion of the *ordre public*, this does not imply that the legal effects of a validly entered polygamous marriage in a country that formally allows polygamy cannot be accepted in Norwegian law.

If, for instance, a Norwegian resident who is married to more than one spouse passes away, the estate of the deceased is, according to Norwegian succession rules, equally divided between the spouses and the children of the polygamous marriages (Thue 2002: 523).[49] As explained above, the consequences of the application of a foreign rule need to contradict the Norwegian feeling of justice, e.g. the Norwegian notion of the *ordre public*, in order not to be applied in the case in question, according to Norwegian private international law principles. The fact that children inherit from their father or the fact that two or more wives equally divide the inheritance after the death of their husband can hardly be considered to contradict the Norwegian notion of the *ordre public* (Thue 2002: 523).

The Norwegian Supreme Court has so far ruled on two polygamy cases. Even though these cases are as similar as two court cases possibly can be, the Supreme Court reached a different conclusion in 1983 than it did in 1977 (Thue 2003: 16–17). In both cases, the husband had domicile in Norway and was thus subject to Norwegian law when entering into a second marriage in his country of origin.

In Rt. (*Norsk rettstidende*) 1977, p. 715 (the Bangladesh case), the facts of the case were as follows: The case involved a Muslim couple who married in 1969 in Bangladesh. Two children were born of this first marriage. During the civil war in Bangladesh, the spouses lost contact with each other and in 1971 the man came to Norway, where he, apart from a few shorter visits to Bangladesh, lived and worked thereafter. During one of these visits to Bangladesh, the man married his second wife, who joined him in Norway. Two children were born of the second marriage. When the second wife returned from a family visit to Bangladesh, she found her husband living in their apartment in Norway with his first wife and their two children. In response, the second wife petitioned the Norwegian court for nullification of the marriage. The Supreme Court concluded that a polygamous marriage was incompatible with the Norwegian notion of *ordre public* and nullified the marriage on the basis of the Norwegian Marriage Act at the time.

In Rt. (*Norsk rettstidende*) 1983, p. 251 (the Pakistan case), the circumstances were more or less the same, apart from the fact that the first wife was still living in Pakistan. When the second wife found out about the first marriage, she petitioned the Norwegian court for legal separation, which she was granted.

It can therefore be asked in what way the 1983 case differed from the 1977 case. In the Pakistan case, the second wife petitioned for legal separation and not for annulment of the marriage, as was the situation in the Bangladesh case. In the Pakistan case, the Supreme Court referred to the Bangladesh case, but was of the opinion that the *ordre public* ban could not be applied as the husband in the meantime – together with the children of his second marriage – had moved back to Pakistan to live with his first wife. Nonetheless, the Supreme Court held that: 'it would not contradict Norwegian legal norms that the applicant in this particular case is granted legal separation, rather than having to petition for annulment of the marriage' [author's translation]. The term 'Norwegian legal norms' was used explicitly to reason in favour of a result that would find support in the 'general sense of justice' in Norway.

The result of the Pakistan case may seem reasonable and pragmatic at first sight, but in legal terms it was in fact rather surprising. According to the Norwegian Marriage Act at the time, a wife was entitled to petition for divorce if her husband married a second wife. Thus, by granting the second wife a legal separation in the Pakistan case instead of declaring the marriage null and void as in the Bangladesh case, the Supreme Court indirectly recognized the polygamous marriage. Most probably, the 1983 Supreme Court ruling never intended to give precedence to the recognition of polygamous marriages in Norway, but was the result of a pragmatic approach in the case in question.

There also is lower court practice regarding polygamy, illustrating the dynamics between legislative measures and legal practice dealing with religious marriages. As a legal source, this lower instance case has little value, but it nonetheless illustrates the problems that Muslim communities in Norway are experiencing with limping situations when entering into and dissolving transnational marriages, as well as the possibilities for forum shopping that these situations seem to create.

On 12 September 2008, the Oslo District Court (TOSLO-2008–97547) concluded that a Turkish man, who in 1999 had entered into marriage with a Norwegian citizen in Norway and later, during the summer of 2003, had entered into a religious marriage in Turkey without informing his Norwegian spouse, was not guilty of polygamy. The facts of the case were as follows: Six months after the religious marriage ceremony in Turkey had taken place, the Turkish man was granted a legal separation in Norway, later followed by a divorce. After the man was formally divorced in Norway, he entered into a civil marriage in Turkey with the woman with whom he already had contracted a religious marriage. Turkish law does not recognize religious marriages as legally valid marriages and entering into a religious (customary *imam*) marriage before a civil marriage is in fact prohibited under Turkish law.[50]

In the case in question, the court had to decide to what extent the religious ceremony performed in 2003 was punishable under section 222 para. 2 of the Norwegian Penal Code, cf. Section 4 of the Marriage Act, which prohibits polygamy. The court correctly concluded that the religious ceremony in Turkey did not establish a legally valid marriage, as 'Turkish law and Norwegian law do not recognize such [religious] marriages or the legal effects deriving from such religious ceremonies. The fact that the shari'a, which is not recognized by either of these two countries, says something else cannot lead to a different result' [author's translation], the court held. Notwithstanding this, the Oslo District Court convicted the man to 30 days imprisonment for giving the police a false statement and for withholding information regarding the religious marriage ceremony when applying for family establishment with his Turkish wife.[51]

In the Borgarting Court of Appeal (RG (*Rettens Gang*) 2009, p. 511), this verdict was overturned. The Court of Appeal was of the opinion that the man had not told the truth about the religious ceremony out of fear that such information could lead to criminal prosecution and that, on these grounds, the man had to be released.

This case therefore not only illustrates that Norwegian courts are granted wide discretion in emphasizing and interpreting the facts of each case, but it also seems to indicate that it may be difficult to make the contracting of religious marriages punishable under current polygamy legislation.

The Norwegian approach regarding the recognition of Muslim divorces

In Norway, legal separations and divorces are, as a rule, granted administratively by a Norwegian county governor. Only in a few, limited situations can divorce be granted by a judge.[52]

It is furthermore an important principle in Norwegian family law that each of the spouses can petition for divorce, irrespective of the consent of the other spouse.[53] This principle is codified in section 7(l) of the Norwegian Marriage Act, which came into force on 1 October 2004. According to this provision, when entering into marriage in Norway each of the spouses recognizes the other spouse's right to divorce.

This amendment was the direct result of a law proposal, which was brought forward in the Norwegian Parliament on 6 June 2003[54] on a private initiative, to guarantee Muslim minority women in Norway a so-called religious divorce, meaning a divorce that also could be recognized by relatives and the local faith community of these women (Innst. O. nr. 132 2002–3; Strandbakken 2004: 69–71).

In the public debate in Norway it is not always quite clear what exactly is meant by a religious divorce and why a Norwegian divorce is not sufficient for Muslim women living in Norway (Salimi 2001: 41–60). As discussed, part of the confusion may be caused by the fact that many mosques in Norway are granted solemnization rights. This may in turn explain why it seems to be a common belief among Muslim communities in Norway that the marriage also has to be dissolved 'religiously', i.e. in compliance with Islamic law. Section 7(l) of the Norwegian Marriage Act is set against the backdrop of these considerations.

Foreign divorces are, as a rule, recognized in Norway, provided that they are not contrary to the Norwegian notion of *ordre public*. The recognition of foreign divorces is governed by the 1978 Recognition Act and is based on the 1970 Hague Convention, which Norway has ratified and which has universal application in relation to foreign decrees on divorce and legal separation.

Foreign divorces that are final and are issued by decree of a competent authority in the country of origin are, as a rule, recognized in Norway by a Norwegian county governor and given legal effect in the realm, provided that human rights principles, such as the right to a fair trial and gender equality, are guaranteed.

Norwegian law and *talaq*

Unilateral repudiation of the marriage by the male spouse (*talaq*) may, under certain circumstances, be contrary to the Norwegian notion of *ordre public*, for instance, when both the parties to the marriage have residence in Norway or when the repudiation has been issued in writing in Norway and sent abroad for further divorce procedures, even when the female spouse lives abroad. However, when a marriage is dissolved before the applicant moved to Norway, the foreign *talaq* is, as a rule, recognized.

However, most problems seem to occur with regard to documentation requirements. In order for a foreign divorce to be recognized in Norway and be given legal effect in the realm, the applicant has to provide a Norwegian county governor with sufficient foreign documentation. At a minimum, the original divorce certificate or an authorized translation of the foreign divorce decree is required, in addition to a certificate confirming that the division of the joint matrimonial property has been finally settled upon divorce. The latter may be particularly problematic with regard to Muslim marriages, where marriage usually does not establish a matrimonial property regime between the spouses.

There are also indications that a Norwegian county governor is likely to be more cautious about recognizing repudiations from Iraq or Pakistan because of the frequency of falsification of documents in these Muslim countries.[55] This may become problematic when, for instance, recognition of the foreign divorce is required to enter into a new marriage in Norway. However, when these refusals by a county governor to recognize Iraqi or Pakistani repudiations are appealed to the court, where other kinds of proof can be accepted, the applicant is usually granted a Norwegian divorce, often at the expense of the foreign party, who usually is not entitled to spousal maintenance or other financial effects of the Norwegian divorce.[56]

The circulars[57] issued by the Directorate of Children, Youth and Family Affairs (Bufetat), on which county governors seem to base their administrative decisions, have no formal status as a legal source of law in Norwegian law, are not fully updated and provide limited information regarding the other forms of divorces that Muslim law allows, such as *khul'*, a divorce initiated by the wife with the consent of the husband in return for compensation.

Norwegian law and *khul'*

The question of the recognition of the foreign *khul'* has not caused the same degree of controversy as the recognition of the foreign *talaq* and its potential infringement on *ordre public* in European jurisdictions (Bogdan 2004: 193–94; Kruiniger 2005: 127–39; Rutten 2002: 81, no. 2; Rutten 2003: 97, no. 4; Pålsson 2006: 67, 71). Discussion of whether a foreign *khul'* can be recognized seems to be nearly absent in Norwegian legal doctrine and administrative and legal practice.[58] In the author's opinion, the *khul'* divorce raises more concerns, especially because this kind of divorce is commonly provided through informal alternative dispute resolution (ADR) mechanisms, for instance, in local mosques in Norway, at diplomatic representation offices of Muslim countries in Europe and in the various departments of the Islamic Shari'a Council (ISC) in the United Kingdom.[59]

It is important to distinguish between foreign divorce judgments that are based on the mutual agreement of the spouses to divorce and *khul'* divorces that are entered into in private and later registered according to local registration procedures in Muslim countries. The latter category of divorces, which are, according to the letter of the law, based on the mutual agreement of both the spouses to divorce, may in reality represent situations where women have been forced to accept conditions that are contrary to European human rights standards of gender equality. This is particularly the case if women accept solutions, according to which they, in addition to giving up their financial claims upon divorce, also give up custody rights of their children, to which they otherwise, according to Muslim law and Norwegian law, would be entitled. Even though Muslim law usually prohibits such *khul'* agreements (Nasir 2009a: 117), they are still contracted in practice and may raise serious concerns with regard to the principle of 'the best interest of the child' enshrined in the Convention on the Rights of the Child, to which Norway is party.

Conclusion

The fact that Muslim spouses in transnational marriages remain subject to their personal status law leaves Muslim citizens resident in Norway with little other choice but to enter into marriage in compliance with both the law of their country of residence and the law of their country of origin. As a rule, Norwegian marriages are recognized in the country of origin of the spouses and registered there, as long as the conditions of the personal status law of the spouses are fulfilled. In practice, this seldom seems to cause problems among Muslim communities in Norway.

Muslim couples may also enter into marriage in the country of origin and later have the foreign marriage recognized and registered in Norway. Foreign marriages are, as a rule, recognized in Norway by competent authorities and given legal effect in the realm, provided that the formal rules of the country in which they took place (*lex loci celebrationis*) are followed and that the spouses were not already married, were not under age at the time of marriage and the marriage was not contracted under coercion or by proxy.

In the case of polygamous marriages that were contracted prior to migration to Norway, only one wife is given a Norwegian residence permit and the choice between the female spouses is left to the male spouse. When there is a legitimate reason to believe that the main objective of the marriage is to establish a basis for residence in Norway for the applicant, a residence permit may be denied.

Irrespective of whether the marriage was entered into in Norway and later recognized and registered abroad or vice versa, the marriage needs to be dissolved both in Norway and in the country of origin because of the transnational nature of these marriages. In the Muslim communities in Norway both the solemnization and the dissolution of transnational marriages are a two-step process.

It is fairly easy under Norwegian law to acquire a divorce, but the Norwegian divorce may not always be recognized in the country of origin of the couple, unless the conditions of the personal status law of the spouses are met as well. This seems to cause problems among Muslim communities in Norway.

The recognition of foreign divorces is mainly an administrative process and is governed by the 1978 Recognition Act. As a rule, foreign divorces are recognized in Norway, mainly in order to enable Norwegian residents to enter into a new marriage. In administrative practice, exceptions are made for repudiations that are (partly) pronounced in Norway or that were performed in Muslim countries, such as Iraq and Pakistan, where there appears to be a high occurrence of falsified divorce papers. However, if the parties appeal the refusal to recognize a foreign divorce, these administrative decisions are often overruled because of the courts are able to take into account additional evidence and proof.

Currently, there is no published practice regarding the recognition of *khul‘* divorces. This chapter has, however, pointed out that there is reason to be cautious about recognizing *khul‘* divorces as it appears that practice in Muslim countries (Mir-Hosseini 2000: 67–70) and among Muslim communities in Europe seems to accept that women, in return for religious divorce, not only give up their claims to the deferred *mahr* and other compensation, but also the custody of their children, despite the fact that the latter is prohibited under Muslim personal status law (Nasir 2009a: 117).

Even though Norwegian law in recent years has become more restrictive with regard to the recognition of transnational marriages and divorces of parties who or whose families have immigrated from a Muslim country, legal practice seems rather pragmatic, so as to enable the parties to remarry in Norway, a fundamental human right to which the Norwegian state is bound. It also appears that Norwegian ministries, departments and other competent authorities lack up-to-date knowledge about Muslim law. As a consequence, decisions may be inconsistent and have discriminatory effects on certain Muslim minorities.

Notes

1 Kjeldstadli contests the myth of the homogenous society, claiming that foreign influences have affected Norwegian society since the 900s, but that foreigners enjoyed a variable social status over time (Kjeldstadli 2003: 149–60).

2 See the *travaux préparatoires* to the Norwegian Nationality Act of 2005: NOU-2000–2032: subsection 2.5.2.

3 Great Britain is the only country in Europe to register the religious dimension of its residents (Dassetto 2000: 33).

4 As at 1 January 2011, the following people from the following 30 countries (in alphabetic order) were among the Muslim population in Norway: Afghanistan, Albania, Algeria, Azerbaijan, Bangladesh, Bosnia-Herzegovina, Egypt, Eritrea, Ethiopia, India, Indonesia, Iran, Iraq, Jordan, Kazakhstan, Lebanon, Libya, Malaysia, Morocco, Nigeria, Pakistan, The Palestinian Territory, Saudi Arabia, Somalia, Sudan, Syria, Tunisia, Turkey, Uzbekistan and Yemen.

5 The author of this chapter (Fredriksen) has adopted the same method as used by Sayed (2009: 82–86).

6 The applicants originated from the following countries (set out in alphabetical order): Afghanistan, Algeria, Bosnia-Herzegovina, Egypt, Eritrea, Ethiopia, Indonesia, Iran, Iraq, Lebanon, Morocco, Nigeria, Palestinian Territory, Somalia, Sudan, Syria, Tunisia and Turkey.

7 See the *travaux préparatoires* to the Norwegian Nationality Act of 2005: Ot.prp.nr. 41 (2004–5): 222–23.

8 Vogt estimated the number of Norwegian converts in 2008 to 500 (Vogt 2008: 24).

9 Statistics Norway uses the term 'immigrants' for first-generation immigrants and the term 'Norwegian-born children with immigrant parents' for second-generation immigrants. For reasons of consistency this chapter will use the terms first- and second-generation immigrants.

10 Pursuant to section 40a of the Norwegian Immigration Act of 2008, a non-EEA sponsor has to have worked or studied for a minimum of four years in Norway in order to be granted family establishment in Norway with a foreign spouse. Exemption from this rule is only granted under very special circumstances. In this chapter a 'sponsor' means the person with whom the applicant for a residence permit to Norway wishes to be reunited or to establish family life (section 39 of the Norwegian Immigration Act).

11 Terms such as 'fake marriages', 'residence marriages', 'bad faith marriages' and 'marriage blanc' are also used to describe what is known in Norway as pro forma marriages. In this chapter the terms 'marriage of convenience' and 'sham or bogus marriages' will be used interchangeably.

12 A complete revision of the Immigration Act and the Immigration Regulations came into force 1 January 2010, replacing the older Immigration Act of 1988 and the Immigration Regulations of 1990.

13 As a rule, after seven years of residence or after four years of marriage with a Norwegian resident and a minimum effective residence time in Norway of three years.

14 As a rule, after three years of residence in Norway.

15 It should be emphasized that the fact that the marriage is dissolved shortly after the foreign spouse has met residency requirements in Norway is not, in itself, sufficient to consider the marriage a marriage of convenience, but may be an indication for other reasons for divorce, for instance, domestic violence.

16 In 2009, the Norwegian Directorate of Immigration assessed 11,168 applications for marriage migration, of which only 1.8 per cent were rejected because they were deemed to be marriages of convenience (Econ Pöyry 2010: 13).

17 Rt *Norsk rettstidende* 2006, p. 1657.

18 LB-2006-093552, LB-2007–156094 and LB-2007-52903.

19 It follows from the *travaux préparatoires* to the new Norwegian Immigration Act of 2008 that there were three particular aspects of transnational marriages that raised concerns: 1) problems related to forced marriages; 2) problems related to abuse, mistreatment or exploitation of women from poor countries who marry men with residence in Norway; and 3) problems related to circumvention of immigration laws through marriages of convenience (Ot.prp. nr. 75 2006–7: 184).

20 Other European countries that practice the 'domicile principle' are Denmark, Iceland and the United Kingdom, even though it needs to be emphasized that the common law concept of domicile differs significantly from the understanding of 'domicile' in the Nordic countries. The Norwegian concept of domicile also differs from the concept of habitual residence, as this generally does not require an intention to stay in the country permanently.

21 The foreign national is not required to actually settle permanently, as long as he or she does not have any concrete plans to leave Norway in the near future (Thue 2002: 76–77).

22 See, for an overview of the Norwegian discussion about the time when a person acquires domicile in Norway: Örenhed 2006: 140–41.

23 There seem to be developments within Norwegian private international law to allow party autonomy in matrimonial property law issues in certain conditions, but there exists no appropriate legislation, and case law is not entirely clear either (Frantzen 2010: 486–89).

24 The only case known to the author is LH-2012–48746, decided by the Hålogaland Court of Appeal, in which recognition of a marriage entered into in 1992 in Gaza was denied.

25 Cf. Ot.prp. nr. 100 (2005–6): 5; Ot.prp.nr. 51 (2002–3): subsection 3.1.1.

26 NOU 2004: 20, p. 241.

27 See, for an explanation of the terms and Swedish legislation regarding forced marriages: Jänterä-Jareborg 2009: 158–63.

28 The Norwegian Marriage Act of 1918 granted a spouse who had been coerced into marriage by the other spouse the possibility of having the marriage declared null and void (section 35, para. 1, no. 6 – revoked), see Ot.prp.nr. 44 (1993–94): 11, 18. However, the Norwegian Marriage Act of 1991 removed this provision due to limited legal practice and the fact that marriage by coercion was considered to be governed by general *ordre public* considerations (Innst. O. no. 105 (1992–93): section 2).

29 See Rt. (*Norsk rettstidende*) 2006 p. 140 (section 25 with further references). Pursuant to Article 23, para. 3, of the International Covenant on Civil and Political Rights (ICCPR) of 16 December 1966, '[n]o marriage shall be entered into without the free and full consent of the intending spouses.' Also Article 16 of the Convention on the Elimination of All forms of Discrimination against Women (CEDAW) contains a provision that both women and men have an equal right to freely choose their spouse and that marriage can only be entered into of their own free will and with their own, unrestrained consent. This provision is also in line with Article 1 of the Convention on Consent to Marriage, Minimum Age for Marriage and Registration of Marriages of 7 November 1962, to which Norway is bound.

30 The right to marry follows from Article 12 of the European Convention on Human Rights (ECHR): 'Men and women of marriageable age have the right to marry and to found a family according to the national laws governing the exercising of this right.'

31 Sima was later reunited with her family and her father dissolved her marriage in Pakistan. However, Sima never received a copy of her Pakistani divorce certificate.

32 See Interview with Sima on 6 April 2009 and later email correspondence with her. She has read and approved the content of this subsection of this chapter.
33 The right to solemnization is stipulated in Section 12a of the Norwegian Marriage Act and follows from the Act relating to Allocations to Religious Communities (AARC).
34 This was confirmed by a Norwegian *imam* in an interview on 20 October 2008.
35 Such legal rights may comprise *mahr* (dower), *nafaqa* (maintenance), and legitimacy of children born from the marriage.
36 See, for instance, the following published cases: RG (*Rettens Gang*)-1999-449 (68–99) from the Fredrikstad City Court and RG (*Rettens Gang*)-2002–2912 (141–2002), decided by the Oslo District Court.
37 See, e.g. LE-2011-97472, in which the Eidsivating Court of Appeal denied annulment of the marriage between two Kurdish spouses on the basis of section 16, para. 4, as the claim commenced after expiry of the six-month period after the coercion had ended and in which the claim had to be made. See also TOSLO-2002–4205, in which the Oslo District Court denied annulment of the marriage between an ethnic Norwegian wife and a Pakistani husband for the same reason, but granted the wife – although the court had some doubt – a divorce on the basis of section 23, para. 3.
38 Prior to 2003, under Norwegian law it was also punishable to coerce a person into marriage, see Innst.O. nr. 106 (2002–3): 2.
39 Cf. ENV-2004-2174, where the offended wife was granted compensation valued at NOK 150,000 for the forced marriage and other circumstances to which she had been exposed.
40 See, e.g. RG (*Rettens Gang*) 1999–449 (68–99), TOSLO-2002–4205, RG (*Rettens Gang*) 2002, p. 981 (151–2002), RG (*Rettens Gang*) 2002–2912 (141–2002), TOSLO-2007-15659; TOSLO-2007–167243, TOSLO-2009-46765, LE-2011–97472.
41 Rt. (*Norsk rettstidende*) 2006, p. 140.
42 The Iraqi court had probably declined the registration of the the 'religious marriage' because the female spouse was under age and/or her father had not been present during the marriage celebration, which according to Iraqi law is a reason to deny validity and thus decline registration (see this chapter on the main rule: *lex loci celebrationis*).
43 The Pakistani Professor Shaheen Sardar 'Ali (who was one of the driving forces behind the agreement) confirmed, during a seminar at the Faculty of Law at the University of Bergen in 13 April 2010, that the steering group had only met once by that date.
44 The following European countries permitted proxy marriage: Italy, Spain, Portugal, Poland, the countries of the former Yugoslavia, Czech Republic, Slovakia and the Netherlands, see Ot.prp. nr. 100 (2005–6): subsection 2.3.2.
45 Cf. Ot.prp. nr. 100 (2005–6): 49.
46 This followed from a telephone conversation with Norwegian Directorate for Children, Youth and Family Affairs (Bufetat) on 20 December 2011 regarding current practice.
47 The main rule is that any person who enters into a marriage contrary to section 4 of the Marriage Act shall be liable to imprisonment for a term not exceeding four years. However, if the spouse was unaware that the marriage was contrary to the said provision, the offender shall be liable to imprisonment for a term not exceeding six years. Any person who aids and abets such an offence shall be liable to the same penalty.
48 With the exception of Tunisia and Turkey, most other Muslim countries formally allow polygamy, even though with restrictions (Nasir 2009b: 25–28).
49 The question of how to divide the estate in the case of a polygamous marriage was also raised in a recent Court of Appeal case (RG *Rettens Gang* 2009: 613), in

which the legal question was whether two wives from Kenya, who both claimed to be married to the deceased, and a son were entitled to inherit the estate of the man. The court could not find proof of the existence of the Kenyan marriages and as the deceased upon marrying his Norwegian spouse declared not to be previously married, the estate was divided between the Norwegian widow and the deceased's sons from a previous relationship.

50 Turkish law is secular and it follows from section 237/4 of the Turkish Penal Code that contracting a *nikah* without first entering into civil marriage is a criminal offence punishable by a prison sentence of two to six months for both the man and the woman. The same section also criminalizes and imposes a prison sentence on persons performing such religious ceremonies without prior verification of the official marriage certificate (Örücu 2010: 276 in n. 9).

51 See section 166, para. 1, of the Norwegian Penal Code.

52 For instance, section 23 of the Norwegian Marriage Act grants a spouse immediate divorce if the spouse or the children have been exposed to violence by the other spouse.

53 See the Norwegian *travaux préparatoires* to the Norwegian Marriage Act, NOU 1986–2: 98.

54 On 16 June 2003 it was suggested that, inter alia, new provision (section 7(1)) be added to the Marriage Act, by virtue of which each spouse would recognize the right of the oterh to divorce. The proposal was accepted by the Norwegian *Odelsting* and three days later by the Norwegian *Lagting* and consequently added to the Norwegian Marriage Act.

55 Cf. Rundskriv Q-19/2004: 12–13, 37, 50.

56 Cf. LE-1986-447, in which a Pakistani man with residence in Norway had divorced his wife in Pakistan in conformity with Pakistani law. The wife contested this and consequently the Norwegian county governor denied recognition. The case was brought before the court and later appealed; the man was granted a judicial divorce and the wife's claim for maintenance was rejected by the Court of Appeal.

57 Circulars have no formal status as legal source of law in Norwegian law.

58 The *khul'* is not discussed in Norwegian private international law or in Rundskriv Q-19/2004, the circular on which Norwegian county governors base their administrative decisions; only a couple of sentences are dedicated to divorce based on mutual consent (*mubara'a*) in Pakistan (p. 50). The only published case, which indirectly concerns the validity of a Syrian *khul'*, is a 2002 Supreme Court case (Rt. *Norsk rettstidende* 2002: 1541).

59 See, for a further discussion of the development of alternative bodies of law outside the formal legal system in Norway and the author's concerns about the legal security of women and children when women settle for a *khul'* divorce, Fredriksen 2012: 503–4.

Bibliography

Bogdan, M. (2004) *Svensk internationell privat-och processrätt*, 6th edn, Stockholm: Norstedts Juridik AB.

Dassetto, F. (2000) 'The new European Islam', in S. Ferrari and A. Bradney (eds), *Islam and European Legal Systems*, Burlington, VT: Ashgate.

Daugstad, G. (2006) *Grenseløs kjærlighet? Familieinnvandring og ekteskapsmønstre i det flerkulturelle Norge*, Oslo-Kongsvinger: Statistisk sentralbyrå, Rapporter 2006/39.

——(2008a) *Ekteskap over landegrensene. Ekteskapsmønster og transnasjonale familieetableringar i perioden 1990–2007*, Statistisk sentralbyrå: Oslo-Kongsvinger, Rapportar 2008/41. Available online at www.ssb.no/emner/02/02/30/rapp_200841/ (accessed 15 January 2012)

——(2008b) 'Transnasjonal kjærleik i globaliseringa si tid', in *IMDi-rapport 6–2008 Integreringskart 2008, Tvangsekteskap – en kunnskapsstatus*, Integrerings-og mangfoldsdirektoratet, 162–72.Econ Pöyry, Pöyry Management Consulting AS (2010) *Marriages of Convenience: a comparative study. Rules and practices in Norway, Sweden, Germany, Denmark and the Netherlands*, Oslo: Utlendingsdirektoratet. Online. Available online at www.udi.no/Global/upload/Publikasjoner/FOU/R-2010-053_SAA_Marriages_of_convenience.pdf (accessed 15 January 2013).

Frantzen, T. (2010) 'Party autonomy in Norwegian international matrimonial property law and succession law', *Yearbook of Private International Law*, 2010 (12): 483–92.

——(2007), 'Tiltak mot tvangsekteskap', in T. Frantzen, J. Giertsen and G. Cordero Moss (eds), *Rett og Toleranse. Festskrift til Helge Johan Thue. 70 år*, Oslo: Gyldendal Akademisk.

Ferrari de Carli, E. (2008) *Religion, juss og rettigheter: Om skilsmisse, polygami og shari'a-råd*, Oslo: Institutt for samfunnsforskning, report no 5.

Fredriksen, K.J. (2012) 'Dommernes uavhengighet og upartiskhet i et multikulturelt samfunn', in N. Asbjørn Engstad, A. Lærdal Frøseth and B. Tønder (eds), *Dommernes uavhengighet*, Bergen: Fagbokforlaget.

Henriksen, K. (2010) *Familieinnvandring og ekteskapsmønster 1990–2008*, Statistisk sentralbyrå: Oslo-Kongsvinger, Rapporter 2010/10.

Jänterä-Jareborg, M. (2009) 'Family Law in a multicultural Sweden – the challenges of migration and religion', *De lege, Juridiska fakulteten i Uppsala årsbok*, 145–72.

——(2010) 'Transnationella familjer ur ett internationellt privaträttsligt perspektiv – särkilt avseende äktenskap', in A. Singer, M. Jänterä-Jareborg and A. Schlytter (eds), *Familj – religion – rätt. En antologi om kulturella spänningar i familjen – med Sverige och Turkiet som exempel*, Uppsala: Iustus Förlag.

Kjeldstadli, K. (2003) 'Innvandring til Norge – en historie om forandring', in B. Hodne and R. Sæbøe (eds), *Kulturforskning*, Oslo: Universitetsforlaget.

Kruiniger, P. (2005), 'De Marokkaanse *khul*' in Nederland: erkenning of verstoting?', *Recht van de Islam*, 23: 127–39.

Kjerschow, A. (2002) 'Minoriteter i et "hvitt" rettsvesen. Flerkulturelle utfordringer for domstolene', in P. Lødrup (ed.), *Rettsteori og rettsliv*, Oslo: Universitetsforlaget.

Koch, K. (2000) *Når mor og far motes i retten – barnefordeling og samvær*, NOVA Rapport 13/2000.

Lindbekk, M. (2013) 'Enforcement of personal status law by Egyptian courts', in E. Giunchi (ed.), *Adjudicating Family Law in Muslim Courts*, Abingdon: Routledge.

Liversage, A. and Jensen, T.G. (2011) *Parallelle retsopfattelser i Danmark. Et kvalitativt studie af privaretlige praksisser*, København: SFI Det Nationale Forskningscenter for velfærd.

Mehdi, R. (2007) 'Arrangerede/tvangsægteskaber og æresdrab under *sharia* og under pakistansk ret og sædvaneret', in R. Mehdi (ed.), *Integration & retsudvikling*, København: Jurist-Og Økonomforbundets Forlag.

Mir-Hosseini, Z. (2000) *Marriage on Trial. A study of Islamic family law*, London and New York: I.B. Tauris.

Nasir, J.J.A. (2009a) *The Islamic Law of Personal Status*, 3rd edn, The Hague, London and New York: Kluwer Law International.

——(2009b) *The Status of Women under Islamic Law and Modern Islamic Legislation*, 3rd edn, Leiden and Boston, MA: Brill.

Naguib, S.-A. (2003) 'Møter i det midtre rom', in Bjarne Hodne and Randi Sæbøe (eds), *Kulturforskning*, Oslo: Universitetsforlaget.

Örenhed, K. (2006) *Bosättningsanknytningar i gränsoverskridande familjerättsförhållanden. En internationellt privat-och processrättslig studie*, Uppsala: Författaren og Iustus Förlag.
Örücü, E. (2010) 'Developments in Turkish family law', in A. Singer, M. Jänterä-Jareborg and A. Schlytter (eds), *Familj – religion – rätt. En antologi om kulturella spänningar i familjen – med Sverige och Turkiet som exempel*, Uppsala: Iustus Förlag.
Østby, L. (2011) 'Muslimsk flertall i Norge i fremtiden? Andelen muslimer i Norge i 2060 kommer til å utgjøre 7 prosent av folkemengden', *Morgenbladet*, 26 August. Available online at www.ssb.no/vis/magasinet/blandet/art-2011-08-29-01.html (accessed 14 November 2012).
Pålsson, L. (2006) *Svensk rättspraxis i internationell famije-och arvsrätt*, 2nd edn, Stockholm: Nordstedts Juridik AB.
Rutten, S. (ed.) (2002) *Recht van de Islam 19. Teksten van het op 8 juni 2001 te Leiden gehouden negentiende RIMO-symposium*, Maastricht: RIMO.
——(ed.) (2003) *Recht van de Islam 20. Teksten van het op 7 juni 2002 te Leiden gehouden twintigste RIMO-symposium*, Maastricht: RIMO.
Salimi, F. (2001) *Til døden skiller oss ad. Ekteskap og skilsmisse i islamsk rettspraksis og norsk lovgivning*, Oslo: MiRA Ressurssenter for innvandrer-og flyktningkvinner.
Sayed, M. (2009) *Islam och arvsätt i det mångkulturella Sverige. En internationellt privaträttslig och jämförande studie*, Uppsala: Iustus Förlag.
Statistics Norway (2011a) 'Members of religious and life stance communities outside the Church of Norway, by religion/life stance. As at 1 January 2005–11. Numbers and percent'. Available online at www.ssb.no/english/subjects/07/02/10/trosamf_en/tab-2011-12-06-01-en.html (accessed 24 May 2012).
——(2011b) 'Population, by Norwegian/foreign citizenship and country background. 1 January 2011'. Available online at www.ssb.no/english/subjects/02/01/10/innvbef_en/tab-2011-04-28-07-en.html (accessed 1 February 2012).
Storhaug, H. (1992) 'Flyktet fra tvangsekteskap', *Dagbladet*, 8 November.
Strandbakken, A. (2004) 'Tiltak mot tvangsekteskap – er en god tanke drevet for langt og fort?', *Tidsskrift for familierett, arverett og barnerettslige spørsmål*, 2: 69–71.
Thue, H.J. (2002) *Norsk internasjonal privatrett. Personrett, familierett og arverett. Alminnelige prinsipper og de enkelte reguleringer*, Oslo: Gyldendal Akademisk.
——(2003) 'Anerkjennelse av ekteskap stiftet i utlandet', *Tidsskrift for familierett, arverett og barnevernrettslige spørsmål*, 1: 5–19.
Vikør, K. (2005) *Between God and the Sultan. A history of Islamic law*, London: Hurst & Company.
Vogt, K. (2008) *Islam på norsk. Moskeer og islamske organisasjoner i Norge*, Oslo: J.W. Cappelen Forlag.
Wikan, U. (2008a) *Om ære*, Oslo: Pax forlag.
——(2008b) 'Tvangsgifte blant muslimer: noen antropologiske perspektiver', in *IMDi-rapport* 6: 2008.

Interviews

Interview with an *imam* in a Norwegian mosque on 20 October 2008.
Interview with Sima (a pseudonym), a woman with a Pakistani background, who had been married off against her will to her cousin in Pakistan, but who later nullified her Pakistani marriage in Norway, 6 April 2009. Later email correspondence in connection with this article.

Norwegian legal sources

Norwegian legislation (in chronological order)

Straffeloven av 22. mai 1902, Nr. 10 (the Norwegian Penal Code).
Lov 2. juni 1978 nr. 38 om anerkjennelse av utenlandske skilsmisser og separasjoner (Act on recognition of foreign divorces and separations of June 2, 1978 no. 38, the 1978 Recognition Act).
Lov om tilskott til livssynssamfunn, 12. juli Nr. 64 1981 (Act relating to allocations to religious communities).
Lov om ekteskap, (ekteskapsloven, el.), 4. juli Nr. 47.1991 (The Norwegian Marriage Act).
Lov-2008-05-15-35 Utlendingers adgang til riket og deres opphold her (Utlendingsloven, utlendl.) (the Norwegian Immigration Act).
Lov om norsk statsborgerskap, 10. juni 2005 Nr. 15 (The Norwegian Nationality Act).

Travaux préparatoires *(in chronological order)*

Ot.prp. nr. 44 (1993–94) *Om lov om endringar i lov 4 juli 1991 nr 47 om ekteskap*
Ot.prp. nr. 51 (2002–3) *Om endringar i straffelova mv. (styrka innsats mot tvangsekteskap mv.)*
Ot.prp. nr. 41 (2004–5) *Norsk statsborgerskap (statsborgerloven)*
Ot.prp. nr. 100 (2005–6) *Om lov om endringer i ekteskapsloven og straffeprosessloven mv. (tiltak for å forhindre tvangsekteskap mv).*
Ot.prp. nr. 75 (2006–7) *Om lov om utlendingers adgang til riket og deres opphold her i landet (Utlendingsloven).*
NOU-1986-2 *Innstilling til ny ekteskapslov – del I.*
NOU 2004: 20 (2004) *Ny utlendingslov. Utredning fra utvalg oppnevnt ved kongelig resolusjon av 14. desember 2001.*
NOU-2000-32 *Lov om erverv og tap av statsborgerskap*
Innst.O. nr. 105 (1992–93) *Innstilling fra forbruker-og administrasjonskomiteen om lov om endringer i lov av 4. juli 1991 nr. 47 om ekteskap.*
Innst.O. nr. 132 (2002–3) *Innstilling fra familie-, kultur-og administrasjonskomiteen om forslag fra stortingsrepresentantene Signe Øye, Karin Andersen, Magnhild Meltveit Kleppa, Anita Apelthun Sæle, Kari Lise Holmberg og Per Sandberg om lov om endring i lov 4. juli 1991 nr. 47 om ekteskap. (Tiltak for å sikre kjønnenes like formelle rett til skilsmisse).*

Court practice

Supreme Court

Rt. (*Norsk rettstidende*) 1977, p. 715 (the Bangladesh case)
Rt. (*Norsk rettstidende*) 1983, p. 251 (the Pakistan case)
Rt. (*Norsk rettstidende*) 2002, p. 1541
Rt. (*Norsk rettstidende*) 2006, p. 140
Rt. (*Norsk rettstidende*) 2006, p. 1657

Court of Appeal

LB-2006–093552 (the Borgarting Court of Appeal)
LB-2007-156094 (the Borgarting Court of Appeal)
LB-2007–52903 (the Borgarting Court of Appeal)
RG *(Rettens Gang)* 2009, p. 613
RG (*Rettens Gang*) 2009, p. 511
LE-2011-97472 (the Eidsivating Court of Appeal)
LH-2012–48746 (the Hålogaland Court of Appeal)

District Court

TOSLO-2002-4205 (the Oslo District Court)
RG *Rettens Gang* 2002, p. 981 (151–2002) (the Toten District Court)
TOSLO-2007–15659 (the Oslo District Court)
TOSLO-2007-167243 (the Oslo District Court)
TOSLO-2008–97547 (the Oslo District Court)
TOSLO-2009-46765 (the Oslo District Court)

6 Islamic family law in the courts

Spain's position with regard to the Moroccan Family Code

Ana Quiñones Escámez

Introduction

This chapter focuses on the judicial practice of Spanish courts and takes into account the new European Union regulations, which are replacing each Member State's private international law. Before embarking on a discussion of this topic, it would be useful to clarify what 'applying Islamic shari'a law' means for Spanish courts and for countries where Islam is the majority religion. The association of 'family law' with 'Islamic law' usually involves invoking religious texts (the Qur'an), but these religious precepts are not directly applicable in most Muslim countries. The law in these countries has family codes and state laws, which can be reformed to some extent albeit within the framework of Islamic orthodoxy, and Morocco, which is the country of origin of most Muslim immigrants to Spain (MESS 2012), is no exception. The Moroccan Family Code was reformed in 2004, half-opening the door of *ijtihad* or legal reasoning (Art. 400), and is the form of Islam-based law that Spanish courts most frequently pronounce on. This chapter therefore focuses on Moroccan law.

Law and religion in internal and international situations

The legal framework enabling Spanish courts to apply a foreign law to legal relationships connected to more than one country or legal system is private international law (PIL), the rules of which are becoming common to European Union Member States. PIL responds to the question of which law is applicable, for example, in the divorce of a married couple who are Moroccan citizens resident in Barcelona and the divorce of another married couple who are Belgian citizens, also living in Barcelona. PIL rules are capable of resolving both situations, but the greater the degree of heterogeneity there is between the law in the country of origin and in the country of residence, the more difficulties there are in applying the foreign law.

Not all Islamic-based national legal systems contain points of conflict, however, and when Muslims invoke these laws it is not always for religious reasons (conflicts of culture), but for their own benefit (conflicts of interest).

The decision about which law from among the same legal family is applicable in one particular case may therefore be a 'conflict' that divides individuals who share a cultural background. A foreign law may be chosen or invoked as part of individuals' legal strategies ('forum shopping'), whether they are seeking a judgment that is more favourable to their interests, or simply one that is effective in both their country of residence and the country of origin with which one or both spouses maintain links. In any event, when PIL applies rules based in a particular culture or religion, it is always because these rules form part of a national law that already regulates family relationships among immigrants or individuals who were once immigrants. That is to say, the foreign law is not applied because the spouses are Muslims but because they were born in or are nationals of a country in which the existence of a state religion means that family law is imbued with religious precepts.

An example will make the situation clearer: the divorce in Spain of a married couple in which the husband is Algerian and the wife Moroccan is regulated by Spanish law as Spain is their place of habitual residence. Although Algeria's and Morocco's legal systems both belong to the Islamic family of laws, in the absence of a common national law Spanish law is applied (Art. 107.2 Spanish Civil Code). The Council Regulation (EU) No. 1259/2010 of 20 December 2010, implementing enhanced cooperation in the area of the law applicable to divorce and legal separation (Rome III Regulation), in force since 21 June 2012, establishes that in the absence of agreement between the parties, the law of the country of residence is applicable.

European responses to the general question about which family law to apply to Muslims (nationals of Islamic countries) resident in Europe have been influenced by abstract immigration theses and models (integration, assimilation, multiculturalism) that go beyond the scope of PIL aims. Some of them advocate a different mode of social organisation, which affects internal rather than international legal relationships. The drawing up of a European code adapted to Muslims residents in Europe has therefore been proposed by the Egyptian professor Fuad Riad, a former judge of the International Court of Justice. In fact, there is something of this proposal in the United Kingdom's religious mediation service and the Qur'anic form of marriage provided for in the 1992 agreement between the Spanish state and the Islamic Commission. However, these solutions are designed for internal situations involving nationals and residents and do not affect family relationships with foreign nationals, which are regulated by PIL, as there is no guarantee of their being recognised in the country of origin. Those would be cases of internal legal pluralism, which would fall outside the scope of PIL.

Support for boosting the application of foreign nationals' national law is linked with multiculturalists' theses, and addresses situations involving foreign nationals with connections to more than one country. As this option carries a cultural or religious element and involves the nationality connection, it initially appears to be a traditional choice and is known in the PIL systems of Spain and other European countries, especially those that were countries of emigration over a long period (Spain, Italy and Portugal) or in which identity or culture carry more weight in nationality acquisition (Germany). The application of foreign nationals' national law has recently been revitalised—particularly by some German authors—with a cultural or religious element (more psychological than geographical). Dr Erik Jayme and his disciples at the University of Heidelberg consider that the nationality connection reflects foreign nationals' cultural and religious identity, and on his 1995 Hague Academy course Dr Jayme argued that when the nationality principle is evoked today it must be done by returning to the original idea of preserving the individual's national, religious and cultural identity (Jayme 2005: 252). In France, D. Gutmann points out that nationality would structure the individual, who is exposed to multiple tensions in an international sphere (Gutmann 2000). Strengthening this classic PIL connection, which looked as though it would be replaced by connections based on domicile, habitual residence or choice of law (*professio iuris*), receives support from certain authors (Foblets and Carlier 2010). However, when a national law is imbued with religious rules, should its implementation be prioritised? This would risk giving preference to the application of foreign legal systems that define the term 'believer' along authoritarian or geographical lines or by birth (*ius sanguinis*). In countries where the constitution includes a state religion (this is still the case in Morocco following the 2011 reform), freedom of worship is guaranteed, but falls short of being freedom of conscience, that is to say, the freedom to opt to change religion or to have no religion. For these reasons, this chapter does not advocate strengthening foreign laws based on religious rules; in fact, such a change would seem to be more of a drawback for their application than a bonus.

The need to try to avoid limping legal situations (valid in one country but ineffective in the other) for families that are caught between two countries or legal systems is an entirely different matter. However, should the spouses (or one of them) not wish to apply a national law imbued with religious rules (if based on sex discrimination and the imposition of beliefs) this desire should be heeded and the focus should be on the individual rights of the men and women concerned.

An example will help to clarify this point. In 2007 a Frankfurt Court of First Instance invoked the Qur'an and the culture of the spouses' country of origin (Morocco) to assess whether the woman had suffered ill-treatment and whether, for this reason, to proceed with a quick divorce provided for in Article 1565 BGB. The individuals concerned were a bi-national married couple, Moroccan and German, resident in Germany. The judge considered that the woman could expect to be badly treated by her husband as both were of Moroccan cultural origin and had been married in Morocco under Islam-based law. On rendering this decision the judge in fact constructed a resolution that complies neither with German law and its PIL nor with Moroccan law. The Moroccan Family Code establishes ill-treatment a ground for dissolving a marriage at the wife's request, and the ill-treatment has to be assessed according to her environment and the country she lives in. Neither German law nor Moroccan law nor PIL invite the judge to put forward a resolution based on the interpretation of archaic religious texts (and contrary to the wife's wishes).

The Rome III Regulation does not change the situation outlined above in any way. Although the new regulation allows spouses to choose the law applicable to their divorce, they will be opting for a national law and not a religious text – the Qur'an, the Bible and so forth. This idea could be concluded by reiterating the different roles played by religious rules and state legal rules in determining the applicable family law, which does not mean that the religious factor, as a sociological fact or piece of data, cannot receive the attention of legislators, judges and administrative authorities. The European Union Civil Service Tribunal considered in the case *W. v. Commission* (F-86/09, 2010) that a same-sex couple has access to a household allowance even if its members are not married so that in this specific case one of them did not have to report his marriage to Moroccan consular officials, given that homosexual sexual activity is prohibited in Morocco (Art. 489 CCM (Civil Code of Morocco)).[1] In the present case, the Tribunal noted that the applicant was a member of the contract staff registered as a stable, non-marital partner in Belgium. Consequently, the couple in question could, in principle, have contracted a legal marriage in Belgium (Art. 46 CPIL). However, the applicant claimed that Morocco was a country with which he had close ties and Moroccan was one of his dual nationalities.

In family immigration contexts involving successive generations the automatic match among individuals, their culture or religion and the law can be a myth that is dispelled when disputes are brought before the courts; the German Constitutional Court's ruling of 30 November 1988 provides an example of this. In this case a woman of German nationality invoked the application of Algerian law which prevented her child's father, with whom she no longer lived, from recognising the child. The Algerian father, meanwhile, considered German law, which permitted him to recognise the child and register himself as the father, to be applicable, and thus asked for Algerian law to be disregarded as being contrary to German public policy.[2] Divorce judgments provide many more examples of disagreements between spouses from the same cultural background over the applicable law, and these were the focus of a previous work, *Derecho e inmigración: el repudio islámico en Europa* (Law and Immigration: Islamic repudication in Europe) (Quiñones 2000). It is not uncommon, for example, for the husband to invoke the law of the spouses' common nationality simply to obtain a divorce that is more favourable to him, while the wife invokes the law of the common country of residence. The point is that the law forms part of private individuals' strategies and they invoke it according to their interests, irrespective of beliefs or cultural patterns. Thus, in court there are not only conflicts of culture among members of the same family or identity group, but also conflicts of interest.

The nationality connection is therefore necessary because it permits the foreign law and past, present and future links with the country of origin to be taken into account, providing the necessary counterweight to the legal system in the country of residence. However, a foreign family code's religious nature (and its application within a collective religious freedom that allows neither individual freedom nor freedom of conscience) is not a value to be protected over and above individuals' own expectations or the need to avoid limping legal situations. PIL aims to guarantee individuals harmonious continuity in their family and personal situations; for instance, individuals whose civil status switches to divorced should receive equal treatment in the countries with which they have special connections so that they do not have trouble crossing borders or with the authorities in their country of origin. However, as the focus has to be on the safeguarding of individual rights, PIL would be critical of the proposal to maintain and strengthen national law as a guarantor of cultural identity.

Private 'inter-national' law has no single national context as its benchmark, aiming instead at the dialogue and coordination between different legal systems. It neither distorts the double belonging of those who were once immigrants, nor does it overstate differences nor assimilate foreigners to nationals. Continuing to underscore international or foreign elements in private family relationships can provide a necessary counterweight to the processes of globalisation, deregulation and acculturation, which are imposing themselves in our cities and which universalise cultural patterns on a superficial level while provoking profound identity-related reactions irrespective of cultural and legal traditions.

Application of the new Moroccan Family Code (2004)

The practice of Spanish courts vis-à-vis the Moroccan Family Code (MFC) will now be reviewed. In Spain this is the most frequently applied national law text from among those based on Islamic law, owing to the presence of a significant number Moroccan families, as noted above. The reformed MFC lies within the bounds of orthodoxy but includes some new elements that favour the application of its rules and the recognition of judgments rendered under its aegis by courts in secular European countries. The broad limits it sets on the personal scope of application (Art. 2) are worth noting here, although its application to cases with a foreign element is less than straightforward in doctrine. Thus, Sarehane does not consider that this provision derogates PIL rules; in any event, its application outside Morocco by foreign authorities depends on each country's PIL rules (Sarehane 2004: 2).

Marriage

An important difference between Spanish and Moroccan law is that the former recognises marriages and unions also between individuals of the same sex; Moroccan law does not.

Other differences pertain to formal and substantive conditions of marriage. As to formal requirements, European countries are divided over the question of allowing religious marriages to have civil effects in their territory. In Germany, Austria, Belgium, France, Luxembourg, Holland and Switzerland, the state has the monopoly over marriages, which have to be performed by the civil authorities and respect the conditions imposed on them by the *lex loci*. The spouses are of course free to hold a religious ceremony as well, but this has no civil effect.

Other countries, such as Spain, Denmark, Greece, Ireland, Italy and Portugal, are open to religious marriage ceremonies and recognise the optional nature of the *locus regit actum* rule; the form of the marriage is subject either to national law or the law of the place in which it is performed. To go into more detail, in 1992, Spain negotiated an agreement with representatives of the Muslim community[3] by virtue of which valid Qur'anic marriages can be performed by accredited or legally recognised Muslim religious authorities. However, whatever religious form the nuptials may take, the capability conditions (age and freedom to marry) are those provided for in civil law (Art. 7). This is one of the forms of marriage permitted by Spanish law and is designed for internal, not international situations (governed by PIL rules). The equality between different faiths is taken into account and a concordat with the Catholic Church has existed since 1979. Where Catholic marriages are concerned, the fact that a religious ceremony was held does not prevent the spouses from filing for divorce under civil law.

As a general rule, Muslim countries consider marriages contracted by their own nationals in foreign countries to be valid. Morocco, on the other hand, in the past refused to recognise marriage ceremonies performed by the designated authorities in European countries because control over the legal requirements provided for in Moroccan law was not guaranteed. However, for the first time, the new MFC now recognises marriages contracted by Moroccans in foreign countries. Where procedural matters are concerned, the applicable conflict rule is the *locus regit actum* (the subjecting of the legal act to the local law in force in the place where the marriage is performed) and such marriages are now recognised in Morocco as long as they fulfil the capacity and consent conditions: that there are neither legal impediments nor waiving of dower rights and that they take place before two Muslim witnesses and the *wali* (the bride's matrimonial tutor) where necessary. The control is now a posteriori. This complexity, together with sociological reasons rooted in the marriage festivities, means that few such marriages are held in Spain.

Let us now turn to the substantive conditions of marriage. Although they are regulated by each party's national law, public policy opposes any foreign law that impedes marriage for reasons of discrimination between the sexes or disparity of worship (*disparitas sexus*). This is the case, for example, when a foreign law prevents a Muslim woman from marrying a non-Muslim man.

Religious impediments

Art. 39.4 of the MFC prohibits Muslim women from marrying non-Muslim men and Muslim men from marrying 'idolatrous' women (that is, neither Muslim nor Christian nor Jewish), but in practice there is no control over these prohibitions, which are in conflict with Spanish public policy. A marriage cannot be refused on the grounds that one or both parties' national law provides for a discriminatory impediment on the basis of sex or religion.[4]

In practice, the husbands-to-be of Muslim women who maintain ties with their family and country of origin may convert to Islam. This act, whether genuine or fictitious, enables the marriage to take place and avoids problems when travelling or should the couple go back to live or spend some time in the country. In such cases any children are considered legitimate and the spouses, as they are deemed to be, are legally related and are counted among the beneficiaries of family inheritance rights in the eyes of the Moroccan authorities.

Polygamy

Where marriages held in Morocco are concerned, a major sticking point for their recognition in Spain is polygamy, or the marital religious privilege of polygyny. Muslim men may have up to four legal wives at once. As the husband is the family breadwinner this means, in theory at least, that he should support all his wives and their children. Polygamy is a taboo institution in Europe, but in practice the taboo is in fact marginal. However, it does constitute a threat for all wives and their children, as the changes in circumstances that it may entail are unlikely to enhance the peace of family life.

It is not possible for either Spanish nationals or foreigners to enter into polygamous marriages in Spain, and Spanish authorities (whether civil or authorised religious) may not perform a second union unless any previous union has been dissolved (an impediment related to the freedom to marry). This ban is firmly established throughout Europe and polygamous marriages cannot be performed anywhere on the territory, even if they are Qur'anic marriages, which are admitted in Spain, as mentioned above.

While a second marriage is thus impossible in Spain, what is possible is the recognition of the validity of a marriage entered into in a foreign country in accordance with each spouse's personal law and with the *lex loci celebrationis*. Recognition of some of the effects of polygamous unions entered into in another country is thus possible in Spain, just as it is in other European countries. While polygamy is not accepted as a marriage model, some of its effects are recognised if the ceremony was performed in another country at a time when the spouses had no links with Spanish territory, and these include inheritance rights, maintenance obligations, the legitimacy of any children born to the couple, and the entitlement to a widow's pension for the surviving wives of a polygamous husband.[5]

It is essential to prevent non-recognition of polygamous marriages from working against the interests of wives and children who are often victims of this family model. However, the solutions provided by jurisprudence can often vary when there is no agreement that provides for them. This is partly because of the diverse nature of the cases dealt with, and it is necessary to distinguish between situations in which actual and not potential polygamy occurred (or did not) before or after the couple entered Spanish territory. The first wife is protected when the married couple lives in Spain and the husband visits his country of origin to bring back a second wife. International public policy acts with greater intensity here. However, in some instances related to the widow's pension the situation results in the pension being divided up between the wives, either on the basis of 50 per cent each or according to the length of the legal relationship. Practice in Spain runs the gamut from denial to selective acknowledgement of the effects of polygamous marriages.

Outside the scope of civil law and family law, in the domain of immigration laws and control over the entry and residence of foreign nationals from non-EU states, there is a generalised rejection of polygamy. The question is not to define who is related to whom but to restrict the relatives who are beneficiaries of the family reunification to one spouse and the children of this union. EU directives on family reunification run along the same lines (Clerici 2009: 197–211 and N. Dethloff 2011 :418). Nevertheless, it should not be forgotten that such restrictions may entail either the repudiation of women and children who are left behind in their country of origin or their illegal entry into Europe and subsequent marginalisation. In the context of immigration, polygyny leads to ghettoisation. It should be noted, moreover, that the immigration laws' entry restrictions mean that polygamists' wives rarely file for maintenance or divorce when they are not resident (or not legally resident) in the country. The immigration law filter also affects access to justice in civil proceedings from a practical or material perspective.

The discrimination existing between children and wives in the context of immigration is at odds with Muslim precepts of the equal treatment of wives. The desirable state of affairs would be the abolition of polygyny, as brought about by the new Tunisian Family Code of 1956. It should be noted that the Tunisian legislators abolished polygyny on the basis of the equality principle affirmed in the Constitution without breaking with cultural and religious tradition. The legislators interpreted the Qur'an's insistence on the equal treatment of wives to impose a mandate on husbands that was impossible for them to fulfil, and on this basis advocated the abolition of polygamy. It is interesting to note that Tunisian jurisprudence invokes public policy to oppose the recognition of polygamous marriages held in Morocco in a more generalised way than Spanish courts (Meziou and Mezghani 1995: 70).

Polygamous foreign nationals have to overcome the obstacle of integration, where acquiring Spanish nationality is concerned. The fundamental problem here is the system's coherence. The personal and family lives of foreign nationals who acquire Spanish nationality are regulated by Spanish laws, which, as previously mentioned, do not allow such marriages although they may recognise their effects if they were contracted by foreign nationals and in other countries. Marriages between Spanish nationals must by law be entered in the civil register. Were polygamous marriages to be registered, it would be tantamount to introducing this marriage model into Spain.[6]

Polygamy is a controversial institution within the Muslim world as well as outside it. Although the new MFC did not abolish this symbolic institution, it does effectively promote monogamy by placing hurdles in the way of second marriages, such as opening up the possibility of divorce to the first wife and encouraging the couple to introduce an anti-polygamy clause into the marriage contract, which is in accordance with Islamic law (Arts 40–41). The effectiveness of the progress made by the 2004 reform lies in the hands of the judges.

Because the new MFC aims to limit polygamy in Morocco, it would seem desirable to have complemented this restrictive system with a PIL provision aimed at making polygamy more difficult for monogamous foreign nationals, specifically with a conflict rule allowing a cumulative application of the couple's personal laws, as proposed by Boye in his 1993 Hague Academy course (Boye 1993: 346). In fact, there is no lack of laws restricting polygamy in this way within the PIL framework, one example being Art. 34 of the Gabon Civil Code (1972), which states that foreign nationals who acquire Gabonese nationality while still retaining their original nationality cannot opt for polygamy if their national law does not allow it or if they have previously renounced it. Should they have lost their original nationality, they cannot marry a second wife if their first marriage was entered into prior to their acquiring Gabonese nationality.[7]

Age and consent

The new MFC establishes that women can marry after they turn 18 years old, the same as for men. It follows from this new legal provision that Spanish public policy intervention over the age of wives has decreased. However, it is possible for judges to grant waivers, as in Spanish law, an example being the decision of DGRN of 20 March 2007[8] regarding the marriage of a Moroccan minor (14 years of age). The real difference lies in the fact that this would be an exceptional situation in Spain compared to the frequency with which marriages of minors occur in rural areas of Morocco. As mentioned above, this provision of Moroccan law is on the face of it no different from Spanish law (Arts 12 and 48, and Art. 75 of the Spanish Civil Code); the real difference lies not in the letter of the law but in the fact that this would be an exceptional situation in Spain compared to the frequency with which marriages of minors occur in rural areas of Morocco.

The new MFC allows women of legal marriageable age to marry without a guardian (*wali*). Art. 24 sets out that women have a right to matrimonial guardianship (*wilaya*), and women of legal age can therefore have a guardian at their marriage if they choose it and it is in their interests.

The mahr *and Muslim witnesses*

In Muslim countries the *mahr* (dower) is an essential condition for the validity of a marriage and is a counterpart to the minimal pecuniary consequences of repudiation. The *mahr* belongs to the woman and is returned to her if she is repudiated by her husband.

Under the new MFC, failure to mention the *mahr* during the marriage ceremony is not a ground for the marriage to be annulled, but the woman is not permitted to waive *mahr*. This provision permits civil marriages performed in other countries by the competent (foreign) authorities to be valid.

The new MFC maintains the requirement of two Muslim witnesses to be present. In practice, this requirement is not demanded when marriages are concluded in Europe. Moroccan authorities make a control a posteriori.

Marital repudiation

Islamic law considers marriage as a contract that can be rescinded by the husband through *talaq* (repudiation). *Talaq* is a religious male privilege and, unlike polygamy, is not only a widespread practice in the Arab world but is in fact the normal way of dissolving marriages. Only a few countries – Turkey, Tunisia, and Central Asian republics – have abolished both marital repudiation and polygamy, raising the barrier of public policy to foreign laws that provide for these institutions, which are deemed discriminatory. Other countries have limited themselves to regulating the repudiation effects, which are controlled by the judge, and broadening the grounds whereby a marriage may be dissolved at the woman's request. This is true of the new MFC.[9] The new MFC has reformed this area, but as it is the result of a variety of compromises the final outcome is complex, introducing as it does new modalities of marital breakdown on top of traditional ones without abolishing any of the latter. This means that every family (or spouse) can invoke the modality that best suits their lifestyle, either more traditional or more modern. Divorce by mutual agreement does not suppress the divorce by *khul'*, the traditional form of repudiation in which the woman buys her freedom by paying her husband a sum of money. This classic modality remains, although the new MFC limits the agreement between the spouses in such a way that issues such as renouncing custody of the children do not enter into the negotiations. Under the new MFC, in cases that involve disagreement over the sum of money to be paid this is set by the judge, along the lines of *khul'*, which may prevent the wife from being blackmailed by the husband (Art. 120). It should be noted that general grounds relating to 'discord' (*shiqaq*) have been added to previously existing grounds; initially designed for the conciliation phase, these are at the judge's discretion and broaden the possibilities for divorce, particularly for the wife. In practice, the discord motive is frequently used by women to obtain a divorce.

MFC is sometimes partially applied by the Spanish authorities in the extinction of relationships. They then turn to Spanish law for some of the effects, particularly where financial benefits and matters of parental responsibility for the children are concerned.[10] The new MFC has been applied along the lines set out in several divorce judgments since 2005, with the aim of providing judgments that are effective in the spouses' country of origin (Quiñones *et al.* 2009: 152). However, public policy in the form of the constitutional principle of the equality of children before the law (Art. 39 Spanish Code) intervenes here to set out the conditions of marital breakdown and the maintenance of children born out of wedlock.[11]

Whether divorce judgments passed in Spain are recognised in Morocco depends on their compliance with MFC dispositions and the control of the Spanish court's international jurisdiction (Art. 128 MFC). However, in 1997, Spain and Morocco concluded two bilateral agreements, concerning the recognition of civil judgments and the custody and illegal movement of minors, that established reciprocal conditions pertaining to recognition.

Several problems may arise concerning public policy limits and when the divorce is irreconcilable with a previous decision:

- The difficulty of having a groundless divorce (according to Spanish law) requested by the woman recognised in Morocco. For this reason, it would be useful for Spanish courts to include the existence of general discord grounds in the divorce decree with the aim of preventing recognition being refused on the basis of Moroccan public policy limits.
- The difficulty of having a marital repudiation (obtained by the husband in a foreign country) recognised in Spain unless the woman consents to its recognition, because she wishes to assert her freedom to marry in Spain (for example, for the purpose of remarrying there) or because the breakdown of the marriage predates her entry into Spain and the divorce's effects are determined.
- The difficulty associated with irreconcilable judgments: the Moroccan authorities will not recognise a Spanish decision on divorce at the woman's request if repudiation has already been pronounced in Morocco, and vice versa.

Repudiations effected in Spain and Morocco

Spain recognises Qur'anic marriage, but religious authorities have no jurisdiction to dissolve the marriage.

Marital repudiation makes the inequality between the sexes in the dissolving of Islamic marriage a structural issue. A husband can repudiate his wife but cannot be repudiated by her. However, it is also true that in certain cases repudiations granted to foreign couples in other countries disguise what are in fact divorces by mutual consent. The spouses may opt for repudiation as a quick and easy way to dissolve their marriage in their country of origin. It may also be the woman who applies for the recognition of the repudiation in Spain (*exequatur*) in order to regain her freedom to marry and to find a new husband there. Although the institution is contrary to the principle of equality between men and women, consistently denying its legal effects may have the perverse effect of actually limiting the woman's ability to remarry or requiring her to file for divorce when she is already in fact considered to be divorced in her country of origin. Spanish courts tend to take a rather pragmatic approach to this question, taking account of the circumstances of the case if it is the wife who applies for the recognition of a judgment passed by a foreign court, or if the repudiation was pronounced some time before the woman became resident on Spanish territory. It follows from this that a selective approach is taken to divorce judgments issued by Islamic countries.

This can clearly be seen from two judgments given in Spain on 21 April and 23 July 1998 in which the Spanish Supreme Court recognised a repudiation *exequatur* pronounced in Egypt but rejected a repudiation pronounced in Morocco, both requested by the woman concerned. In the first case, however, the husband had already remarried in Egypt, while in the second the husband was a Spanish national at the time of the repudiation, which was an impediment to its recognition (Quiñones 2000: 164–72). Equality can be restored if the woman applies for the recognition of the repudiation, thereby preventing non-recognition from being detrimental to her (Déprez 1988: 170).

Household management, parenting orders and *kafala*

The 2004 MFC enshrines the principle of equality between men and women in the area of household management and the spouses' rights and duties (Art. 51). However, legal guardianship of children (*wilaya*) is conceived of as a male prerogative (agnatic) and pertains to the father, who has to support them. The father's authority in this area limits the mother's custody (*hadana* or care of young children) if the couple divorce, for example with regard to fixing the minors' place (country) of residence.

The MFC also strengthens children's rights. Should their parents divorce, children have the right to a domicile independently of maintenance payments. This indirectly provides a way for the mother, who usually has custody of young children, to avoid being turned out of the family home when it is owned by the husband. However, this measure actually aims to protect the children and not the divorced mother who looks after them.

The new MFC also introduced the recognition of children conceived during courtship, although this is not an acknowledgement of natural parentage outside marriage. The principle of equality among children is an obstacle to the application of foreign laws that discriminate against them, although the courts do sometimes make distinctions based on special connections between the case and the territory.

Morocco has ratified the United Nations Convention on the Rights of the Child of 20 November 1989 and the Hague Convention of 19 October 1996 on Jurisdiction, Applicable Law, Recognition, Enforcement and Co-operation in Respect of Parental Responsibility and Measures for the Protection of Children. Both Conventions cover the Muslim institution of *kafala* (a substitute for adoption, which is prohibited in Islamic law), and because of its inclusion Morocco was the first country to sign. However, private *kafala*, when there is no court ruling, is excluded from the Convention, and as it is a private notarial act there are obstacles to its recognition in Europe, particularly when it allows the father to decide on the children's *kafala* without the mother's consent. More detailed discussion of this complex issue can be found in previous works (Quiñones *et al.* 2009).

Inheritance rights

The principle that daughters (or women) should receive only half of what sons (or males) are entitled to acquire or that non-Muslims cannot inherit from Muslims prevents non-Muslim wives from inheriting part of their husband's estate (the opposite does not apply because Muslim women cannot marry non-Muslim men). These sex- or religion-based differences in treatment are deemed contrary to public policy. There is some debate over whether the discrimination in wills can be addressed. The MFC reform contains just one very timid step forward in this area. Grandchildren of both sexes on the mother's side can now inherit from their grandfather (Art. 369).

Islamic family law and the new Rome III Regulation

In order to achieve the integration (and assimilation) of foreign nationals it is usually proposed that the law applicable to their family relationships should be determined according to the domicile of choice and the ordinary residence (presence and *animus menendi*). Favouring the law of the place of residence has been reinforced in the latest national PIL codifications (e.g. Belgium in 2004), in the international conventions and in the European Union PIL.

The general principle of party autonomy (*profesio iuris*) has been added to this trend, which is to say that the spouses can choose which family law is applicable to them. This solution is fully in line with a liberal conception of private law in which homogenous legal systems are involved, but it is not appropriate when religion-based non-EU states are involved. It allows spouses to settle the conflict of laws (cultures) between the law of their country of origin (nationality) and the law of their host country (residence, and generally of the court seized) for themselves, but if they opt for a foreign law that is contrary to public policy this law may be disregarded. Religion-based laws permit the parties to negotiate agreements (private autonomy), but it is not possible to choose the applicable law if this allows the religious law to be disregarded (mandatory rules). Choice of law is not a definitive solution

(Quiñones 2000: 32–40 and 176–78), but it does allow the parties to weigh up the consequences of choosing a limping law and it is therefore vital for foreign nationals to have good legal advice before making their choice. The validity of the choice of law must be controlled by the authorities and it must be the genuine outcome of free and informed consent on the part of both spouses, reached without pressure from their cultural group, family or husband when the law favours the woman. With regard to the material validity of the content (Art. 6, Rome III Regulation), the solutions that it puts forward are based on the dispositions of the Rome I Regulation on the law applicable to contractual obligations.

The difficulties that arise in this situation are illustrated by the Rome III Regulation. The new text regulates the breakdown of marital relationships, but questions concerning maintenance payments and the care and custody of children are excluded and are subject to other Council Regulations and Conventions of the Hague Conference on PIL. Two new Proposals for Council Regulations of 16 March 2011 on jurisdiction, applicable law and the recognition and enforcement of judgments in matters of matrimonial property and the property consequences of registered partnerships[12] will soon be added to these texts.

Autonomous free will in the new regulation on the law applicable to divorce

Art. 5 of the Rome III Regulation allows the spouses to choose the law applicable to their divorce. Introducing this provision into the regulation was not a straightforward matter. Common law countries brought pressure to bear in favour of applying the law of the court, as this is the traditional solution in their systems and the one that leads to Member States' laws shutting out non-EU states' laws, notably Islam-based laws. In any event, the spouses are not actually choosing a religious law (shari'a, canon law, etc.), but the law of a state (Morocco, Algeria and so on) to which they are bound by geographical (nationality or residence) ties.

Relative limits of international public policy

The Rome III Regulation strengthens the use of public policy with the aim of establishing equality of the spouses in the access to divorce. Together with the standard public policy clause (Art. 12), the regulation provides for a special clause (Art. 10), the drafting of which is imperfect, as it contains no other proximity requirements than the forum. However, it is still a public policy clause because it depends on the conflicts of laws rules.

Note that this aim could only be achieved with the general clause of Art. 12 or the regulation that gives judges more flexibility than the special clause of Art.10 of the regulation. Obstacles to the recognition of the divorce in the wife's country of origin must not be underestimated if she maintains contact there. The aim of the special clause is to ensure that the designated, chosen or objectively applicable law allows the spouses equal access to divorce. Its use, though, needs to be measured: if it is possible to apply one of the grounds for divorce (at the woman's request) with the chosen or objectively applicable foreign law, this must be heeded, with the aim of ensuring that the judgment is recognised and the divorce is effective in both countries to which the spouses have connections.

Problems relating to the recognition of judgments on divorce when the applicant is the wife

It is not uncommon for Spanish courts to apply Spanish law to the divorce of a Moroccan couple when divorce can be applied for in compliance with Moroccan law. However, if the law of the country of origin is applied to the divorce judgment, it is more likely to be recognised in Morocco. Art. 23 of the above-mentioned 1997 bilateral convention between Spain and Morocco does not require control of the law applied in the scope of the exequatur (the Art. 16(g) of the bilateral Spain-Algeria Convention does provide for such control, as does Art. 16(g) of the bilateral Spain-Mauritania Convention). In such case a certain equivalence in the outcome must be attempted, at least when the divorce is applied for by the woman (without her husband's consent), to smooth the way for the judgment to be recognised in the country of origin.

The problem of recognition arises now more than ever because divorce without grounds, although not without reasons, has been allowed in Spanish law (and the laws of some other Member States) since the 15/2005 reform. If it were obtained by the woman, any such 'groundless divorce' may be denied in the country of origin. Belgian academics Claire Foblets and J-Y Carlier (2005: 545 and the judgments in note 67 therein), point out that in a case subsequent to the reform of the Family Code the Moroccan Supreme Court, applying the law of the forum, did not recognise a judgment on a divorce applied for by the woman, obtained outside Morocco and opposed by the husband. Drafting judgments to take into account a general discord reason could facilitate their recognition in the country of origin, and this could certainly be said to be one of the challenges and problems that the new regulation faces with respect to Islam-based laws. The spouses must therefore weigh up their options carefully and be well informed of the risks of a limping judgment, in particular for the wife when she is the party applying for the divorce. Access to justice is facilitated by the rules of international jurisdiction (Art. 3 CE 2201/2003 Regulation). The courts of EU Member States can declare themselves competent to deal with a divorce when the applicant spouse is a foreign national who has been resident on the territory for a year (or six months if he or she is a national or has dual nationality). However, recognition of the judgment in the other spouse's country of residence and nationality is not guaranteed. It is necessary for judges to justify their judgments, seeking some sort of equivalence in the outcome.

Conclusion

The solution to most of the problems discussed here entails the avoidance of abstract deductive judgments about what are known as 'conflicts of culture' and the parties' expectations. Modern society increasingly requires judges to come up with *ad hoc* creative solutions, causing them to assume responsibilities in the effective rather than abstract protection of fundamental rights. It is true that the law rests on the principles of legality, hierarchy of rules and legal certainty, but these parameters must not be understood as a hurdle to adaptation and the need to pursue fair outcomes. It is important not to tie judges' hands too tightly in the assessment of the application of a foreign law and to leave some application of the public policy clause to their discretion, a task that needs to be undertaken with a certain dose of pragmatism, attention to details and awareness of the variables of each particular case, as an adaptation mechanism for the foreign law. The judges' task may seem excessive (Dworkin's Judge Hercules) as they are not required to judge foreign legislators or legal systems (in such cases their institutions would always or never be contrary to public policy) but to render decisions *in casu* on whether a foreign law can be the basis of a fair and effective solution, if possible not only in the forum but in another country to which the spouses have ties.

Judges need to be aware that the discrimination between the sexes in Islamic family codes is a structural matter and that it is projected onto the recognition of foreign judgments. Applying the foreign law is therefore advisable whenever possible; or, when a European Union Member State law is applied, judges should at least draft their judgments to include a justification based on the grounds for divorce provided for in the family code of the country in question and focusing on the protection of the individual rights of the men and women who find themselves caught between two legal systems. This may not be an easy task, but it is well worth a try.

Notes

1 *W/Com.*F 86/09.
2 (1989) *IPRax*, 298, note Siehr.
3 26/1992 of 10 November Act (*BOE*, 272, 12 Nov., 38214).
4 RDGRN, 27 April 1999 (BIMJ no. 1857) and RDGRN 4 June 2001 (BIMJ no. 1989)
5 TSJ Cataluña (Social), 30 July 2003, (*AS* 5255/2003); TSJ Galicia (Social), 13 July 1998, (*AS* 1998, 1493); TSJ Galicia 2 April 2002 (*AS* 2002, 899) and TSJ Madrid, 29 July 2002 (AS 2002, 3324).
6 Tribunal Supremo, 26 February 2010, (2010) *REDI*, I, 245–48, note A, Quiñones.
7 *JO Rep. Gabon*, 20 December 1972, p. 1.
8 BOE n° 96, 21.4. 2007.
9 SAP Barcelona no. 611/2009, 29 September 2009 (vlex-71101773).
10 SAP Barcelona no. 515/2009, 16 June 2009 (vlex-77144459).
11 SAP Baleares, no. 198/2011, 1 June 2011 (vlex-351723094).
12 COM (2011) 126/2 and 127/2.

Bibliography

Aldeeb Abu-Sahlieh, A.S. and Bonomi, A. (1999) *Le Droit musulman de la famille et des successions à l'épreuve des ordres juridiques occidentaux*, Zurich: Schulthess.

Boye, A.K. (1993) *Le statut personnel dans le droit international privé des pays africains au Sud du Sahara*, Cambridge: Martinus Nijhoff Publishers

Carlier, J.Y. and Verwilghein, M. (1992) *Le statut personnel des musulmans*, Brussels: Bruylant.

Clerici, R. (2009) 'La compatibilità del diritto di famiglia mussulmano con l'ordine pubblico internazionale', *Famiglia e Diritto*, 2: 197–211.

Dethloff, N. (2011) 'Polygamie-Wer definiert Ehe und Familie in Europa?', *Festschrift für Ingeborg Schwenzer*, Cambridge: Intersentia: 409–25.

Déprez, J. (1988) *Droit international privé et conflits de civilisation*, The Hague Academy Collected Courses, The Hague: Martinus Nijhoff Publishers.

Foblets, M. Cl. and Carlier, J.Y. (2005) *Le Code marocain de la famille*, Brussels: Bruylant.

Foblets, M. Cl. and Carlier, J.Y. (eds) (2010) *Islam & Europe: crises are challenges*, Leuven: Leuven University Press.

Gutmann, D. (2000) *Le sentiment d'identité*, Paris: LGDJ.

Jayme, E. (2005) *Identité culturelle et intégration*, The Hague: Martinus Nijhoff Publishers

Lagarde, P. (2005) 'Différences culturelles et ordre public en droit international privé de la famille', *Institute of International Law Yearbook*.

Meziou, K. and Mezghani, A. (1995) 'Les musulmans en Europe', *Cahiers des Droits Maghrébins*, 1(1), 65–79.

Ministerio de Empleo y Seguridad Social (MESS) (2012) *Stadistics*. Available online at http://extranjeros.empleo.gob.es/es/Estadisticas/operaciones/con-certificado/index.html#Principales (accessed 10 December 2012).

Quiñones Escámez, A (2000) *Derecho e inmigración: el repudio islámico en Europa*, Barcelona: Fundación La Caixa.

——(2012) *Inmigración e integración en la UE: dos retos para el s.XXI*, Bilbao: EUROBASK.

Quiñones, A., Rodríguez-Benot, A., Berjaoui, K. and Tagmant, M. (2009) *Matrimonio y divorcio en las relaciones hispano-marroquíes* (Arab & Spanish), Madrid: FIIAP. Available online at www.fiiapp.org/uploads/publicaciones/MATRIMONIO_Y_DIVORCIO_vol_I.pdf (accessed 15 March 2013).

Quiñones, A., Rodríguez-Benot, A., Zekri H. and Ouhida, J. (2009) *Kafala y adopción en las relaciones hispano-marroquíes*, (Arab & Spanish), Madrid: FIIAP. Available online at www.fiiapp.org/uploads/publicaciones/kafala_y_adopcion.pdf (accessed 15 March 2013).

Rodríguez-Benot, A. (ed.) (2002) *La multiculturalidad: especial referencia al Islam*, Madrid: Consejo General del Poder Judicial.

Rosander, E.E. (2002) *Getting a Divorce in Spain: gender, migration and legal pluralism*, Uppsala: Uppsala University. Available online at www.ku.dk/satsning/Religion/sekularism_and_beyond/pdf/Rosander_Paper.pdf (accessed 15 March 2013).

Sarehane, F. (2004) 'Le nouveau Code marocain de la famille', *Gazette du Palais*, 58(11) 247.

Vargas, M. (2006) *La reagrupación familiar de los extranjeros en España: normas de extranjería y problemas de Derecho aplicable*, Navarra: Aranzadi.

7 An analysis of British judicial treatment of Islamic divorces, 1997–2009

Al-Rahim Moosa and Denise Helly

Introduction[1]

The assertion of the primacy of state justice stems from the idea of an integral link between the state and the law. According to this idea, the law has no social reality other than that assigned to it by state laws – mainly national ones – and cannot be multifaceted. Yet, the multiplicity of norms, rationalities, and justice mechanisms in all societies, as well as the existence of international treaties on fundamental rights that put national laws into perspective, have been undermining this notion for more than 20 years. National laws, it seems, can no longer ignore other normative orders at the risk of contravening principles that have already been acknowledged: the dignity of actors, the legitimacy of their self-identification, and their necessary adherence to state authority. In this context, our goal is to analyse how judges view family norms and values adhered to by Muslims, specifically the approach of British judges to the recognition of Islamic divorces.

This article's central issue – the British recognition of Islamic divorces – is not a new one. With almost three million Muslims residing in the United Kingdom as of 2010, this issue is very familiar to British judges and policy-makers. Indeed, some of the most important developments in the British recognition of Islamic divorces occurred in the early 1970s and 1980s, in the form of judicial decisions and legislation meant to clarify this area of the law. However, as recent case law suggests, the law lacks clarity for multiple reasons, one of which is the focus of this study.

The purpose of this study is to examine British judicial treatment of Islamic divorces through both a legal and anthropological lens. The cases considered, all from between the years 1997 and 2009, concern divorces obtained in Islamic jurisdictions under Islamic (shari'a) law. The focus is to assess how judges in British courts perceive Islamic law in their decisions of whether or not to recognize the validity of Islamic divorces. The cases are summarized as concisely as possible, with emphasis upon the facts most pertinent to the purpose of the study (i.e. those portions of the judgments that concern Islamic law, customs, and values). Before engaging in an analysis of the case law, a brief summary[2] of Islamic law and British law as they pertain to divorce law is presented, followed by relevant legislation for British recognition of foreign divorces.

The Islamic concept of divorce

Under Islamic law, a man may divorce his wife by a pronouncement known as the *talaq*. Generally speaking, the *talaq* may be pronounced three separate times – after the first two times, reconciliation between the spouses is permissible should relations turn for the better, but upon the third pronouncement, the marriage is irrevocably terminated. In its classical form, the *talaq* is not meant to be subject to the enquiry of any external body or person (Pearl 1984). It is intended to be a personal decision arrived at through man's relationship with God. Certain countries preserve the validity of the unrestrained *talaq*, for example India, where a *talaq* pronounced three times successively[3] will render a marriage legally nullified (known as a 'bare *talaq*'). However, many Islamic countries have subjected the *talaq* to various legal reservations with the effect of curbing a man's absolute power to divorce his wife unilaterally at whim. For example, in the Islamic Republic of Pakistan, the *talaq* is regulated by s. 7 of the MFLO (Muslim Family Laws Ordinance), which requires that the *talaq* be registered with an official of the local council and that the wife receive notice of it, both of which are not required under its classical interpretation.

A wife may petition for divorce in Islamic jurisdictions by pursuing a *khul'*. Unlike the unilateral right of a husband to issue a *talaq* to nullify a marital bond, in many jurisdictions, for example, Algeria and Singapore, the *khul'* must be agreed to by the husband. Alternatively, where a husband refuses to agree, a *khul'* may be obtained by the wife with the permission of a *qadi*[4] who may be empowered to overrule the refusal of the husband in certain jurisdictions, for example, Egypt, Bangladesh, and Pakistan.

The British concept of divorce

In contrast to the 'bare' or regulated *talaq* permitted under Islamic law, divorces in the United Kingdom (as well as marriages) are heavily regulated by legislation and the courts. Marriage and divorce in the UK result in significant legal rights and responsibilities, from financial to familial, and regulation of marital status is designed to administer these rights and responsibilities as objectively as possible (i.e. devoid of factors such as gender and religion insofar as they are irrelevant). Consequently, divorce law in the United Kingdom is governed by the Matrimonial Causes Act 1973 (MCA 1973), as amended, which requires the divorcing person to state one of the grounds for divorce under on the 'irretrievable breakdown of marriage' (MCA 1973 s. 1(1)); these are adultery, unreasonable behaviour, desertion, two-year separation with the consent of the respondent, and five-year separation.

British law, both case law and legislation (and including family law), is influenced by the concept of 'reasonableness', a notion deeply embedded in the common law. Reasonableness gives legal effect to the ordinary conduct of human affairs, so that actions well outside the normal conduct of a 'reasonable man' cannot be justified in law. Though a concept that works relatively well within the jurisdiction where it was conceived, understanding 'reasonableness' against the philosophy and practice of entirely different jurisdictions, such as those under Islamic law, becomes far more complicated, as will be explored.

The recognition of foreign divorces

British recognition of foreign divorces is governed by ss. 44–54 of the Family Law Act 1986 (FLA 1986). Relevant provisions (which will be cited and referred to throughout) are paraphrased below:

i) s. 44 – no divorce will be effective within the British Islands unless granted by a court of civil jurisdiction
ii) s. 45 – the validity of an overseas divorce (that is, one obtained outside the British Islands) will be subjected to ss. 46–49 of the FLA 1986.
iii) s. 46(a) – the validity of an overseas divorce obtained by means of proceedings will be recognized if it was effective in the country in which it was obtained, and if either of the parties to the marriage were habitually resident or domiciled in that country when proceedings commenced.
iv) s. 46(b) – the validity of an overseas divorce obtained otherwise than by means of proceedings will be recognized if it was effective in the country in which it was obtained and, at the date it was obtained, each party was domiciled in that country or another country that would recognize the divorce as valid, and neither party was habitually resident in the United Kingdom for up to one year prior to the date it was obtained.
v) s. 51(3)(a) – the validity of a divorce obtained by means of proceedings may be refused recognition (i) without such steps having been taken for giving notice of the proceedings to a party to the marriage as, having regard to the nature of the proceedings and all the circumstances, should reasonably have been taken; or (ii) without a party to the marriage having been given (for any reason other than lack of notice) such opportunity to take part in the proceedings as, having regard to those matters, the party should reasonably have been given.
vi) s. 51(3)(b) – the validity of a divorce obtained otherwise than by means of proceedings may be refused recognition if (i) there is no official document certifying that the divorce, is effective under the law of the country in which it was obtained; or (ii) where either party to the marriage was domiciled in another country at the relevant date, there is

no official document certifying that the divorce is recognized as valid under the law of that other country.

vii) s. 51(3)(c) – refusal to recognize the divorce may be exercised if doing so would be manifestly contrary to public policy.

Methods used to acknowledge and/or recognize foreign law

This section considers cases where judges have acknowledged and/or recognized the validity and implications of divorces obtained under Islamic law, in accordance with the laws of the country where they were obtained.

In *Wicken*,[5] the wife, a Gambian Muslim, was validly married under Gambian law to her husband in 1989. A year later, she claimed he had sent her a letter of divorce that was effective to dissolve the marriage in that jurisdiction. She married another man in a civil ceremony of marriage in England two years later, in 1992, which was followed by a Muslim ceremony of marriage in the Gambia later that year. In 1996, the wife petitioned in England for a divorce from her second husband, to which the husband responded with a declaration of nullity on the grounds that the letter that had dissolved her first marriage was in fact a forgery, which he was told of by the first husband. Holman J. cites the relevant provisions of the FLA 1986, and categorizes this particular situation as falling within the definition of an overseas divorce obtained 'otherwise than by means of proceedings', which leads to recognition only if 'effective under the law of the country in which it was obtained'.[6] The judgment then considers the evidence as to whether the wife was 'free to marry' in 1992, when her second marriage was contracted. Holman J. finds that the letter had been procured and delivered by the first husband. In discussing whether the letter of divorce was sufficient to be effective under Gambian Mohammedan law, he points to the various ways that a divorce can be obtained, such as via *talaq*, by letter of divorce addressed to the wife or her parent, or by a deputation sent to the parents of the wife. With regard to registration, Holman J., citing a *qadi* of an Islamic court in Gambia, states that it is not necessary for marriage or for divorce; it simply serves as testimony to the execution of either a marriage or a divorce. In fact, 'most Gambian couples do not register their marriage or divorce'. Holman J. then addresses the issue of witnesses to the divorce, with experts from the husband's and wife's sides disagreeing over whether a divorce delivered by letter can be valid without witnesses. Holman J. references the *qadi* again, stating that in a situation where a woman claims to have been divorced by a letter but where that is denied by the first husband, the *absence* of two witnesses will result in her 'being returned to the former husband and the second marriage … void'. Therefore, the husband submitted that in an Islamic court, according to what the *qadi* said, the divorce could not be held valid without the testimony of two witnesses to affirm it and, accordingly, that Holman J. could not hold whether it was effective without those testimonies. Holman J. replies as follows:

> What the law of The Gambia requires is that in the event of a dispute in The Gambia the authenticity of the document be proved by the testimony of two righteous male witnesses. But the dispute is not in The Gambia. The dispute is here. Proof of authenticity is a matter of evidence rather than of substantive law and the relevant rules of evidence are those of England and Wales where the dispute arises and is being determined (the *lex fori*) rather than of The Gambia.

Holman J. then looks at the evidence of the divorce alone, without testimony of two male witnesses, and finds that it did take place, further stating that it is possible that the *qadi* would come to the same conclusion, though via 'different forms of proof of authenticity'. Holman J.'s judgment concludes by contemplating a refusal to recognize the divorce due to lack of an official document (because it could not be produced at the proceedings) under s. 51(3)(b)(i) of the FLA 1986, but in rejecting that option, he states:

> One would hope that an English court is unlikely to deny recognition if it is satisfied as to the effectiveness of the divorce, etc. even though no certificate is forthcoming. If that is so, it is hard to see what real purpose this provision serves.[7]

As required by s. 1(3) (1) of the MCA 1973, Holman J. traces the petitioner's evidence comprehensively when coming to his decision. His judgment thoroughly accounts for Islamic law and custom (as seen by his consultation of the *qadi*) which ultimately influence his decision, and takes into account the various means by which a divorce can be obtained in The Gambia, including by letter, which is recognized as a valid means of divorce for the purposes of English proceedings. Although the authenticity of the divorce letter is subject to English evidential procedure (as opposed to the requirement for two righteous male witnesses in the Gambia), this is simply the procedure of the English judicial system and is effectively the only difference between an Islamic court and an English court in the context of this particular case. Thus, Holman J. in essence, substitutes English equivalent for the 'two male witness' requirement and finds that it would lead to the same outcome. Finally, Holman J. refuses to employ the provisions of s. 51(3)(b)(i) of the FLA 1986 (that is, to refuse the divorce because of the lack of physical proof of the divorce letter), which displays his willingness to look beyond the prescriptions of legislation that would otherwise deny an Islamic divorce that, in his eyes, had legitimately taken place.

The case of *El Fadl* in 2000 concerns similar issues. The husband and wife, both Lebanese, underwent a polygamous marriage in accordance with the local law of Lebanon in April 1981. In December 1981, the husband executed a *talaq* in accordance with Lebanese law, in the presence of two witnesses and registered with the shari'a court in Lebanon. The wife was not initially notified of the *talaq* by the husband or any other body, nor was this a requirement under Lebanese law. Hughes J. is convinced that the wife came to know of the *talaq* by the end of 1987. The husband provided financial support for the next 16 years until withdrawing it in 1997, whereupon the wife brought a petition for divorce in England. The husband submitted that, having issued the *talaq* in 1981, there was no subsisting marriage to dissolve. The central issue for consideration in this case was whether the husband's *talaq* would be recognized in the United Kingdom, thereby leaving no marriage left to be dissolved under the wife's petition. Hughes J. was assisted in his judgment by a Lebanese lawyer, Mr Kabrossi, and an English barrister and expert on Islamic law, Mr Edge. Though representing the wife and husband respectively, both agreed that the rules applicable to *talaq* procedures vary across different Islamic jurisdictions. Therefore, Hughes J. states that it would not be appropriate to extract any generalizations from the rules that apply in Lebanon. He then compares and contrasts the Lebanese system of divorce with those of other jurisdictions, such as Pakistan, noting that the Lebanese *talaq* procedure requires it to be pronounced before two witnesses and registered with a shari'a court. He also notes that there is a parallel system in Lebanon for the civil registration of marriages and divorces, but neither the marriage nor the ensuing divorce were registered in this case, nor were there any legal ramifications for failing to do so – the only registrations were with the shari'a court that, in Lebanon, is responsible for all matters falling within the domain of personal status.

Hughes J. establishes that both husband and wife were domiciled in Lebanon in 1981 – when the *talaq* was issued – and then moves on to assess whether the *talaq* qualifies for recognition under English law. He comprehensively outlines the evolution of case law and legislation leading to the current provisions, in particular ss. 44–54 of the FLA 1986 and then marks the difference between divorces 'obtained by means of proceedings' (s. 46(1)) and those 'obtained otherwise than by means of proceedings' (s. 46(2)). The latter provides for the recognition of divorces that are not obtained through judicial means (for example, the validation by a judicial organ of the state), which becomes a point of contention in the case at hand. Section 51 provides the grounds for refusal of recognition of an overseas divorce. For those divorces obtained via proceedings, the grounds include steps for giving notice to one of the parties not been reasonably taken (s. 51(3)(a)(i)), followed by a broader provision that captures reasons, other than lack of notice, that may inhibit one party's participation in the proceedings (s. 51(3)(a)(ii)). Where no proceedings took place, neither notice nor participation is a consideration at all – what is required is official documentation certifying that the divorce was valid in local law. Thus, the legislation appears to embrace different approaches to overseas divorces, including those without any judicial involvement. However, for divorces, both where there were proceedings and where there were no proceedings, there is a provision that allows the judge to exercise his discretion to refuse divorces that are 'manifestly contrary to public policy'.

Hughes J. draws on the case of *Quazi v Quazi*,[8] which held that a divorce may be a proceedings divorce even though no judicial process is involved and where the proceedings do not involve any decision-making power as to the permissibility of a divorce. However, the subsequent case of *Chaudhary v Chaudhary*[9] (binding on *El Fadl*) held that a *talaq* that 'depended for its effectiveness solely upon the pronouncement in front of witnesses' would not constitute a proceedings divorce due to the lack of the participation of state machinery in the process. Therefore, Hughes J. finds *in El Fadl* that, despite the shari'a court having no judicial authority to decide whether a divorce had occurred, the presence of a court, judge, and clerk, alongside a duty to record formal declarations in a register, constituted proceedings for the purposes of ss. 46 and 51. With that established, Hughes J. engages s. 51(3)(a) to discuss refusal of recognition on the grounds of lack of notice and/or insufficient participation. He states:

> It is plain to the English lawyer, or indeed layman, that a wife should be divorced without knowing it is contrary to all instinct. Even if such a wife cannot resist the divorce, she needs to know what has happened. First, she needs to know out of common humanity. Next she may be entitled to some form of maintenance. Thereafter, she may wish to enforce a marriage contract for deferred dowry, and, indeed, she may wish to marry again, or simply to know whether she is in peril of an accusation of adultery, with all that brings in Islamic countries. Notification after the event meets her needs, as does prior notice.

At first sight, Hughes J. appears to be refusing to recognize the divorce by considering it next to the British divorce procedure, and highlighting its relative inequities. However, in his decision to ultimately recognize the divorce, he finds that prior notice, as opposed to notice after the *talaq*, would have served no practical function to the wife; her rights would remain the same regardless. Further, the *talaq* was the prescribed form of divorce in the country that both parties were domiciled – that is, both parties are taken to know the personal status laws that applied to them upon marriage (and subsequently in the event of divorce). He also qualifies his own stance on the decision by stating that even if he was wrong in his classification of this case, and that it was a divorce without legal proceedings, notice would, as stated above, not be a requirement under the appropriate legislation. As a result, he states, '[t]hat confirms my decision that recognition should not be refused on the basis of an *English-imposed requirement* for notice or participation which is wholly foreign to the law of the domicile of both parties' (emphasis added). The next issue considered is whether recognition of the *talaq* would be manifestly contrary to public policy. Counsel for the wife submitted that this type of *talaq* is neither regular, nor 'consistent with Muslim concepts of personal responsibility'. In essence, counsel was arguing that if the shari'a court had any ability to refuse the *talaq*, it would have done so. Hughes J. dismisses this argument, stating that the correct question to ask is whether such a divorce is contrary to English public policy, not whether hypothetically it would be against Islamic public policy within that state. The judgment concludes with another hypothetical scenario – whether recognition of the divorce ought to be denied if the wife legitimately did not have notice at any point (though Hughes J. is convinced she did). Hughes J. speaks to this issue by addressing the relationship between different types of jurisdictions more generally:

> I am satisfied that however much a unilateral divorce without notice may offend English sensibilities comity between nations and belief systems requires at any rate this much, that one country should accept the conscientiously held but very different standards of another where they are applied to those who are domiciled in it.

This case speaks extensively to two matters of historical significance concerning the recognition of Islamic divorces in the United Kingdom – first, whether a *talaq* constitutes proceedings or 'non-proceedings' for the purposes of English law and, second, the role that notice to the spouse subsequently plays in question of whether it should be recognized. With regard to the latter, Hughes J. makes it clear that despite how irreconcilable the failure to give notice may be with English standards, of seminal importance is the comity between nations and belief systems. For Hughes J., then, the domicile of the parties constitutes the most important aspect in the decision to recognize an overseas divorce, and if the domicile remains with the foreign country, any English-imposed requirements should not apply.

Abassi v Abassi,[10] an appeal case, concerned a couple of Pakistani origin, married in 1988. It is not explicitedly clear, but the presumption is that the couple was married in the UK and moved to Pakistan where the husband alledgedly issued as *talaq*. The wife presented a petition for dissolution of the marriage in the United Kingdom, which culminated in a *decree nisi* of divorce, but was not made absolute as the husband claimed the marriage had been dissolved via *talaq* much earlier, in 1999. The husband sought a declaration under s. 55(1)(d) of the FLA 1986, claiming that the divorce by *talaq* in Pakistan should be recognized as a valid foreign decree. The wife argued that there had been no valid *talaq* proclaimed in 1999 and, had there been, the documentation relied on by the husband was 'bogus, forged or otherwise improperly procured'. The Attorney General, along with experts consulted by him and those jointly instructed by both parties, agreed broadly that the *talaq* would qualify under Pakistani law, despite some inconsistencies. In a course of action that was welcomed by counsel for the husband and opposed strongly by counsel for the wife, Wood J. ordered that validity of the *talaq* '[be deferred] to the Pakistani court [for] the determination of what was essentially a Pakistani issue'. The wife applied for permission to appeal against Wood J.'s decision to defer to the Pakistani court, on the ground that the decision was an improper exercise of the judge's discretion 'and that he had placed too much emphasis on the availability or convenience of witnesses, all of whom were resident in Pakistan'. Thorpe L.J. begins deliberation on the case by first considering the details of the order to defer, particularly the undertakings given by the husband to the British court. He notes that they required the husband to pursue the matter expeditiously (within 28 days) and to give due consideration to a set of criteria in order to validate the divorcc, including whether formalities for the divorce were complied with, whether the documents relied on were valid, whether notice of it was required, and, if so, if it was properly given to the wife. In accordance with the Matrimonial Clauses Act 1973, the order also recorded a concession made by the husband to provide due ancillary relief to the wife, regardless of the outcome of the case.[11]

Thorpe then considers the exercise of the judge's discretion. He notes that Wood J. took into account that both parties were of Pakistani origin and both had family in Pakistan, and that there would be grave repercussions for the wife if the British court too quickly allowed the husband's application. This would convey that she had been cohabiting for 'some years' with the husband under the same roof 'and holding herself out to be his wife' despite the husband's *talaq.* Thorpe L.J. also recalls Wood J.'s concern that, because much of the case dealt with issues of fact – evidential issues surrounding apparently fraudulent documentation presented by the husband – it would be far better for a court in Islamabad to deal with these issues, in particular because 'the judge would be familiar with the language, with the law and with the local customs'. Counsel for the wife also attacked Wood J.'s reliance on the availability of ten witnesses as support for the pronouncement of the *talaq*, in that none of them were used at trial to support the husband's contentions – indeed, all there had been were his statements alone, alongside the opinions of three experts. Thorpe L.J. dismisses counsel's argument that this should not have factored into Wall J.'s discretion, stating that 'once the reference to the ten available witnesses is fully explained', it would fall within the judge's discretion whether it should inform his decision. Finally, counsel for the wife submitted that there had been insufficient evidence before Wood J. as to 'the nature of the application that might be brought in Pakistan or the likely duration of Pakistani proceedings' as well as 'the wife's difficulties in participating in the Pakistani proceedings'. Thorpe L.J. dismisses this argument on the grounds that these concerns, if true, need not necessarily pave way to proceedings in the United Kingdom. There are alternatives available, such as adjourning proceedings for further investigation, or direct communication between London and Islamabad via a liaison judge to ensure a proper trial. In ultimately finding that the judge did not overstep his discretion, Thorpe L.J. comments on the changing nature of international family law proceedings:

> In an international family law case such as this, opportunities and practices which exist for the judge of today were simply not there for the judges of decades earlier ... My final observation is that ... it is becoming

increasingly common to have regard to the sensible transfer by the court, acting on its own motion.

Thorpe L.J. comments directly on the strong relationship between the family law courts of the United Kingdom and the judges of Pakistan, stating that 'the collaboration between the two judiciaries has had its most obvious expression in the Pakistani protocol of January 2003'[12] which, Thorpe L.J. suggests, could have been used to facilitate collaboration in this case.

Wood J.'s decision to defer the case to the courts of Pakistan is the product of a careful balancing act between the need to acknowledge the cultural and social repercussions for the wife if the courts in Pakistan decide in the husband's favour, and the acceptance that given the case's complex evidential problems, it would be better dealt with in Pakistan. The undertakings by the husband to the British court at Wood J.'s behest are not intended to impose English criteria for the valid recognition of a divorce onto the Pakistan legal system. Rather, they are meant to ensure that the criteria for divorce under Pakistan's own family laws – the MFLO[13] – are validly met, primarily due to the fact that much of the wife's case concerns issues not of law, but of evidence, which she feels may be improperly handled by the Pakistani family law system. As Thorpe L.J. elaborates, advances in international family law proceedings have given rise to new means – the use of a liaison judge, for example – to address such concerns. The strong links between the two judiciaries that Thorpe L.J. refers to further show a confidence in the Pakistani legal system that it will yield the appropriate outcome, whatever that may be.

K v K[14] is the most recent case in the timeline of this chapter, and draws on cases prior to guide its decision. The husband and wife married in Pakistan and arrived in the United Kingdom in 1966. The wife petitioned for divorce in England in January 2004, which was met by an affidavit from the husband in August 2004 stating that he had divorced his wife via *talaq* in Pakistan in March 1987. He claimed he had delivered her notice personally in 1987, but the wife stated that she had never received it. A *decree nisi*[15] was granted in the UK in October 2004, which was met by a petition by the husband in 2005, giving rise to the current proceedings. The issue at substance is whether the divorce took place as set out in the husband's affidavit. Sumner J. traces the relevant law under the FLA 1986, noting also that he has been referred to *El Fadl* to inform his decision. He highlights that it was not necessary for the wife in that case to have notice of the *talaq* in order for it to have effect, and that it would not be a proper exercise of discretion on the part of the judge to refuse a divorce that was valid by the personal law of both parties and that had been known to them for many years. The balance of the judgment explores whether the husband had obtained a proper divorce in accordance with Pakistani law, and whether he had served a copy of the divorce decree on the wife in 1987. Mr Edge (an expert in Islamic law) is consulted once again; he explains that notice is required under the MFLO 1961 (which applies in Pakistan). Mr Edge concludes that a Pakistani court would accept that a *talaq* had been proclaimed by the husband, with notice given to the Chairman of the Union Council (Union Councils are local government bodies in Pakistan) as required, effective in April 1988. About this, Sumner J. notes, importantly, that 'it was fatal to a valid *talaq* if there was no notice to the chairman. It was *not* fatal if there was no notice to the wife.' Sumner J. ultimately prefers the evidence of the husband to that of the wife, finding a stream of inconsistencies in her submissions, alongside evidence that the *talaq* had likely been declared. He takes into account a variety of considerations apart from those extracted from the evidence. These include a consideration that if the husband had not obtained a divorce, his second marriage in 1992 under shari'a law would have been considered adultery for which there were 'social and legal consequences … and severe penalties'. Further, he finds that it would be unlikely for the husband to contract a second marriage without divorcing his wife 'in particular when he was going to continue living in the community where he was known. I do not consider that he would have run the risk associated with such a course.'

The judgment concludes with a consideration of past cases, first with a recitation of the findings in *Chaudhary* to the effect that 'proceedings' requires the involvement of some form of state machinery to be involved in the divorce process. Sumner J. also produces the statements of Lord Scarman in *Quazi* which states that any act(s) that lead to a valid divorce in a country where it was obtained would be capable of qualifying as proceedings within the British jurisdiction. Finally, he reiterates the position of Hughes J. in *El Fadl* and finds that, in *K v K*, the situation is not irregular, and indeed ought to be valid for reasons affecting international relations:

> There are a great many people living in the UK from Pakistan and many move freely between both countries. Where there are as here close links to each country, it is important that marriages and divorces recognised by the country where they take place should be recognised in the other country unless there are good reasons for not doing so.

Sumner J. essentially follows the decision of Hughes J. in *El Fadl* when arriving at his decision, notwithstanding that the decision in *El Fadl* is not binding upon him. Taking into account the evidence of Mr Edge, he accepts that while the lack of registration would affect the validity of the divorce under Pakistan's MFLO, the lack of notice to the wife would not invalidate it, and applies this to the case at hand. He does note one particular difference between the facts in *El Fadl* and in the case at hand; that is, in the case at hand the wife had been away from Pakistan for 25 years when the divorce occurred and her domicile was therefore likely to be in England. Yet, that said, Sumner J. elevates the fact that she was 'born, brought up and married in Pakistan to someone of the same background' above the location of her (likely) domicile, considering these aspects to be most important in his decision.

Methods used to ignore, misapply or undermine foreign law

The following section presents cases where judges have ignored or misapplied Islamic laws, custom, and values in order to provide rulings that indicate a preference for, or the superiority of, British law.

In a case from 2002, *Sulaiman v Juffali*,[16] the couple was domiciled in Saudi Arabia, where they were married in accordance with shari'a law in 1980. The wife filed a petition for divorce in England on 22 June 2001, which was followed by a bare *talaq* pronounced by the husband in England the next day. The *talaq* was registered with the shari'a court in Saudi Arabia on 26 June and the marriage was finally and irrevocably terminated in that jurisdiction. The husband applied to the UK court for an order to decide whether the marriage was subsisting or had been validly dissolved by his *talaq*. The wife submitted that the *talaq* executed by the husband was a paradigm of a 'non-proceedings divorce' and did not accord with s. 44(1) of the FLA 1986, which states that no divorce obtained in any part of the British Islands would be regarded as effective unless granted by a court of civil jurisdiction. Further, despite being registered with the shari'a court in Saudi Arabia, it had been 'obtained' within England and Wales, therefore the wife contended that it would not meet the criteria for an overseas divorce as per s. 45(1)(a) of the FLA. She also argued that the *talaq* did not amount to 'proceedings' – judicial or otherwise. The husband submitted that the *talaq* ought to be recognized because it was properly registered in Saudi Arabia and met all the necessary formalities required in that jurisdiction. It was effective and recognized in the society from which both parties came from, were nationals of, and domiciled in. It was argued that the wife took steps that were alien to the parties' culture and traditions. In reaching his judgment, Munby J. was assisted by two experts in Islamic law, Dr Al-Sawwaf and Mr Edge. Both stated that registration of the *talaq* is not a formal requirement in Saudi Arabia, and the presence of witnesses to testify to the pronouncement makes no material difference to its validity. Additionally, they clarified that the location of the *talaq* pronouncement under Islamic law is immaterial as well – 'The validity of a divorce is … a matter between man and God.' Munby J. turned to the relevant provisions of the 1986 FLA. Section 44(1) disallows any divorce obtained within the UK and not granted by a court of civil jurisdiction. Section 45(1) permits overseas divorces provided they meet the criteria listed in ss. 46(1) and (2), but Munby J. highlighted one particular section of s. 45(1) – that it needs to be 'obtained in a country outside the British Islands'. Therefore, despite having provided notice to the wife and registering the *talaq* with the shari'a court (which would normally meet the requirements of s. 46(1) or (2), depending on whether these acts are construed as 'proceedings' or 'non-proceedings'), the physical act of the pronouncement of the *talaq* needs to have taken place outside the British Islands. Therefore, preferring the statement of Dr Al-Sawwaf, Munby J. states that the effect of the *talaq* is to dissolve the marriage 'as soon as' the *talaq* was pronounced, devoid of any participation or authorization of judicial authorities in the UK. Munby J. clarifies that, had this issue been regulated by common law as it had been prior to 1973, it is likely that the *talaq*, pronounced within the UK in this case, would have been recognized as a valid divorce. Section 16(1) of the Domicile and Matrimonial Proceedings Act 1973, ancestor to s. 44(1) of the FLA 1986, was meant to reverse the outcome of *Qureshi*, Munby J. explained.

Munby J. then supplements his decision by stating that it is not 'founded upon any lack of respect for the husband's religion or culture'. He clarifies his position as a 'secular judge … sworn to do justice "to all manner of people", though religion 'is not the business of government or of the secular courts. So the starting point of the law is an essentially agnostic view of religious beliefs.' Munby J. refers to an extract of Sir Jocelyn Simon P. from *Qureshi* where he stated, 'the rule of foreign law under which the husband has proceeded has the authority of the holy scriptures of the common faith of himself and the wife', but Munby J. refuses to give effect to this 'informal divorce' on the grounds of policy that he was bound to follow.

Munby J.'s concluding comments regarding Islam and Islamic law are significant when placed into context. The judgment in this case was handed down on 9 November 2001, shortly after the beginning of the war in Afghanistan. The judgment also served to clarify for many Muslims across the country the legal status of a *talaq* obtained in England. It is notable that the triple (bare) *talaq* procedure was denied as an effective means of divorce within the United Kingdom despite the fact that both parties were domiciled within Saudi Arabia and that the divorce was registered with a shari'a court in the country of domicile. The judge's consideration seems to have prioritized the physical location where the divorce was 'obtained' above all else. This indicates that he considered the pronouncement of the *talaq* in Saudi Arabia as the equivalent of obtaining a divorce in the civil courts of England and Wales, which then begs the question as to what purpose, if any, the registration of the *talaq* in the shari'a court of Saudi Arabia had on the overall case. Would the triple *talaq* have been validly recognized in the United Kingdom if the husband had taken an overnight flight to Saudi Arabia, pronounced it, and then returned the United Kingdom (presuming registration in the shari'a court also took place)?

In *Na v Mot*,[17] a case from 2004, the husband and wife were both Iranian by nationality, Muslim, and bound by the code of shari'a law. The husband had lived in the United Kingdom since 1978. They married in Iran in 1998, with provision in the marriage deed for capital for the wife, which would be her property upon marriage and thereafter. They settled in the United Kingdom, but within weeks the wife moved back to Iran and began proceedings for divorce, seeking her marriage portion in its entirety. The Iranian court ordered the husband to pay the marriage portion, but based on evidence it would have been difficult for the wife to obtain a divorce (*khul'*) according to Iranian law; she would have instead needed the husband to grant her a *talaq* to receive her full portion. The wife sought divorce proceedings in the United Kingdom instead, and claimed ancillary relief in the sum of the marriage portion she claimed to be entitled to. The wife's application was permitted, and the order of a lump sum (which was a fraction of the marriage portion) would have been granted if she had dropped all proceedings in Iran on the basis that the husband had granted a *talaq,* without which she would not have been entitled to the full amount.

An expert on the Iranian law of divorce, jointly instructed by the parties, highlighted that according to shari'a law as applied by Article 6 of the Iranian Civil Code, 'Iranian nationals remain subject to the laws of Iran in respect to matters of their personal status, even if they have gained a second nationality and are resident abroad', which suggested that Iranian courts would be unlikely to recognize an English divorce and any orders ancillary to it. Baron J. explains the difference between a *khul'* and *talaq* – specifically, the difficulties facing the wife in obtaining the former. Though the wife has a thorough set of protections in her marriage contract to obtain her marriage portion upon divorce, the husband must agree to the *khul'* and the courts must be shown that she has proven, to high standard of proof, one of the grounds specified in her contract. Baron J. also lays out the consequences of not obtaining a *khul'*, which would be to live as a married, but separated woman – that is, with restrictions on her remarriage, physical relations, and freedom to travel. In the event that she were to obtain a *khul'*, it would be subject to renegotiation with the husband (again, who must consent first) and would likely result in a lesser amount than the marriage portion initially agreed to. Baron J. finds her motive for seeking a divorce in the UK to be to obtain a set of divorce conditions that would be more favourable than those under Iranian law. Likewise, the husband would not want to issue a *talaq* because doing so would require him to pay her the full sum of the marriage portion.

Baron J., when applying the law, acknowledges that the cultural background against which the case was set would be a decisive factor in his judgment. Baron J. refers to a prior case[18] where the application of s. 25 of the MCA 1973 called for the judge to:

> give due weight to the primary cultural factors, and not ignore the differential between what the wife might anticipate from determination in England as opposed to determination in the alternative jurisdiction, including that as one of 'the circumstances of the case'.

He accepts that if the wife did not secure a religious divorce, her 'long-term prospects are bleak', and that even upon its success, she would have to start anew in England or Tehran.

Baron J. orders the husband to grant the wife a *talaq* and to pay the wife slightly over half of the stipulated marriage portion, arriving at that figure by accounting for the husband's wealth and the period of time for which the husband and wife cohabited. He orders the husband to pay this portion within 28 days; if he did not, the wife would be entitled to the full amount stipulated in the original marriage contract, all contingent upon her dropping proceedings in Iran.

Baron J.'s judgment exhaustively traces all relevant aspects that need to be considered under Islamic law, drawing particular attention to the legal ramifications for the wife in her attempt to obtain her promised marriage portion through the Iranian judicial system. In his decision, Baron J. effectively engineer the relevant Islamic legal mechanisms to work in the wife's favour in order to create an outcome he considered appropriate, but one that would not, it seems, be served by the courts in Iran. His decision elevates the cultural aspects of being a Muslim wife in Iran over the religious decrees of the Islamic legal system. While the decision visibly serves the needs of the wife who would have had no other recourse, it must be noted that the decision contradicts the value system of the country in which the wife married, along with the code that was intended to bind the parties to the marriage under Islamic law regardless of their physical locations and nationality.

Our analysis concludes with the 2005 case *Duhur-Johnson v Duhur-Johnson*.[19] The husband and wife, both Nigerian, married in Nigeria before coming to England. The wife issued an English divorce petition based on his unreasonable behaviour and received permission to proceed despite the husband's failure to acknowledge the petition. When the *decree nisi* was about to be pronounced, the husband interrupted proceedings to declare that he had already obtained a divorce in Nigeria, based on the wife's unfaithfulness while they lived there (as well as unreasonable behaviour, such as 'going to nightclubs and other such matters'). The husband did not inform the wife of the Nigerian divorce when they met the year before to discuss child support. Further, the husband did not inform the Nigerian court or his lawyers in Nigeria that the wife had any connection – residence or otherwise – with England; therefore the bailiff in Nigeria was unable to serve the wife's notice of the Nigerian proceedings. The Nigerian court instead ordered substituted service, pasting the petition to a property where the wife supposedly lived, and proceeded to grant the divorce in the wife's absence. The husband sought a stay of the English divorce, arguing that the English court was bound to recognize the Nigerian divorce as a valid overseas divorce.

The husband's case for recognition of the Nigerian divorce relied on s. 46(1) of the FLA 1986. The Attorney General (AG), intervening on behalf of the wife, submitted that no decision on that point could be made in the absence of expert evidence pertaining to Nigerian law. The AG further submitted that even if the Nigerian decree is effective under Nigerian law, it should have been refused according to s. 51(3) of the FLA on the basis that the husband had not taken reasonable steps to notify the wife of the Nigerian proceedings. Mr Richardson QC (sitting as a Deputy High Court Judge) accepts that s. 46(1)(a) binds him to acknowledge overseas divorces, but only if they were effective in the jurisdictions in which they had been obtained. In order to do so, evidence of that effectiveness is required, evidence that he did not have before him. Notably Mr Richardson choses not to adjourn the case in order to obtain that evidence, seeking to decide the case by reference to s. 51(3) alone. He refers to *El Fadl*, *Wicken*, and to *D v D* (a case outside of the time period considered in this chapter) to guide his decision. In *D v D*, a Ghanaian divorce questioned in the English courts was held to be ineffective due to the interpretation of s. 53(1)(a), which states that a divorce may be refused 'without such steps having been taken for giving notice of the proceedings'. In that judgment, Wall J. states that what constitutes 'reasonable steps must be a matter of fact in each case' and that, technically, it could be possible for a divorce to be permitted *without* such reasonable steps. However, this is subject to 'English standards of reasonableness, having regards to the nature of overseas proceedings'. The same point is found in *El Fadl* where Mr Richardson highlights Hughes J.'s comments stating that the lack of notice to a wife was 'contrary to all instinct' and that she needed to know 'out of common humanity'. Again, Mr Richardson points to the 'wide judicial discretion' that could be used to refuse recognition under s. 53(1)(a).

Mr Richardson observes that the 'nature of the proceedings in the High Court of the Delta State of Nigeria is very similar to divorce proceedings in this country' and that 'what is utterly clear is that the Nigerian procedure ordinarily requires notice of the proceedings to be given to the other party'. He accepts that the Nigerian court and lawyers did attempt to serve notice on the wife. Therefore, he categorizes the Nigerian court's decree as a 'proceedings'-style divorce, which may have been recognized had the Nigerian court not been misled by the husband when he failed to inform the court that the wife may have been resident in England. Mr Richardson concludes that the divorce should not be recognized because the Nigerian court had been critically misled by the husband's failure to inform the court about the wife's residence in England. This is a technical matter of procedure, required under s. 53(1)(a), that was not met. Had it been met, and had the husband taken those reasonable steps, it seems likely that Mr Richardson would have recognized the overseas divorce. In fact, he highlights that the Nigerian court system was familiar to English lawyers, and was one that, like the British system, required notice to be served on the spouse. Ultimately, his judgment incorporates the evidence that was lacking in the Nigerian court proceedings, and therefore arrived at the decision that the Nigerian court would have had if it had not been misled.

Additionally, Mr Richardson speaks broadly on the issue of overseas divorce recognition. His intention in referring to the *El Fadl* case is to convey the fundamental role that notice plays in British divorce proceedings, and he emphasizes that judges are equipped with wide discretion to refuse recognition where, in an overseas divorce proceeding, reasonable steps to notify are not taken. However, he subjects these steps to English standards, an approach that was *not* advocated by Hughes J. in *El Fadl*. Hughes J. focused on the 'comity between nations' as preferable to any attempts to 'impose' English standards onto the legal procedures and philosophies of other jurisdictions. While one cannot presume the approach Mr Richardson would have taken if he had presided over a case such as *El Fadl*, it seems as though the wide judicial discretion enjoyed under s. 51(3)(a) would have been exercised with more favour towards British legal procedures than those of the foreign jurisdiction.

Conclusion

Although this chapter has placed the above cases within two categories – the acknowledgement and/or recognition of foreign laws, and the ignorance, undermining, and/or misapplication of the foreign laws – the individual judgments reveal very different means by which to achieve each end. Therefore, for judgments that ultimately respect legal pluralism and strive to move away from the 'positivist centrality'[20] of the British legal standard, the question of *how* the judgment will arrive at such an outcome remains difficult to predict. The lack of consistency in approaches to the recognition of Islamic divorces can be attributed to multiple reasons. In a comprehensive report compiled by Women Living Under Muslim Laws (WLUML) (2006)[21] the following reasons were identified:

- The lack of knowledge regarding the law on the part of all actors.
- The lack of clarity in the law of the country of origin.
- Mutual mistrust between the British legal system and Muslim communities subject to that system.

Such reasons have always characterized the dynamics of overseas divorce recognition and transnational family law issues more generally – the period that this chapter covers, 1997–2009, is only a small segment of a much longer history plagued by the same issues. However, judges now have plentiful access to resources to better educate themselves and to inform their decisions with regard to foreign laws. As British law constantly evolves, so should British legal academics, policymakers, and judicial authorities acknowledge the inherently pluralistic nature of Islamic law(s) and that a universally just outcome can be achieved through either, if not both, lenses. Consequently, greater dialogue between traditionally opposing legal systems becomes ever more important in order to exchange ideas with the ultimate goal of coming closer to this universally understood notion of justice. This is particularly relevant for the higher courts, as precedent in judgments serves not only to set the stage for subsequent cases, but also has an impact on relations between countries.

Notes

1 We would like to acknowledge the grant from SSHRC in 2007 for a research project entitled: Différence de valeurs et de normes. Des pratiques familiales musulmanes

selon des juges au Canada, en Espagne et au Royaume Uni [Difference in values and standards: Muslim family practice according to judges in Canada, Spain and the United Kingdom]. The authors would also like to express their gratitude to Professor Werner Menski, School of Oriental and African Studies, University of London.

2 Please note that British and Islamic family law(s) are summarized as they relate to the content of the chapter. Wider theoretical debates about how the Islamic and British divorce laws operate independently of one another are not within the scope of this chapter.

3 *A* talaq recited three times successively is is generally referred to as 'triple *talaq*' or *talaq-ul-bidat.*

4 Generally, a *qadi* is considered the equivalent of a judge in the Islamic (shari'a) legal system.

5 *Wicken v Wicken* (1999) Fam 224.

6 Section 46(2)(a) Family Law Act 1986.

7 Citing *Cheshire and North's Private International Law.*

8 [1980] AC 744, [1979] 3 WLR 833, [1979] 3 All ER 897, HL.

9 [1985] Fam 19, [1985] FLR 476, [1985] 3 WLR 350, [1984] 3 All ER 1017, CA.

10 (2006) EWCA Civ 355, (2006) 2 FL 415.

11 In accordance with the HCA 1973.

12 'In January 2003, judges from Pakistan and the UK signed a "judicial protocol". This is an understanding between the two countries which aims to secure the return of an abducted child to the country where they normally live, without regard to the nationality, culture or religion of the parents. The judges agreed that the child's welfare is a priority and that the courts of the country where the child normally lives are usually in the best position to decide on matters of custody and where a child should live.' Full protocol available online at www.reunite.org (accessed 20 November 2013).

13 The MFLO 1961 is one of the central pieces of legislation governing family law in Pakistan. It is available online at unhcr.org/refworld/pdfid/4c3f1e1c2.pdf (accessed 20 November 2013).

14 (2007) EWHC 2945 (Fam).

15 If a party to a marriage does not defend the other party's divorce petition, the party seeking divorce can apply for a decree nisi. A decree nisi is a conditional confirmation that the divorce can be granted (i.e., in practice, it means that the court cannot see any reason why the divorce cannot be granted). It will become a decree absolute after a certain time period (six weeks plus a day) during which the other party can bring forward any objections to the divorce.

16 (2002) 2 FCR 427.

17 EWHC 471 (FAM), [2004] All ER (D) 238 (Mar).

18 *Otobo v Otobo* EWCA 2002.

19 [2005] 2 FLR 1042.

20 While legal positivism has several meanings, most of its followers would accept two basic propositions. First, the definition of 'law' should not depend on questions of moral validity. Second, law should only be identified in terms of tangible formal provisions, such as legislation, case law, and customary traditions. As a result, positivists refuse to incorporate any moral assessment in their definition of law (Menski 2006: 152).

21 Women Living Under Muslim Laws 2006: 2.

Bibliography

Burton, F. (2012) *Family Law*, Abingdon: Routledge.

Menski, W. (2006) *Comparative Law in a Global Context: the legal systems of Asia and Africa*, Cambridge: Cambridge University Press.

Pearl, D. (1984) 'Recognition of the talaq. Some recent cases', *The Cambridge Law Journal*, 43(1): 49–54.

Women Living Under Muslim Laws (2006) *Recognizing the Un-Recognized: inter-country cases and Muslim marriages & divorces in Britain*. Available online at www.wluml.org/node/566 (accessed 15 November 2012).

Cases considered

D v D (Recognition of Foreign Divorce) [1994] 1 FLR 38, FD
Wicken v Wicken (1999) Fam 224
El Fadl v El Fadl (2000) 1 FLR 175, [2000] 1 FCR 683, [2000] Fam Law 84
Sulaiman v Juffali (2002) 2 FCR 427
Na v Mot EWHC 471 (FAM), (2004) All ER (D) 238 (Mar)
Duhur-Johnson v Duhur-Johnson (2005) 2 FLR 1042
Abbassi v Abbassi (2006) EWCA Civ 355, (2006) 2 FL 415
K v K (2007) EWHC 2945 (Fam)

8 Can there be a compromise?

Australia's confusion regarding shari'a family law

Ann Black

Setting the scene

Twenty-first century Australia is a multicultural, multilingual and multifaith nation in which Muslims are a recognisable minority group, estimated at approximately 500,000 (ABS 2011). A distinguishing feature is Muslim heterogeneity. The 100 different nations from which Muslims have immigrated are both monocultural and multicultural societies, operate under shari'a law or apply only secular law, or are legally pluralistic. Australia is home to Muslims from Sunni and Shi'a traditions, each with their own subgroupings, and because of the dynamic nature of *ijtihad* (reasoning) they hold wide-ranging views on legal, theological and doctrinal matters. The term 'Islams' rather than 'Islam' has been coined to capture this intra-plurality (Glenn 2004: 203). Most are Muslim by birth, but there is a growing number of converts; conversely, others who were born Muslim have either left the faith as apostates, or are now non-practicing, or identify themselves as 'secular Muslims'. Of Australian Muslims, 62 per cent were born overseas (ABS 2011) and hold different attachments to their countries of origin, cultural practices and traditions. These factors directly inform perceptions of law, both shari'a and secular law. Such differences have led legal academic, Jamila Hussain, to conclude that it is 'probably more correct to speak of Muslim communities in Australia rather than *the* Muslim community' (Hussain 2004: 203). The absence of Muslim homogeneity in Australia can be contrasted with Britain where there is a concentration of Muslims (75 per cent) from South Asia (Moore 2010:17) and also Singapore where most Muslims are Malay, sharing the same language, culture and history. Intra-pluralism in Australia is a significant contributor to the confusion enveloping the future direction for Islamic family law: Australian Muslims conceive Islam and Islamic law in multiple and varied ways and divide on the role it should have in secular Australia.

Australia's legal culture is a creation of its distinctive historical and political trajectory. Muslims now comprise 2–3 per cent[1] of the population, which is numerically similar to the Torres Strait and Aboriginal people, the descendants of the continent's first peoples. When the British government colonised this land in the late eighteenth century, it introduced into New South Wales, and then into each of the subsequent five colonies, the common law of England. Unlike other British colonial possessions in South Asia and the South Pacific, the colonial government did not consider any form of legal pluralism for Australia. In nearby Singapore, Brunei and Malaya, the British recognised the right of Malays to be governed by personal status laws embodying Islamic law principles. No similar recognition was afforded the traditions, customs and practices of Australia's indigenous peoples, nor was there a treaty negotiated. This was justified on the basis of the legal concept in international law – *terra nullius* or land belonging to no one. The validity of *terra nullius* in Australia was not rejected until 1992 with the landmark decision of *Mabo v Queensland*.[2] This historical context is important because right from the earliest days of first settlement Australia has been a 'one law for all' country. When the six colonies federated in 1901, the Australian Constitution omitted any recognition or acknowledgement of the first peoples of Australia, and even though Christians made up over 90 per cent of the population, the Constitution did not establish a state religion, opting instead for a de-establishment provision. While s. 116 of the Constitution provides for 'free exercise of any religion', de-establishment has meant that a separate system of religious courts for personal status matters is contrary to Australian practice and constitutional ideals. From inception, anti-sectarianism informed Australia's secularism (Voyce and Possamai 2011: 339). At federation, mosques coexisted with churches, synagogues and temples, but the cultural preference for secularism to be prioritised over religiosity (Bouma *et al.* 2010: 4–14) meant that religious law, like religious practice, was to be voluntary, independent from government, and not contrary to secular law.

Labour Prime Minister Gillard, Attorneys-General Roxon and McCelland, also Minister Bowen, along with their Liberal and National predecessors have all been unequivocal in reaffirming that there is 'no place in Australia for shari'a law'. This bipartisan position has proved a significant obstacle for those Muslim Australians who advocate that multiculturalism should lead to legal pluralism (AFIC 2011) and who desire full legal autonomy over family matters be given to either a formally recognised system of shari'a courts/tribunals, or to the legal enforcement of arbitral decisions applying shari'a law. Without official recognition along these lines there are two main consequences. First, in the suburbs of Australian cities and towns, many Muslims do turn to *imams*, sheikhs and informal councils, variously called Imam Councils, Tribunals or *Majlis Ulama*, to apply shari'a family law. For Muslims who choose this avenue, the imperative to live according to shari'a law is too strong to be displaced by Australian secularism. However, as it is applied only in the private, unofficial and unregulated realm it is difficult to know exactly who is using these services, what legal advice if any the parties are given, the types of decisions made regarding marriage, divorce, custody and property settlement, and the protections afforded to parties. The anecdotal reports of inconsistencies and unaccountability in the decision-making adds to the confusion regarding shari'a family law in Australia, and gives rise to concerns that patriarchal and conservative interpretations dominate, leaving some

Muslim women quite disadvantaged (Essof 2011:184). The second consequence is that Australian courts, in particular the Family Law Courts and the Federal Magistrates Courts, are now finding that they are faced with deciding cases brought by a Muslim party or parties, where the marriage was solemnised under the Islamic law, but subsequent disputes have arisen on the validity of the marriage itself or on matters pertaining to separation, divorce, property settlement and parenting arrangements. While the 'one law for all' approach does govern court decisions, when there is an element of Islamic law embedded in the dispute, it is complex and at times confusing for the parties and for the judges.

The case of *Mohamed v Mohamed*[3] illustrates the complexity when there is interplay between shari'a and Australian law and gives insight into how the 'one law for all' approach plays out in Australian judicial thinking. Faced with paying *mahr*, the appellant husband argued from an Australian law perspective that the marriage contract was contrary to Australian law on public policy grounds and, conversely, that the issues involved the applicability of Islamic law that could only be determined by Islamic law. It also highlights that engaging with shari'a law is new territory for our courts as Harrison AsJ. noted when concluding her judgment in the appeal:

> As this appeal raises the current issue of the way agreements based on religious or cultural tradition should be dealt with in our society, and it appears that there is not Australian case law on this topic, I shall refer this question to both the Australian Law Reform Commission and the NSW Law Reform Commission for their consideration as to whether this topic is suitable as the subject of a term of reference.

Case study: *Mohamed v Mohamed*

In 2009, Neima Mohamed brought a claim to the New South Wales Local Court for enforcement of $50,000 *moackar sadak* (*mahr*), referred to by the court as her dower. This was the first time an Australian court had to determine whether a term of an Islamic marriage contract could be enforced under Australian law.

In 2004, Mostafa Mohamed (Mostafa) and Neima Mohamed (Neima) married under Islamic law. The marriage was confirmed by a signed agreement stating that they were in a 'relationship blessed by Islamic shari'a' and that it was a relationship within the meaning of the Property Relationships Act 1984 (NSW). It stated they intended to marry at a future date under Australian law. Within the contract there was recognition of both secular and Islamic law. The agreement was that each of them would keep their assets if the marriage were to end, in line with the NSW and the Family Law Act 1975 (Cth). The contract was signed and its terms understood by both parties. One key term in clause 11 stated that if Mostafa 'initiated separation and/or divorce' he would pay Neima's *moackar sadak* of $50,000 but if she initiated divorce, or there was mutual agreement, no money was to be paid (clause 12). The couple never married under Australian law. Three year later, the marriage was in trouble. It culminated in police being called in April 2007, when Neima alleged her husband threatened her with a knife. She claimed that she moved out of the apartment a few days later at the behest of Mostafa and after his daughter (from an earlier marriage) told her to leave and set out how their division of their property would occur. Each attempt at reconciliation was unsuccessful. In September 2008, during an argument, Neima claimed that Mostafa Islamically divorced her by saying 'You are divorced'. Mostafa disputed that he had pronounced *talaq* and claimed that Neima initiated the separation by taking his key and leaving. Under the terms of the marriage agreement, whether Mostafa would have to pay $50,000 depended on the question of who initiated separation and/or divorce. It is not mentioned in the judgment whether the couple tried to have the matter resolved informally through an Islamic tribunal. No expert evidence on Islamic law was presented.

At the hearing in the New South Wales Local Court, Magistrate Trad found that the couple separated in April 2007, with Mostafa the initiator, and gave a judgment in Neima's favour for the $50,000. Mostafa was also ordered to pay her costs. Mostafa appealed to the NSW Supreme Court on five grounds, including that the magistrate erred 'in not finding that the agreement was unenforceable because it was against public policy' and in 'not finding that the relevant separation did not have to be in accordance with shari'a law'.

Was the contract against public policy?

Counsel for Mostafa submitted that clause 11 of the agreement containing the *moackar sadak* was against public policy for two reasons. First, it amounted to an agreement for servitude as its sole purpose was to compel Mostafa to remain in a relationship with his wife, which, in effect, amounted to a penalty clause. The clause and contract, it was argued, should be rendered void for illegality. As neither counsel could find a case in Australia that had previously determined this point, Harrison AsJ. turned to other common law jurisdictions and surveyed American and Canadian decisions as to whether a *mahr* – or *moackar sadak* – clause was enforceable. She found favour with the view expressed by Moen J. of the Alberta Court of Queen's Bench in *Nasin v Nasin*,[4] that *mahr* agreements could be enforced as long as they 'complied with the formalities of the applicable Canadian legislation' and so a religious component in the contract did not make a case 'non-justicable'.[5] It was held that the contract could not be constructed as one of servitude. The second argument was that in the Australian family law context of no-fault divorce, it was against public policy for a court to determine which party left the relationship and then impose a financial penalty. Harrison AsJ. reasoned, judges are often called on to 'determine sensitive factual matters such as when a relationship has ended, or whether it was indeed a de facto relationship' and so it did not constitute any breach of the principles of 'public policy recognised by law or by the community' (pp. 50–51).

When the law of the marriage is shari'a law, does a court have jurisdiction to make a decision that is not in accordance with shari'a law?

Counsel for Mostafa argued that the Magistrate did 'not have jurisdiction to make a decision in accordance with shari'a law' stating that 'what constitutes an initiation of Islamic divorce or separation proceeding is something distinct to Islamic law and could only be determined by an Islamic Court' (p. 55). However, as their agreement made express reference to several pieces of Australian legislation and included an intention to have the marriage solemnised under Australian law, Magistrate Trad read the words 'divorce' and 'separation' to be concepts that operate under Australian law. Accordingly, to determine when the separation occurred, Magistrate Trad did not rely on Islamic family law but sought to factually determine the issue under applicable Australian law. The Supreme Court noted that Mostafa had not, at first instance, challenged the jurisdiction of the local court or sought to bring in shari'a expert evidence. The agreement was silent regarding the application of shari'a law with no requirements for religious mediation or other process. More specifically, Harrison AsJ. opined that the agreement did not require the meaning of 'separation' or 'divorce' to be interpreted in accordance with Islamic law, and if that had been so intended it should have been specified in the contract. The lower court's finding that shari'a law was not required to properly interpret the marriage contract was affirmed.

Mostafa's counsel also submitted that under the terms of the contract, marriage under Australian law was a condition precedent to the enforceability of the contract, specifically for clause 11. Harrison AsJ. agreed that s. 90B of the Family Law Act 1975 (Cth) only applies in the event of 'the breakdown of a marriage' and as no marriage under Australian law between Neima and Mostafa occurred, the Act had no application and the separation occurred before the 2009 de facto relationships provisions. However, the agreement itself did not specify that marriage under Australian law was a condition precedent to its enforceability, and any resultant ambiguity allowed for evidence of surrounding circumstances (including their significant financial assets and the need for certainty in their financial affairs). This enabled the court to find that separation could apply to a de facto as well as a marital relationship. The appeal was dismissed on all grounds. Mostafa was required to pay Neima the *moackar sadak* of $50,000 and pay all her costs.

The significance of the case is threefold. First, because an Australian Court found an Islamic marriage contract with a *mahr* clause can be legally enforced, which will act as a precedent for subsequent cases. However, it was a contract that expressly referred to Australian law. If the contract had instead specified Islamic law the outcome may have been different. Second, it is significant because the Muslim couple were only married under Islamic law, yet the contract was decided by applying Australian contract law. Islamic law did not inform the reasoning. The husband's submission that the Australian court lacked jurisdiction for matters involving shari'a law failed, thereby signalling that Australian courts will not cede jurisdiction because a religious dimension is involved. Harrison AsJ. cited Black and Sadiq's view that 'shari'a family law cannot be relegated exclusively to a religious tribunal, court or other body to apply and enforce as it is the right of all citizens to being family matters to the courts of law for determination and have the general law of the land apply' (p. 49) (Black and Sadiq 2011: 406). Third, Neima said in an interview after the decision that it is 'important for Muslim women to fight for their rights' (Berkovic 2012). The case is seen as confirming that the secular courts may provide better and fairer outcomes for Muslim women than many of the informal shari'a tribunals where conservative and more patriarchal views prevail.

Yet, for Neima, if she wishes to remarry within the Islamic faith she will need to ensure that she was in fact Islamically divorced. Mostafa disputed her evidence that he pronounced *talaq* in 2008 and if the case were to come to an informal shari'a tribunal or to a local *imam*, his willingness to agree to divorce by mutual consent (*mubaret*) or to pronounce *talaq* would be crucial. A *khul'* divorce is unlikely because of the protracted dispute over the *mahr*. Although some *imams* will take into account the fact that a couple is divorced under Australian law, many will not, leaving the wife in the 'limping marriage' situation of having a civil divorce but not a religious one.[6] Without the religious divorce, she remains married to her Muslim husband. A remarriage would be seen by her community as adulterous and any children deemed illegitimate. The husband, however, can remarry as a polygynist marriage is lawful in Islam and the children legitimate. Awareness of such outcomes and the perception that Australian *imams* apply conservative shari'a interpretations act as significant disincentives for Muslim women wanting to leave an unhappy, even a violent, marriage. Recent immigrants can be especially vulnerable to spousal, religious and community pressures to resolve the marital dispute within the Muslim community and accept the *imam*'s ruling.

Marriage

Australia's Marriage Act 1961 (Cth) is accommodating of Islamic marriages. It enables Islamic marriage ceremonies to be performed and registered by an authorised marriage celebrant, which, for Muslims, will usually be an *imam* from their mosque. If the requirements of the Act are adhered to, and the *imam* is authorised, then the Islamic marriage can be valid under both sets of laws. The marriage can be registered with the relevant state government office for births, deaths and marriages. As was seen in *Mohamed v Mohamed*, some Islamic marriages will not be registered. This can be an overt rejection of the secular and an affirmation of the Islamic union (*nikah*) as the sole foundation for their marriage. At times, non-registration occurs as an oversight, or one or both of the spouses believe that the marriage is going to be registered and the *imam* fails to do so, or cannot as he is not an authorised celebrant, and some couples erroneously assume that an Islamic marriage is automatically a state marriage. In *Oltman & Harper*,[7] there was a mix of these circumstances at play. The wife, a non-English speaking immigrant from Somalia told the court that: 'When we married I trusted the husband had organised our marriage so that it would be recognised in the eyes of Allah and in Australian society' (p. 27). However the sheikh was not authorised under Australian law as a celebrant, a fact known to the husband but not the wife. The sheikh said he had no knowledge of Australian law as this was the first marriage he had conducted. The Court invoked s. 48 Marriage Act 1961 (Cth), which provides that a marriage can be valid despite procedural non-compliance. It rejected the husband's evidence that he only wanted a religious marriage and found instead that both had intended for the marriage to be legally valid under Australian law. Given there was a religious ceremony with an intention for it to be a registered marriage, Young J. applied the common law presumption of marriage.

In the case of *Wold v Kleppier*,[8] the *imam* told the court he did not always register marriages because 'when couples go back home the civil marriage certificate may not be accepted' and so only the Islamic certificate is needed. He explained that Islamic marriages are 'very, very quick to perform' as the one-month notice period of intention to marry is not required,[9] nor are birth certificates and other forms of identity required. In *Wold & Kleppir*, the Court had to decide whether a ceremony performed by an *imam* was an Islamic marriage ceremony or not. Kleppir, the husband, claimed the ceremony was merely one converting the woman with whom he was living to Islam, and not a marriage ceremony. The *imam* gave evidence that the ceremony was a '*nikah* conducted in the presence of others' (p. 28) in which he spoke in both Arabic and English so both would understand what was occurring and that he did pronounce them husband and wife. The wedding apparel worn, the exchange of rings, an Islamic marriage certificate and a post-ceremony, celebratory feast were held to be supportive evidence of marriage. Barry J. rejected the husband's claim that he believed the ceremony by the *imam* was merely a ceremony of conversion and held that there was s. 45 compliance. The judgment noted that it is the 'responsibility of the *imam* to comply with Australian law'. The non-registration of Islamic marriages leads to quite different versions of events given in evidence to Australian courts that have to decide whether there was in fact a marriage before deciding any property and parenting arrangements.

There are no restrictions on inter-faith marriages in Australia and it is inevitable in a multifaith society that couples of different religions fall in love and marry. Rarely will an *imam* officiate at such marriages and if he does, it will typically include a conversion to Islam ceremony, or the fact one party is not Muslim will be kept secret. When there is deception of this type, it can unravel later. In *H v H*,[10] the *imam* and the wife's Lebanese family were unaware that the man she was marrying in the Islamic ceremony was a Maronite Christian. The marriage would be void under Islamic law, and the relationship fractured when their baby son was baptised and the father sought a Christian upbringing for him.

Age for marriage

The lawful age for marriage in Australia is 18 years or older. A person who is 16 or 17 years of age and who has parental approval to marry can apply to a judge or magistrate for an order authorising his or her marriage to a person who is of marriageable age (Marriage Act 1961 Cth, s. 12). This is limited to situations where there are exceptional or unusual circumstances to justify the order.[11] The Act does not spell out what makes circumstances 'so exceptional and unusual' but case law indicates that the courts are reluctant to consider cultural practices of ethnic groups as exceptional circumstances. The test for 'exceptional' is that it must relate to the particular parties and not the class of persons to which they belong.[12] Australian courts have not been sympathetic towards the cultural or religious traditions of ethnic groups that allow young marriage in countries of origin, generally holding that an order is not justified simply because a proposed marriage would be acceptable under the cultural norms of another country or religion. 'Underage' marriages are void (s. 23(1)(e) and s.23B (1)(e) Marriage Act 1961 (Cth)) and may constitute an offence under s. 95 by the person conducting the marriage. In Muslim migrant communities where marriage between children under 16 years is an accepted practice in some overseas countries, young marriage continues to have particular appeal as a way to preserve the integrity and virginity of girls, especially as Australian society is viewed as morally lax. It seems that when such marriages take place the approval of the Australian court is not sought (unless there are immigration implications) and the families facilitating the marriage are content with the Islamic *nikah*. *Imams* have indicated that when the couple attains marriageable age they may then ask their *imam* for the marriage to be registered under Australian law. The extent of underage marriage in Australian Muslim communities is unknown but it can be linked to the practice of 'servile and forced marriages'.

Consent

One of the known contributors to non-registration of Islamic marriages is the *nikah* taking place without full consent of one party, usually the bride. In Australia these marriages are called 'forced' or 'servile' marriages as distinct from arranged or facilitated marriages, the latter being lawful and frequently practised amongst Muslim and also Hindu families. Forced marriage is defined as the absence of full and free consent by both parties, often as the result of coercion or deceit. Servile marriage refers to situations in which a person is considered a chattel that can be sold, transferred or inherited into marriage (A-G Dept 2011). The victim of a forced marriage may be taken overseas to wed under the law of another country, but marriages where there has been physical, emotional or financial duress or deception do take place onshore. Forced marriage is, of course, contrary to Islamic law but such marriages do occur, officiated by Muslim sheikhs and *imams* in Australia, possibly in the misguided belief that the marriage is 'protecting their child or preserving cultural or religious traditions' (A-G Dept 2011). The Australian government believes cases of forced marriage are widely under-reported and in 2011–12 conducted an enquiry into the problem. The report estimated that 1,000 such marriages occur annually. A bill was introduced into the Federal Parliament that proposes criminalizing forced marriage with a seven-year maximum imprisonment term.

The cases of forced marriages that do come to the court have been mainly dealt with by injunctions issued pursuant to s. 68B of the Family Law Act 1975 (Cth). The child has contacted the police or a person whom she trusts, which leads to an application being made to the court seeking the court's protection. In *Madley & Madley & Anor*,[13] a 16-year-old girl expressed her fear that her parents were forcing her into an arranged marriage with a man in Lebanon who she had met only once. After telling her parents she did not want to go to Lebanon, nor marry, she feared for her personal safety. Harman F.M. noted that he was not judging the cultural basis upon which the mother sought to force the marriage, but that 'the child being an Australian citizen as well as being raised in, and no doubt continuing to be part of, a Lebanese Islamic culture, is in some real conflict … that should, at least in the short term, be the subject of this court's assistance and intervention through injunctive relief' (p. 18). The court must 'protect a child from physical or psychological harm in circumstance whereby a young person does not wish to proceed with a wedding … and is being forced to do so – a principle that is contrary to all our legal processes hold dear and which would indeed, under Australian law, render the marriage void, as it is absent genuine consent' (p. 27). Harman F.M. conceded that the court was interfering with this family unit and the familial relationship between the child and parent, and that these arrangements should not be 'judged or criticised from a western perspective, but must be viewed through the eyes of those who live and appreciate that culture'. Although the daughter 'straddles both cultures', it was significant that she sought the protection of the court, which showed 'she clearly embraces and understands her independence under her Australian citizenship and lifestyle' (p. 32). In cases such as this, the injunctions issued are to restrain family members from assaulting, threatening, harassing or intimidating a minor child[14] and to prevent the child being taken out of the country. The court will usually put the child on the Airport Watch list and order that the passport be retained by the court registry. Arrangements for protection of a child can be made and also counselling given to the child and family.

Another issue regarding consent to marriage is when it has been fraudulently obtained (s. 23 Marriage Act). This arises particularly when the marriage has been entered into by one party with the sole, and undisclosed aim of obtaining residency status in Australia, which the courts have indicated is an increasing problem not only amongst Muslim immigrants but also all the migrant groups. There are a series of cases in which Muslim women sponsored their future husbands to immigrate to Australia for marriage, but once the Islamic marriage ceremony was conducted and registered, the husband ceased contact and refused to cohabit. Australian courts are generally reluctant to annul marriages involving fraudulent misrepresentation of this type unless, as in the case *In Marriage of Deniz*,[15] it goes to the 'root of the marriage contract'. A Muslim schoolgirl was convinced that a man from Turkey loved her and she agreed to leave school and marry him. With her parents' consent she married, to be told shortly afterward he married her only to obtain permanent residency in Australia. The girl was distraught and attempted suicide. Frederico J. found her husband did not have the slightest intention of fulfilling any of his marital obligations and declared the marriage void. Annulments were not given in other cases where the fraudulent misrepresentation was held not to constitute fraud sufficient for a decree of nullity.[16] These cases turn on their own facts and highlight a 'difference of opinion amongst the judiciary' in Australia (Parkinson 2012: 355).

Polygamy

Just as polygamy, or more accurately polygyny, is not widely practised in Muslim nations, it is not common amongst the Muslim diaspora in Australia. Australia legally recognises polygamist marriages lawfully contracted in an overseas country (Family Law Act, s. 6) provided neither party was domiciled in Australia at the time. They are deemed to be marriages, which enable the co-wives to be recognised as lawful wives for the purposes of the Act. The wives can apply to the court for maintenance, property distribution, a parenting order or injunctive relief and are equally entitled to government welfare benefits. However, if either party is domiciled in Australia at the time of the marriage ceremony, it is a ground for nullity of the marriage and constitutes the criminal offence of bigamy (Marriage Act, s. 94). However, polygynist relationships, as opposed to marriages, are recognised and accrue the same legal benefits and recognition as monogamist marriages. This arises as a consequence of s. 4AA(5)(b) Family Law Act, which states that a de facto relationship can exist even if one of the persons is legally married to someone else or in another de facto relationship. So if a married Muslim man marries another wife under Islamic law, the marriage cannot be registered but it will nonetheless be recognised as a lawful de facto relationship and providing the wife can establish that the relationship is one of 'a couple living together on a genuine domestic basis' then she and other co-wives will have the same rights to property division and maintenance as if they had been legally married.

However, this consequence has not yet been applied by an Australian court (Richards and Esmaeili: 2012).

In the case of *Wold & Kleppir* mentioned earlier, the Family Court was also required to consider the potentially polygamous nature of Islamic marriage. The husband had submitted that his unregistered Islamic marriage in Australia should be declared invalid as it was a 'potentially polygamous union' that would allow him to take up to four wives. Counsel for the husband argued that an Islamic marriage should therefore be denied the status of a marriage under the Marriage Act 1961 (Cth). The judge, Barry J., noted there were several 'insurmountable difficulties with this submission', including that if a Muslim male contracts a second or subsequent marriage by the rites of Islam, or any other religious ceremony, it exposes him to the crime of bigamy. The husband's submission was dismissed as *reductio ad absurdum*. The courts also turn a blind eye to evidence of polygyny when it arises as an ancillary matter in a case. In *H v H*,[17] evidence was given by the first wife that the husband entered a second marriage with a Muslim wife while still married to her, which the Magistrate dismissed as not one of the issues 'that are of true concern in a parenting case' (p. 27).

Polygamy is one aspect of Islamic family law that divides Australia's Muslim communities (O'Brien 2008). It is also seen as alien to Australian culture and Western traditions, even though extramarital affairs are commonplace and accepted as inevitable. In modern Western contexts, it is difficult to replicate and oversee that the Islamic requirements of equal support, lodging, time and expenditure are fulfilled, and concerns are expressed that the expense incurred in educating children and managing more than one household means the children can be disadvantaged and that exploitative arrangement of second wives occur in Australia (Sayit 2011). However, social security support goes some way to alleviating financial disadvantage. It has been argued by Muslim community spokesmen, such as Keysar Trad of the Islamic Friendship Association (Trad 2008), that polygamous Muslim marriages should be lawful, although the contrary view possibly dominates (Hussein 2008). Academics Richards and Esmaeili submit that while the potential of the courts to protect the interests of Muslim women in de facto polygamous relationships exists, this does not extend to actual recognition of shari'a law. If s. 4AA(5) of the Marriage Act were changed to recognise all Muslim polygnist marriages as lawful (not only those contracted overseas), it would ensure full protection under Australian family law, which the authors contend is 'appropriate in an Australian society which regards all men and women as equal, and respects all religious traditions' (Richards and Esmaeili 2012: 13).

Mahr

When Australian courts are required to assess disputes over *mahr* they do so either using the Australian law of contract, as in *Mohamed v Mohamed*, or apply the provisions of Part VIII Family Law Act 1975 (Cth). In Australian contract law, *mahr* can be held as an enforceable term of a contract and the husband ordered to make the payment. Whether the outcome would be different if determined by a shari'a court is irrelevant. Similarly, when *mahr* provisions are raised in the context of a post-divorce property settlement, the court will treat *mahr*, either paid or deferred, as part of the combined asset pool to be distributed in line with spousal and child maintenance needs and property distribution. Parties will usually try to work out these matters without recourse to litigation, but some cases will require resolution by the Family Court.

In *Hashim v Hashim*,[18] the Family Court had to determine the property settlement for the divorcing couple, as well as make parenting orders detailing with whom the children would live and the arrangements for spending time with each parent. For the property settlement the court accepted that the *mahr* in the marriage contract was $70,000, with $25,000 paid at the time of the wedding and the additional $45,000 was outstanding. The mother disputed ever receiving the $25,000, however the court regarded this as inconsistent with the contract with her signature. The financial records were not conclusive and the Court noted deficiencies in the evidence of both parties. The *mahr*, however, was not dealt with as a separate item to accrue to the wife but was seen as part of the overall available asset pool, including home, cars, superannuation and bank accounts, all of which was to be divided under the formula of a just and equitable division of the matrimonial assets. The *mahr* as a term of the marriage contract had no independent standing.

In the Australian context, there is uncertainty as to the current role for *mahr*. One of the difficulties in the Australian context is that *mahr* functions as a financial safety net to enable a wife to manage financially should the marriage end. A husband's right to pronounce divorce by *talaq* without citing grounds means he would have to pay any remaining *mahr* and maintain his wife for the three month *'idde* period. His financial obligations to her then cease. However, in Australia, *mahr* is not a divorced woman's only avenue for financial support post-divorce. She is entitled to take her case to the Family Court for spousal maintenance, which does not end after three months, and for property settlement. Depending on the circumstances, she may also be entitled to government paid social security benefits. As far as the Australian courts are concerned, it does not matter who initiated the divorce or who was 'at fault', so the Islamic differentiation of *talaq*, *khul'*, *faskh*, *taliq* forms of divorce and the *mahr* implications are rendered meaningless. Australian courts will not defer to such distinction just because the parties are Muslim. Instead, all assets and contributions are taken into account in order to produce an outcome that addresses the future needs of both parties.

It can be frustrating that if a Muslim party seeks divorce in an Australian court there can be a quite different outcome from what would have occurred in a shari'a court in a Muslim country, or if the issue was informally determined by a tribunal in Australia. There are two consequences. The first is that the informal shari'a system is preferred especially by Muslim husbands and if the case is brought to the Family Court the secular nature of jurisdiction is called into question. The second is that, as couples know that in Australia a wife's financial security will not depend on the *mahr*, increasingly they are specifying small sums of money ($100–$1,000) or symbolic items (jewellery or a Qur'an). The role for *mahr* is being redefined.

Divorce

Regardless of whether the parties are Muslim, Australian courts do not apply Islamic criteria in divorce cases. Australian law stipulates only one ground for divorce, which is irretrievable breakdown of the marriage[19] evidenced by 12 months continuous separation of the parties. It is no-fault divorce and the court is unconcerned about the cause of the marriage breakdown. The court's focus will be on establishing the period of separation, as was seen above in *Mohamed v Mohamed*. The evidentiary relevance of a husband's pronouncement of *talaq* will be only for a factual determination regarding the date of separation. The Islamic practice or legal requirements, as with any religion, will have no bearing on divorce decrees and post-divorce settlements issued by Australian courts. For this reason, some Muslim parties will try to reject the jurisdiction of the secular court. In *Shible & Mead*,[20] the wife applied for a divorce decree citing that their separation commenced with a phone call from her husband in Lebanon saying: 'We are not married!' The husband's response was that her application should be dismissed on the ground that it was against his 'religious beliefs' to divorce in a 'secular court system'. Any divorce, he submitted, should be in Lebanon, 'in the same religious court system the marriage took place in'. The wife did not want a shari'a court in Lebanon to make the decision, submitting that 'it is almost impossible for a woman to be granted a divorce if the husband does not consent to it'. While the Family Court did not remit jurisdiction to Lebanon, the case was dismissed on the factual ground that the 12-month period of continuous separation had not been established.

As with marriage, a couple can comply with both shari'a and Australian divorce law. Under Islamic law a husband has to wait three months before a *talaq* divorce takes effect but then can remarry in accordance with shari'a. In Australia, he needs to be separated from his wife a further nine months before he can lawfully remarry. For some Muslim men, this is seen as an unfair, onerous and unwarranted requirement imposed by the state. The Australian system also has requirements for mediation and counselling that are similar to the Islamic law process, and culturally appropriate options exist.

Islam is not the only faith tradition requiring a religious divorce for its adherents. Other religions also do not accept a secular divorce as dissolving a marriage that took place under their religious law. Roman Catholics and Jews in Australia have ecclesiastical and rabbinical courts respectively to make such determinations. These matters remain internal to the religion and are separate and independent from the government and the state legal system.

Although there have been recommendations (Family Law Council 2001) that Australian courts should not grant a divorce until Muslims (or Jews) have first obtained an Islamic (or Jewish) divorce, this has not been implemented into law, and is unlikely to be. To address the problem of recalcitrant Muslim husbands and to ensure equality between Muslim spouses, Essof has argued that the Australian government should set up an Islamic divorce council and amend the Family Law Act to require Muslims married in a religious ceremony to first obtain an Islamic divorce before a decree absolute can be granted (Essof 2011: 186). The proposal would mandate a separate stream of law for Muslims. However, to deny any party access to the state court on the basis that he or she was married under an Islamic rite would be problematic. Advocates for a dual court system so argue on the untested assumption that most Muslims, including Muslim women, would give up their right to have direct access the Family Court. The Director of the Islamic Women's Council of Victoria, Joumanah El Matrah, finds it 'entirely bewildering' that:

> our [Muslim] ... religious recognition is now measured by the extent to which the government is prepared to set us apart from the rest of Australian society. The legal ghettoization of Muslims does not recognize their difference: it would simply allow a government to delegate its responsibility for ensuring the rights and protection of people who are different ... Establishing parallel system for Muslims does not ensure a culturally appropriate response to justice: it fundamentally locks out Muslims from services they as citizens have a right to access.
>
> (El Matrah 2009)

It is acknowledged that in Australia's current *ad hoc* system, a wife seeking a shari'a divorce has to find someone or some organisation she believes can grant a divorce in accordance with Islamic law. As well as leading to inconsistent outcomes and possible bias, this *ad hoc* system is said to allow 'recalcitrant husbands' to refuse to finalise their divorces' (Essof 2011: 182). However, there is no guarantee that a government-run statutory Islamic council would consider Islamic divorce decrees in any way different from, or more favourably for women, than the current informal practice. In Singapore, Abdul Rahman found that its Muslim minority encounters 'significant problems' arising from 'traditionalism' in the judicial interpretations of Singapore's Syariah Courts, and that the contemporary needs of Muslim women in divorce and custody matters were eroded by dogmatic attitudes 'that cling firmly to old ways, resisting innovations or accepting them only unwillingly' (Abdul Rahman 2006: 416). It would seem that internal reform within Muslim organisations in Australia is the better option for review of Islamic marriage contracts in Australia to ensure wives have greater, or even equal, divorce powers. The marriage contract could specify that the husband delegates to his wife the right to pronounce divorce (*talaq-i-tafwid*), whether or not he consents to it, which would place both husband and wife in the same position regarding divorce. This right is already found in some Australian Islamic marriage contracts. It brings an end to the limping marriage problem and allows greater equality in the marital relationship.

Parenting orders and *kafala*

Of all the issues that will bring divorcing Muslim couples to the Family Court, the most frequent one is a dispute over the care of their children. Muslim parents can bypass the Australian system in favour of settling the matter according to the established Islamic principles of custody based on the presumption of *hadana*, with guardianship going to the father. As the courts in Australia do not recognise or apply these Islamic principles, one parent may submit their dispute to the secular system hoping for an order that will be more favourable. At a personal level it can be incredibly emotive, and tactics of discrediting the other party are common. The current Australian position is that concepts of guardianship, custody and access are outdated and have been replaced by parental responsibility, residence and contact. These new concepts highlight the duties and responsibilities parents have to their children, and negate any concept of parental rights over children. This was the rationale underpinning the Family Law Reform Act 1995 (Cth), designed to reflect the principles contained in the United Nations Convention on the Rights of the Child (1989) ratified by Australia in 1990. The overriding objective is to ensure that the 'best interests of the child' guide the court and any parenting order must have this as the 'paramount consideration' (s. 43C Family Law Act 1975 Cth). The best interests of the child are determined 'in light of the particular facts and circumstances of the case' and not 'from the viewpoint of the standards of particular parents or of one section of society' (Harland *et al.* 2011: 146). In a multicultural society, the court strives to be impartial regarding the 'relative merits of the practices, beliefs and ways of living of different cultural, ethnic, social minority and religious groups within society' (Harland *et al.* 2011: 146). Judges are mindful of the directive in s. 60B(1)(e) of the Act that 'children have a right to enjoy their culture (including the right to enjoy that culture with other people who share that culture)'. Muslim practices and beliefs are not seen as superior or inferior to those of any other religion. As Muslims see transition of Islamic values and practice to their children as crucial, the application of the neutral best interests of the child test can be perplexing. This is especially true in cases where a parent has left Islam as an apostate, or where a mother has remarried or is deemed *nusyuz* (disobedient). In a shari'a setting this would be relevant. In Australian courts, who was 'at fault' in ending the marriage and whether a parent is lax in his/her adherence to Islam has no bearing on the parenting orders given.

This was a significant issue in *Heiden & Kaufman*.[21] The mother unilaterally left the marriage of four years, took the two children and renounced Islam. In an Islamic system an apostate, and one who also failed to follow her husband's directions, would lose custody. In this case, evidence was given by the husband and other Muslim witnesses that as an apostate she would not 'bring up these children in the faith and that the children really would be better off living with their father' (p. 132). However, there was a record of violence in the marriage and the court was concerned by the husband's 'extremist views' and his membership in an extreme Islamic organisation. He had required his wife to wear a *burqa*, be segregated from males and not to leave or have guests in the home without his permission. His Honour was particularly concerned for the welfare of the children as the father had pronounced *du'a*s (prayers of supplication) that his children die 'as martyrs in the cause of Islam' (p. 54). The court found it was in their best interests to reside with their mother. Best interests of the child can include stability of lifestyle, so when the father in *W v W*[22] converted to Islam and took on a new Islamic lifestyle and a Muslim wife, that break in continuity was held as detrimental to their child's development. The parenting order confirmed the continuance of the prior arrangement. Ryan F.M., in *H v H*,[23] affirmed that 'it is not the judicial role to prefer one religion over another' (p. 29) and while cases involving religion often involve one of the parents arguing that being brought up in a particular faith is fundamental to a child's best interests, courts try to avoid this kind of argument and 'religion is only considered relevant when it is detrimental to the child' (p. 28). Here, a Muslim mother and a Maronite Catholic father were in dispute about the school their child should attend. The court decided that it was in the best interests of the child to go to a secular government school, rather than a Catholic school, provided the secular school did not create a bias in favour of Islam as against the father's Catholicism. Religious holidays are usually allotted to the parent of that faith, but, in *Eriksson v Tinkham*,[24] Monahan FM found that the importance the Christian mother gave to Christmas was cultural, not religious, so the order was for her to have the children only for every second Christmas and in the alternate year, the children would be with their Muslim father.

Some cases engender such high level of conflict between the parties that the secular court can be called on to decide, amongst other things, a Muslim baby's name. In *Mohammed Salah & Gastana*,[25] both parents were Muslim of Arab ethnicity. The father opposed the Muslim name chosen by the mother, stating that it was 'blasphemous in the Islamic religion' and insisted on another Muslim name. The mother submitted an affidavit from the Imam Council that the name was neither blasphemous nor offensive. The *imam* was called to give oral evidence in court to clarify 'that in shari'a law there was no problem with the name'. The dispute meant that for two years the child's birth had not been formally registered. Forrest J. held that it was in the child's best interests to be registered and should be registered in the name chosen by the mother. This was because the mother was caring single-handedly for the child, the child was widely known by that name (save for the father's household) and it was an acceptable name for a Muslim girl.

Naming of children is important in Islam and is part of the reason Western-style adoption is rejected. Adoption throughout Australia is declining with less than 50 adoptions a year, so the issue of recognising an Islamically acceptable form of adoption, *kafala*, is not a significant issue. However, adoption laws in several states now support 'open' as well as traditional 'closed' adoptions. Open adoptions allow adopted children to know their lineage and cultural heritage and, importantly, to have contact with their birth parents, to the extent that all parties agree. In New South Wales, it is possible for the child to retain their birth family's surname when requested, and where possible Muslim children will be adopted by Muslim families so their faith is preserved (DOCS 2007). However, the adoptive parents remain the legal parents of the child.

Conclusion

Muslims in Australia have choices. Choice can lead at times to confusing and conflicting outcomes. A Muslim couple can marry according to Islamic law and have a valid *nikah*, which is also a state registered marriage; they can choose just the Islamic marriage; they can bypass a religious ceremony in favour of a secular one; they can cohabit without marriage; even enter a same-sex civil union. Australian Muslims are afforded the same relationship choices as other Australians: the decision is theirs to make. If they choose the unofficial shari'a route, more confusion can arise as in a land of many 'Islams' and many distinct Muslim communities. Again they have choices as to which *imam* or which Council to turn to for a ruling, aware that inconsistency is commonplace. Despite advocacy by some Muslim leaders for a separate official stream of family law, or for secular court jurisdiction to be secondary to an Islamic Council, the 'one law for all' approach remains well entrenched and is supported by many Muslims who argue that formalised shari'a law is neither needed nor wanted as, in effect, Australian law meets the higher objectives of Islamic law (Rane 2011). While it would be unconscionable to deny a Muslim access to any Australian court of law, the secular judges need always to be cognisant that they operate within a multicultural and multi-religious nation. It is evident from the judgments that they try to do. With some Muslim parties now framing their submissions using Islamic legal concepts and norms, secular judges face new challenges. Muslims also have adjustments to make when deciding whether to stay within the more familiar shari'a law paradigm or trust the secular courts or alternate between the two. That is the current direction of compromise in Australia.

Notes

1 An overview on the Muslim population is available online at ww.immi.gov.au/media/publications/multicultural/pdf_doc/Muslims_in_Australia_snapshot.pdf (accessed 10 December 2013).

2 (No 2) (1992) 175 CLR 1.
3 (2012) NSWSC 852.
4 2008 ABQB 219.
5 Citing *Marcovitz v Bruker* (2007) 3 SCR 607 at 12–13. Contra *Kaddoura v Hammoud* (1988) OJ No 5054 (24).
6 An analogous because under Jewish law divorce is delivered by the husband, and is accepted by the wife. A wife cannot remarry without the husband pronouncing divorce (Williamson 2004: 7).
7 (No. 2) (2010) FamCA 1360 (3 September 2009). In this chapter, the names of cases are pseudonyms approved by the court pursuant to s. 121(9)(g) Family Law Act 1975 (Cth).
8 2009 FamCA 178.
9 *Marriage Act 1961* (Cth), s. 42, requires written notice of the intended marriage to be received not later than one month before the date of the marriage.
10 (2003) FMCAfam 31.
11 Re SG 1968 11 FLR 326, 327.
12 (2011) FMCAfam 1007.
13 *Kandal & Khyatt & Ors* 2010 FMCAfam 508.
14 (1977) FLR 114.
15 *In the Marriage of Osman & Mourrali* (1990 FLC 92–111).
16 2001 FMCAfam 192.
17 (2012) FamCA 135.
18 Section 48 (1).
19 (2010) FMCAfam 354.
20 (2011) FMCAfam 478.
21 (2001) FMCAfam 192.
22 (2003) FMCAfam 31.
23 (2011) FMCAfam 341.
24 (2011) FamCA 440.
25 [2011] FamCA 440.

Bibliography

Abdul Rahman, N.A. (2006) 'Traditionalism and its impact on the administration of justice: the case of the Syariah Court of Singapore', *Inter-Asia Cultural Studies*, 5(3): 415–432.

Attorney-General's Department (2011) 'Forced and Servile Marriages'. Discussion paper. Available online at www.ag.gov.au/www (accessed 15 January 2013).

Australian Bureau of Statistics (ABS) (2011) *Census Data*. Available online at www.abs.gov.au/census (accessed 12 December 2012).

AFIC (Australian Federation of Islamic Councils) (2011) 'Embracing Australian Values – Maintaining the Right to be different'. Submission to Australian Government Enquiry on Multiculturalism. Available online at www.aph.gov.au/house/committee/mig/multiculturalism/subs/sub81.pdf (accessed 6 December 2012)

Berkovic, N. (2012) 'NSW court tells man to pay Islamic dowry', *The Australian*, 1 August. Available online at www.theaustralian.com.au/news/nation/nsw-court-tells-man-to-pay-islamic-divorce-dowry/story-e6frg6nf-1226439836081 (accessed 10 December 2013).

Black, A. and Sadiq, K. (2011) 'Good and bad shari'a: Australia's mixed response to Islamic law', *UNSW Law Journal*, 17(1): 383–412.

Bouma, G.D., Ling, R. and Pratt, D. (2010) *Religious Diversity in South East Asia and the Pacific*, Dordrecht: Springer.

DOCS (Department of Community Services, New South Wales) (2007) *Adoption in New South Wales: information for the Muslim community*, Ashfield: Department of Community Services.

El Matrah, J. (2009) 'A shari'a tribunal is a contradiction of Islam', *The Age*, October 20. Available online at www.smh.com.au/federal-politics/society-and-culture/a-sharia-tribunal-is-contradiction-of-islam-20091020-h59c.html (accessed 10 December 2013).

Essof, I. (2011) 'Divorce in Australia from an Islamic Law perspective', *Alternative Law Journal*, 36(3): 182–88.

Family Law Council of Australia (2001) *Report on Cultural Community Divorce and the Family Law Act 1975*, Executive Summary, Family Law Council: Barton ACT.

Glenn, H.P. (2004) *Legal Traditions of the World*, 2nd edn, Oxford: Oxford University Press.

Harland, A., Cooper, D., Rathus, Z. and Alexander, R. (2011) *Family Law Principles*, Pyremont: Law Book Co.

Hussain, J. (2004) *Islam: its law and society*, 2nd edn, Leichhardt: Federation Press.

Hussein, S. (2008) 'Something borrowed, something blue', *The New Matilda*. Available online at http://newmatilda.com/2008/07/09/something-blue (accessed 21 December 2012).

Moore, K.M. (2010) *The Unfamiliar Abode: Islamic law in the United States and Britain*, Oxford: Oxford University Press.

O'Brien, N. (2008) 'Muslim leaders split on polygamy', *The Australian,* 1 July. Available online at www.theaustralian.com.au/news/nation/muslim-leaders-split-on-polygamy/story-e6frg6nf-1111116783413 (accessed 10 December 2013).

Parkinson, P. (2012) *Australian Family Law in Context*, 5th edn, Pyremont: Lawbook Co.

Rane, H. cited in Merritt, C. (2011) 'Debate on Shari'a a sign of a healthy democracy' *The Australian*, 3 June.

Richards, J. and Esmaeili, H. (2012) 'The Position of Australian women in polygamous relationships under the Family Law Act 1975 (Cth): Still "taking multiculturalism seriously"?', *Australian Journal of Family Law*, 26 (2): 142

Sayit, K. (2011) cited in Merritt, C., 'Shari 'a law at work in Australia', *The Australian* 20th July. Available online at www.theaustralian.com.au/national-affairs/sharia-law-at-work-in-australia/story-fn59niix-1226097889992 (accessed 10 December 2013).

Trad, K. (2008) 'Women deserve better', *The New Matilda*. Available online at http://newmatilda.com/2008/07/07/women-deserve-better (accessed 21 December, 2012).

Voyce, M. and Possamai, A. (2011) 'Legal pluralism, family personal laws and the rejection of shari'a in Australia: a case of multiple or clashing modernities', *Democracy and Security*, 7(4): 339–43.

Williamson, A. (2004) 'An examination of Jewish divorce under the Family Law Act 1975 (Cth)', *James Cook University Law Review*, 7(11): 132–58.

9 Islamic family law in American courts

A rich, diverse and evolving jurisprudence

Abed Awad[1]

> Clearly, the Mahr Agreement in the case at bar is nothing more and nothing less than a simple contract between two consenting adults. It does not contravene any statute or interests of society. Rather, the Mahr Agreement continues a custom and tradition that is unique to a certain segment of our current society and is not at war with any public morals.
>
> (Odatalla v. Odatalla 2002)

Introduction

In the past few years, the American right has found its new 'red menace' – Islam. Described as 'a totalitarian ideology', 'an exitential threat' and 'a mortal threat', shari'a has become the focus of the American right as a 'stealth *jihad*' to take over America (Awad 2012c).[2]

The politicization of shari'a has created much confusion and misunderstanding about Muslims and Islam, fueling the rapid spread of Islamophobia around the country (Awad 2012b, 2012c). Over the past few years, legislators in 32 states have introduced legislation seeking to ban state courts from considering foreign law, international law and religious law. The foreign law ban has passed in five states: Oklahoma, Kansas, Louisiana, Tennessee and Arizona (Wajaht 2011). While most of these laws on their face are religiously neutral, there is no question that the target of the ban is specifically shari'a (Awad 2012c).

The proponents claim that Americans need the foreign law ban to protect women and fundamental rights from the 'creeping shari'a'. The ban however does not do this. In fact, it has the exact opposite effect. For instance, in a recent Kansas case a Muslim woman was prevented from enforcing her greater than $600,000 dower provision in her Muslim marriage contract because of the Kansas foreign law ban (Zakaria 2013). More seriously, the ban on foreign law (including shari'a) in state courts is unconstitutional for many reasons. The foreign law ban violates Article IV of the US Constitution – the supremacy clause – which provides that treaties 'shall be the supreme law of the land'. The ban is unconstitutional because the legislature is encroaching on the judiciary's independence by divesting judges of their authority to determine the law that applies to a matter according to century-old conflict of laws jurisprudence and by limiting a judge's fact-finding authority to better understand the circumstances of the disputes in order to adjudicate them fairly and justly. In so doing, the ban violates the separation of powers. The ban also restricts Americans' freedom to contract by invalidating choice of law clauses in contracts. Most significantly, the ban in many circumstances interferes and restricts Americans 'free exercise' of their religion in direct violation of the First Amendment of the United States Constitution (Zakaria 2013). Once challenged, these bans will be found unconstitutional. It is only a matter of time (Awad 2010a, 2010b).[3] Be that as it may, the ban has not passed in all states, so courts around the country continue to consider shari'a when adjudicating disputes.

What is shari'a?

Shari'a is relevant in the lives of an estimated 3 to 7 million Muslims living in the United States, irrespective of their religiosity (Pew Research Center 2007). In the realm of marriage, Muslims, like the majority of Americans, choose a religious minister to solemnize their marriages. It is not a surprise that Islamic law, customs and/or traditions have routinely surfaced in family-related litigation in American courts. Whether it involves the enforcement of a Muslim marriage contract, the religious-rearing of children, the recognition of foreign Muslim divorces, marriages and custody decrees or the distribution of a decedent's estate, Islamic family law in American courts is a rich, diverse and evolving jurisprudence.

Shari'a is more than 'law' in the prescriptive sense. It also includes the methodology and process of ascertaining divine meaning. It is a legal system based on the general principles contained in the Qur'an and Sunna.[4] Shari'a thus forms the moral and legal anchor of a Muslim's total existence. Everything, from the way Muslims marry and dissolve their marriages, to the way they eat, to how they treat animals and protect the environment, to the way they conduct commercial trade, and to the way their estate must be distributed at death, is governed by shari'a. Whether it is a commercial transaction or a divorce settlement or one's relationship with parents, the elderly and children, it is governed by the same degree of honesty, good faith, an eye to fairness, social responsibility, and equity – an ethical life seeking to please God (Awad and Michael 2010).

Shari'a dictates every aspect of an observant Muslim's moral life, to varying degrees depending on the level of one's religiosity of course. Nonetheless, it is extremely personal to the majority of Muslims (Elliot 2011; Awad 2012c). The nature of one's religious beliefs is personal and private to Americans of all religious faiths. Many Jews submit to the jurisdiction of Rabbinic courts, Christians submit to Christian conciliation tribunals and Muslims submit to Muslim arbitration panels. Religious beliefs are quite pronounced in American political activism. American political activists advocate a religious position on abortion, capital punishment, sex education, same-sex marriage and many other issues. That religion and religious law have been alive and thriving in America since its founding is undisputed. The role of religious law or religious principles in American courts, naturally, has always been subject to public policy and constitutional constraints – that is, the United States Constitution is the law of the land.

The classical interpretive methodology of shari'a (Hallaq 2009)[5] disappeared – to all intents and purposes – with the emergence of the nation-state (technically, shari'a was not a nation-state/emperor law but an independent jurist-made law: Hallaq 2012).[6] Despite this, the modern manifestations of shari'a are either a source of legislation or actual nation-state law in many Muslim-majority countries (more than 40 countries with an estimated 1.2 billion adherents). For example, shari'a is the supreme law of the land in Saudi Arabia, and is a primary source of the family law codes in the majority of Muslim-majority countries.

The next section surveys many cases from around the United States to better understand how American judges consider Islamic family law in adjudicating disputes.

Islamic family law in American courts[7]

As an attorney, consultant and expert witness, I have handled more than 100 matters involving a component of shari'a or the laws of the Middle East. It is clear, from both my first-hand litigation experience and from the published United States cases, that shari'a is relevant in American litigation, either as a foreign law or as extrinsic evidence. Extrinsic evidence means as a source of information to aid in the interpretation of a contract or dispute (for example, to understand the expectations of the parties in a dispute, to clarify an ambiguous term, to correct mistakes, to determine established custom and the like). The cases considered below are organized according to these two categories.

Shari'a as extrinsic evidence

Mahr *is a prenuptial agreement*

In the following cases, the courts construed the Muslim marriage contract as a prenuptial agreement. The unique facts of each case combined with the state of prenuptial jurisprudence in the jurisdiction determined whether the *mahr* was enforceable or not.

In *Afghani v. Ghafoorian* (2010)[8] and *Akileh v. Elchahal* (1996),[9] the relevant parties' marriage contract provided for a substantial *mahr*. In both cases the courts construed the marriage contract as a valid premarital agreement that did not violate public policy and, therefore, awarded the wives their deferred *mahrs*. In *Akileh*, the Appellate Court held that marriage was sufficient consideration and that the parties agreed to the essential terms of the contract in contemplation of their forthcoming marriage. The parties' conflicting interpretation about the *sadaq* (dower) had no impact on the enforceability and validity of the document as 'a subsequent difference as to the construction of the contract does not affect the validity of the contract or indicate the minds of the parties did not meet with respect thereto'. Unlike in *Afghani* and *Akileh*, where American substantive law governed the validity of the contract, in *Chaudry v. Chaudry* (1978),[10] the enforcement of the Muslim marriage contract turned on the application of substantive Pakistani law. The parties married in Pakistan in 1961. In 1963, they moved to the United States, where they lived until they returned to Pakistan in 1968. Shortly thereafter, the husband returned to the United States without the rest of the family. Through 1973 the husband visited them in Pakistan a few times. But at the end of that year when he returned to the United States, he filed for divorce in the Pakistani consulate in New York City. Divorce litigation commenced in Pakistan and the wife actively participated. The Pakistani trial court confirmed the Pakistani consulate divorce in New York City. She appealed but the Pakistani Appellate Court affirmed the validity of the Pakistani consulate divorce. The wife later filed for divorce and alimony in New Jersey. The court granted comity to the Pakistani divorce as a final, valid decree that adjudicated the financial claims of the parties and was not contrary to public policy, noting that the parties' marriage contract was akin to a prenuptial agreement under Pakistani law.

As in *Afghani* and *Akileh*, the courts in *Ahmed v. Ahmed* (2008)[11] and *In re Altayar and Muhyaddin*,[12] determined that the Muslim marriage contract was a prenuptial agreement. Unlike *Afghani* and *Akileh*, the *Ahmed* and *Altayar* courts found the prenuptial agreement invalid under state law. In *Ahmed*, the trial court awarded the wife $50,000 dollars as liquidated contract damages, as it construed the mahr to be a valid, binding and enforceable premarital agreement under Texas law. The Appellate Court reversed the decision, holding that the parties' valid civil wedding ceremony occurred six months before signing the *mahr* agreement, i.e. they were not 'prospective spouses'[13] entering into their agreement 'in contemplation of marriage'. Finding that the trial court erred in enforcing the *mahr* agreement as a 'premarital agreement', the Appellate Court remanded the matter to allow the wife to present evidence that the *mahr* agreement was enforceable as a simple contract as opposed to the premarital agreement theory. Similarly, in *Altayar*, the court described the *mahr* as a prenuptial agreement but established that it was invalid under state law. The Appellate Court affirmed the lower court's decision holding that a '[p]renuptial agreement is valid only when it is plainly shown that the transaction was fair'. In this case, the court found that 'the exchange of 19 pieces of gold for equitable property rights under Washington law is not fair … . Even if it were a fair agreement, there is no evidence that he disclosed his assets or that [wife] received any independent advice during the three days between their initial meeting and marriage.' Similarly, in *Zawahiri v. Alwattar* (2008)[14] and *Ahmad v. Ahmad* (2001)[15] the court agreed that the Muslim marriage contract was a prenuptial agreement but held that the agreement was invalid as it did not comply with the requirements of premarital agreements: advice of counsel and full and complete financial disclosures.

In *Zawahiri*, the Appellate Court found that the husband had entered into the marriage contract as a result of overreaching and coercion by his wife because the *imam* raised the *mahr* provision only two hours prior to the ceremony after guests were already present, placing the husband under the pressure of embarrassment. Furthermore, the husband had not consulted with an attorney prior to signing the marriage contract.[16]

As in *Zawahiri*, the court in *In re Marriage of Dajani* (1988)[17] refused to recognize the Muslim marriage contract on the public policy ground that the *mahr* allowed the wife to profit from filing for divorce to obtain her 5,000 Jordanian dinars dower. Like the courts in *Zawahiri* and *Dajani*, the court in *Ahmad* confirmed that a valid premarital agreement requires advice of counsel and financial disclosures. But in *Ahmad*, the court also pierced through the husband's attempt to circumvent state law by obtaining a foreign divorce by taking jurisdiction based on Ohio's residency requirements. The parties had resided in Ohio for eight years. During a visit to Jordan, the husband filed for divorce in Jordan. Upon her return to Ohio, the wife filed for divorce seeking alimony and equitable distribution. The trial court held that it had jurisdiction over the matter, based on the fact that the parties had been residents of Ohio six months prior to the filing of the divorce complaint. The Court further held that 'the Jordanian court did not have personal jurisdiction over [wife] and that the *sadaq* or antenuptial agreement was unenforceable under Ohio law because at the time the agreement was entered into, [the wife] was not represented by counsel, there was no disclosure of [the husband's] assets, and the agreement did not take into consideration the assets subsequently acquired in Ohio during the eight-year marriage'. Interestingly, the court utilized a creative approach by recognizing the foreign divorce only to the extent that it severed the marital relationship, but took jurisdiction to adjudicate the financial aspects under state law.

The court in *Shaban v. Shaban* (2001)[18] did not even reach to the fairness of the Muslim marriage contract, as it held the contract too vague and indefinite to be enforcable. Unlike in most of the marriage contract cases where the wife sought the payment of her *mahr*, in *Shaban* it was the husband who asked the court to recognize his Egyptian marriage contract with a nominal *mahr* as a prenuptial agreement barring the wife from sharing in the marital estate and receiving alimony. The court simply held the contract was too vague and indefinite to be enforced. It then rejected the husband's argument and divided the marital estate according to California law. On appeal, the Appellate Court affirmed the decision, holding that the document signed by the parties providing that their marriage shall be governed by the laws of

Islam and the traditions of the Prophet alone was 'hopelessly uncertain as to its terms and conditions' to satisfy the statute of frauds on its own.

Mahr *is a simple contract*

In the following cases, the courts construed the Muslim marriage contract as a simple contract. As long as the contract had all of the elements necessary for a valid contract and there was no valid defence, the court enforced the *mahr.* The simple contract approach is less burdensome for enforcement compared to the prenuptial agreement approach. In addition to satisfying the basic contract elements, the prenuptial agreement requires additional safeguards such as advice of counsel and financial disclosures, which are seldom included in the religious wedding ceremony.

In *Abdallah v. Sarsour* (2006),[19] *Aziz v. Aziz* (1985)[20] and *Odatalla v. Odatalla* (2002),[21] the courts found that the *mahr* agreement satisfied the elements of a valid simple contract and thus enforced the *mahr.* In *Abdallah*, the court held that the contract was not void for vagueness, explaining that 'where an agreement is to pay money and no time is specified, it is interpreted as being an agreement to pay the same on demand; and if it is an agreement to do something other than to pay money, it is interpreted as a promise to do it in a reasonable time'. Similarly, in *Aziz*, the court awarded the wife her $5,000 *mahr*, holding that the Islamic marriage contract conformed to the requirements of New York contract law and was 'enforceable as a contractual obligation, notwithstanding that it was entered into as part of a religious ceremony'.

Similarly, in *Odatalla*, the trial court enforced the dower provision, holding that applying neutral principles of law (i.e. the principles of contract law in New Jersey) to the mahr agreement satisfied all the elements of a valid civil contract. The evidence showed the husband freely making an offer to the wife by signing the *mahr* agreement, the wife accepting the offer by signing the agreement and the husband intentionally binding himself to the agreement by making the payment required by the mahr. The court utilized parole evidence to interpret the meaning of the written words of the contract, concluding that the $10,000 deferred portion of the mahr was due on demand or upon the death of the husband or dissolution of the marriage. It is noteworthy that the court, while not stating so in the published decision, equitably distributed the marital property, assets and debts and made a finding as to alimony.

Finally, in *Obaidi v. Qayoum* (2010)[22] and *Rahman v. Hossain* and *Habibi-Fahnrich v. Fahnrich*, while the marriage contract was construed as a simple contract, the courts found that the parties did not have a meeting of the minds and that the contract was entered into under duress and overreaching. In *Habibi-Fahnrich v. Fahnrich* (1995),[23] the court acknowledged that '[t]his Court has already determined in this case that as a matter of law, on the basis of *Aziz v. Aziz* … a religious agreement may be enforceable if it conforms to the requirements of [New York contract law].' But the court concluded that the '*sadaq* being a ring and half of husband's possessions' was undefined, indefinite and not specific and thus could not meet the requirement of a valid contract under New York law.

In *Obaidi*, the Islamic marriage contract included a *mahr* provision written in Farsi. The Appellate Court held that neutral principles of contract law governed the interpretation of the contract and concluded that there was no meeting of the minds because the husband was advised of the *mahr* ceremony 15 minutes before he signed the document; in addition, he did not read, write or speak Farsi and was pressured to sign the agreement by the families.

In *Rahman v. Hossain*,[24] the court found that fault for the divorce impacted the entitlement of the wife to her deferred dower and even required her to return the immediate payment. The trial court granted the husband a divorce on the basis of extreme mental cruelty – the wife's failure to engage in sexual relations, her lack of personal hygiene and her abandonment of the marital residence. Finding that fault impacted the entitlement to the postponed dower, the trial court also ordered the wife to return the $12,500 *mahr* because she did not disclose important information at the time of the marriage ceremony, such as her pre-existing mental illness, which had contributed to the demise of the marriage.

Analysis

The cases mentioned above pertain to the question of whether the *mahr* agreement is a prenuptial agreement or a simple contract. In both theories, the agreement must comply with state contract law. If construed as a prenuptial agreement, in addition to basic contract elements and traditional contract defences, the court enquires whether the parties had the advice of counsel and made financial disclosures before signing the agreement (Awad 2002).

The simple contract approach articulated in *Odatalla* is in my opinion the best approach to adjudicate Muslim marriage contract cases. A *mahr* provision in the marriage contract is not a prenuptial agreement. A latter is an agreement between prospective spouses made in contemplation of marriage. The agreement then becomes effective upon marriage. In essence, a prenuptial agreement is an agreement between the bride and groom to resolve all the financial issues arising out of the prospective marital relationship in the event of divorce or death of either party. The financial terms of a prenuptial agreement are set up to function in lieu of any inheritance or other community property, equitable distribution or alimony laws otherwise applicable to the couple. Unlike a prenuptial agreement, *mahr* is an obligation upon the husband that serves as a supplement to, not a substitute for, other legal obligations between the spouses. In addition, a Muslim wife under Islamic law has a right not only to the *mahr*, but also to alimony (although for a short duration) and if the husband predeceases her, she has a right to inheritance.

The primary purpose of a prenuptial agreement is to determine property and support rights upon the death of the spouse or the dissolution of the marriage. In other words, prenuptial agreements attempt to alter the state-imposed statutory default formula for spousal rights. The fact that the validity of prenuptial agreements in American jurisprudence prior to the 1970 was suspect – and in many jurisdictions outright void – further supports my conclusion that a Muslim marriage contract is not a prenuptial agreement. Prenuptial agreements were created in the twentieth century to address objective social and economic circumstances of modern American society: marriage at older ages, prevalence of divorces, remarriage, children from different spouses and protection of premarital wealth (Cahn II 1992; Younger 1992; Marston 1997). The simple contract approach protects Muslim women and is fair to Muslim men. The family court is a court of equity. Whether sitting in a community property state or equitable distribution state, judges are required to consider the financial positions of both spouses (Awad and Mawla 2013). For example, if the entire marital estate is $100,000 and the wife's *mahr* is $50,000, the judge must take into account the wife's receipt of the $50,000 *mahr* when he determines how to equitably divide the remaining marital estate. The simple contract approach provides the court with the necessary flexibility to fashion a fair and equitable distribution of the marital estate. Finally, given that the majority of American jurisdictions have adopted the Uniform Premarital Agreement Act (2001)[25] or the principles therein, the validity of a Muslim marriage contract under the Act is suspect. The Act requires, at the very minimum, advice of counsel and full and complete financial disclosures – both requirements that are rarely followed by Muslim couples, especially in first marriages.

Shari'a as foreign law

In the following cases the courts refused to recognize foreign divorces obtained unilaterally/*ex parte* by husbands. In *Rahawangi v. Al-Samman* (2006),[26] the parties, both Syrian citizens, were married in Syria in 1991. They had two children born of the marriage and lived in Ohio. In 1997, the husband accepted employment as a physician in Saudi Arabia and the family moved there. In 1999, after marital disputes, he told his wife to return to Syria with the children. She did not do so, but instead moved to Kuwait with her sister. During this time period, the husband obtained a divorce decree from Syria. It was obtained via proxy, with the husband appointing a family member to represent him.[27] The wife returned to the United States in 1999 and filed for divorce in Ohio. After the Syrian decree became final, the husband remarried. In April 2000, the wife filed a complaint for divorce in Ohio again and the husband moved to dismiss the complaint. The trial court held that the Syrian divorce decree was not entitled to comity because it was issued *ex parte* and without notice to the wife.

Similarly, in *Tarikonda v. Pinjari* (2009),[28] the parties were married in India under Islamic law. Subsequently, they moved to Michigan. Several years later, the husband traveled to India and obtained a divorce or *talaq*[29] certificate

(Awad and Mawla 2013). The wife in response filed for divorce in Michigan. The trial court found that the *talaq* certificate was valid under Indian law and recognized it. On appeal, the Appellate Court reversed that decision, holding that the wife was not afforded the basic rudiments of due process, she was not present in court and no hearing on the merits was held. Furthermore, it would be against public policy to recognize the Indian divorce because Islamic law differs substantially from Michigan law in regards to property distribution.

In *Hashime-Bazlamit v. Bazlamit* (2009),[30] the court recognized a unilateral foreign religious divorce. The recognition was on a technical procedural ground rather than on the legal merits of the case. The parties got married in 1993 in Jordan. Around 2007, the husband traveled to Jordan and filed for divorce. Shortly thereafter, the wife was issued a revocable divorce by proxy by a shari‘a court. Several months later, she filed for divorce, custody and equitable distribution in Ohio. The trial court recognized the Jordanian divorce and dismissed the wife's complaint for divorce in Ohio, holding that all related issues, such as custody, child support, visitation, alimony and dower had been resolved by the Jordanian divorce proceeding. As the wife did not file an objection to the magistrate's decision, she was barred from objecting to the decision on technical grounds, not on its merits.

In the following cases the courts recognized foreign divorces. In *S.B. v W. A.* (2012),[31] the parties were married in 1998 in New York. Their marriage contract provided a *mahr* in the amount of $255,000 – $5,000 of which immediate and $250,000 deferred. Two children were born of the marriage. In 2006, the parties' moved to Abu Dhabi for work. During their stay in Abu Dhabi, the husband physically assaulted the wife. She filed for divorce in an Abu Dhabi court based on cruelty and requested custody, her *mahr* and other financial relief. The Abu Dhabi court entered a divorce decree and awarded the wife custody of the children and her $250,000 postponed dower, among other financial relief. The parties proactively litigated in Abu Dhabi in connection with the divorce, custody and the proceedings against the husband. In 2011, the wife commenced enforcement proceedings in New York, seeking the recognition of the Abu Dhabi court decisions. The trial court recognized the Abu Dhabi decisions, finding that the divorce decree was obtained after trial and two appeals. There was no question that the Abu Dhabi court had jurisdiction over the parties and the divorce because the parties resided in Abu Dhabi at the time. The New York court found nothing in the divorce decree that would violate New York's public policy.[32] Therefore the divorce decree was deemed valid. The court next addressed the money judgment in the sum of $250,000 for the wife's dower. Finding that the Abu Dhabi court had jurisdiction and complied with US notions of due process and provided an impartial proceeding combined with the proactive litigation between the parties, the court applied neutral principles of law to the contract, concluding that it did not violate New York public policy. Therefore, the New York granted comity to the Abu Dhabi money judgments.

Also in *Aqel v. Aqel* (2005),[33] the court recognized a foreign divorce decree obtained in Jordan. The husband married his second wife in 1996 in Kentucky but the marriage was annulled in 1997 because the husband had not divorced his first wife in Jordan. He filed for divorce in Jordan and was granted a three-month revocable divorce decree. During this period, the husband remarried his second wife. A few years later, the second wife filed for annulment of her marriage. She argued that because the husband had remarried her during the *'idda*[34] his divorce was not valid or final in Jordan (Awad 2013). Affirming that the second marriage was valid, the Appellate Court cited a Board Immigration Appeal decision (1965)[35] that held that divorce was effective on the date that the revocable divorce decree was granted as long as the parties did not reconcile during this three-month period.

In the following cases the validity of the foreign divorce turned on whether the parties were residents in the foreign country. In *Husein v. Husein* (2001),[36] the husband married his first wife in Palestine sometime in 1970. Later that year, the couple moved to Ohio where they had three children. He had an extramarital affair producing two children from that relationship. In 1992, the husband traveled to Palestine for three weeks to divorce his first wife and obtained a shari'a court divorce without the presence of, or notice to, his first wife. After obtaining a divorce, he returned to Ohio, married his second wife, a third woman, and stated on his marriage licence that he was divorced. Up until this point, his first wife was not aware that she was divorced in Palestine. The husband was later murdered in front of his convenience store. His surviving children sought the distribution of their father's estate. The trial court granted comity to the Palestinian divorce and concluded that the second wife was the surviving spouse. The Appellate Court reversed the decision, holding that the Palestinian divorce decree was not entitled to comity because the husband did not reside in Palestine and did not provide notice to the first wife.

In a case similar to *Husein*, a Maryland court, in *Aleem v. Aleem* (2006),[37] refused to recognize a Pakistani consulate divorce when the parties had residence continuously in Maryland for over 20 years. In response to the wife's filing for divorce in Maryland, the husband filed for divorce with the Pakistani Embassy in Washington DC and performed a *talaq* in accordance with Pakistani law. The divorce was valid under Pakistani law, and his expert witness testified that under Pakistani law the wife had no rights to property in her husband's name. The trial court rejected the Pakistani divorce and adjudicated the matter according to Maryland law, thus granting the wife 50 per cent of the marital estate. On appeal, the Appellate Court affirmed the decision, concluding that the Pakistani divorce was contrary to Maryland public policy, both on due process and financial rights grounds, and thus not entitled to comity.

Similarly, in *Mir v. Birjandi* (2007),[38] the court found that the wife's Iranian divorce decree, secured while a resident of Ohio and at the same time the Ohio divorce action was pending, was invalid. The court adjudicated the matter in accordance with Ohio law, awarding the husband equitable distribution and alimony.

Unlike in *Husein*, in *Sherif v. Sherif* (1974),[39] the parties were in Egypt at the time of the divorce. While in Egypt, the husband obtained a divorce consistent with Egyptian law. The wife then filed for spousal support in New York, though conceding that her Egyptian divorce was valid under Egyptian law. The trial court recognized the Egyptian divorce as a matter of comity and dismissed the wife's spousal support action.

Analysis

Religious divorces (*talaq*) taking place in the United States are not valid. A divorce must be a judicial divorce. However, an American court is likely to recognize a religious divorce obtained from a foreign consulate if the divorce complied with basic due process, if it was mutual and both parties appeared. Of course, if the divorce did not resolve the financial and non-financial aspects arising out of the marriage – alimony, equitable distribution, child support and custody – either spouse is able to commence an action to determine these open issues, as the few cases above have confirmed.

In religious divorces taking place abroad, the standard comity factors must be considered: due process, notice, fairness, opportunity to participate and the like. Furthermore, the residency and marital domicile of the parties is a major factor courts consider before granting comity to a foreign divorce decree. It is clear from a survey of our jurisprudence that travelling abroad to obtain a divorce while your spouse remains in the United States is suspect and the divorce not likely to be recognized by US courts. But the judicial interpretive flaw is in understanding the effect of the husband's unilateral exclusive right to *talaq* under Islamic law. *Talaq* is only one method of dissolving a marital relationship under Islamic law. Many Muslim women include their right to unilaterally divorce in their marriage contracts. Several other methods to terminate or dissolve a marriage are *tafriq* (judicial divorce based on various grounds by either spouse), *khul'* (divorce upon mutual consent) and *faskh* (annulment by either spouse) (Awad and Mawla 2013). Be that as it may, *talaq* does not foreclose the wife's financial rights under Islamic law. Furthermore, because of the husband's exclusive right to dissolve the marriage in the *talaq* setting, his financial obligations are actually triggered. This means that an American court can accept the *talaq* but proceed with the financial aspects under state law.

The norm in today's global village is that couples have multiple residences. *Talaq* becomes much more complex when the domicile and/or residence of the parties is in both the United States and a Muslim country. How should a court deal with cross-border divorces, assets in multiple jurisdictions and income from more than one jurisdiction? Which country has jurisdiction? Does the first filer have an advantage? If the matter is pending in one country, should the other country stay its proceedings pending an outcome? Our common law has yet to clearly answer these questions. In my opinion, prohibiting courts from considering the foreign law elements of these matters stunts the development of our jurisprudence.

Religious marriages and marriage licences

The following cases examine the different approaches taken by US courts to determine the validity of religious marriages that do not comply with all of the state law formalities. In *Yaghoubinejad v. Haghighi* (2006),[40] the parties were married in an Islamic ceremony in New Jersey without obtaining a marriage licence. Several years later, the wife filed for divorce. The trial court held that the Islamic marriage was valid and granted the wife a divorce. The Appellate Court reversed that decision, holding that the parties were never legally married because under New Jersey law it is an absolute requirement that the parties obtain a marriage licence in order to validate their marriage. Similarly, in *Ellehaf v. Tarraf* (2006),[41] the parties were married in an Islamic ceremony in Michigan without obtaining a marriage licence. The husband filed a complaint seeking custody of their children and a declaratory judgment that the parties were never legally married. The trial court ruled in his favor. On appeal, the Appellate Court affirmed the trial court decision, holding that the parties were never legally married because they did not obtain a marriage licence.

In *Farah v. Farah* (1993),[42] the parties married via proxy in England under Islamic law – neither the husband nor wife was present in England at the time the marriage was solemnized. The parties had a wedding in Pakistan and then moved to the United States. The husband filed to have the marriage voided and the wife filed for divorce and equitable distribution. The trial court held in favor of the wife, granting the parties a divorce and equitable distribution. On appeal, the Appellate Court reversed the decision, holding the marriage to be void ab initio under British law, the law of the place where the marriage occurred, because the parties did not meet the formalities required under British marriage law.

In *Mussa v. Palmer-Mussa* (2011)[43] and *Matter of Farraj* (2009)[44] affirmed 72 A.D.3d 1082 (2010), the absence of a marriage licence did not render the marriage void. In *Mussa*, the defendant/wife married the first husband in an Islamic ceremony held in Maryland. However, neither party obtained a marriage licence as required under Maryland law and they never consummated the marriage. Shortly thereafter, the wife obtained a religious divorce from the first husband. That same year, the wife met the plaintiff/second husband. After they obtained a marriage licence, they got married in 1997. The couple had three children and remained married for 12 years. In 2008, the wife filed for divorce. The trial court found that her first marriage was invalid; therefore, her marriage to the second husband was valid. The second husband appealed. On appeal, the Court of Appeals reversed the trial court's decision, holding that the wife's marriage to the first husband was voidable because the parties had not obtained a marriage licence. Unlike a void marriage, a voidable marriage has all of the legal rights of a valid marriage until it is legally dissolved by a court of law. Here, the alleged dissolution of the first marriage was a religious dissolution; it was not a legal one. Therefore, the wife's marriage to the second husband was void because the first voidable marriage continued to have legal effect.[45] Similarly, in *Farraj*, the wife resided in New Jersey and the husband resided in New York. He traveled with an *imam* to the wife's home to perform the religious marriage. They did not obtain, however, a marriage licence. After the religious solemnization, they had a wedding and lived as husband and wife in New York for several years. The husband died intestate and his children petitioned the court as the only surviving heirs because they claimed that the wife's marriage with their father was not valid. The trial court had to determine whether New Jersey law – the place of the marriage – or New York law – the marital domicile – governed the validity of the marriage. The trial court held that under New York law the presumption of validity of marriages is strong and thus allowed the court to choose between the law of the place of marriage or the law of the marital domicile to determine validity. While the marriage would be void under New Jersey law without a marriage licence, the wife's marriage was valid under New York law without a marriage licence. The Appellate Court affirmed holding that the marriage was valid under New York law.

Domestic religious divorces

In *Mussa* and *Shikoh v. Murff* (1958),[46] the court made clear that religious divorces in the United States are not a substitute for civil divorce judgments. A religious divorce in the United States without a civil divorce is invalid and does not dissolve the marital relationship. For example, in *Shikoh*, the parties married in Pakistan. The husband moved to the United States while his wife remained in Pakistan. After 11 years in the US, he went to his local *imam* in New York and obtained a religious divorce. Subsequently, the husband married a US citizen and applied to adjust his status to a permanent resident. The United States Immigration and Naturalization Service denied his request, concluding that his divorce was invalid, thus rendering his second marriage void. The court explained that non-judicial divorces are recognized, but only as long as they are valid where performed. While in this case the divorce may have been valid in Pakistan, it was not valid where it was performed, in New York.

Analysis

Muslim marriages are valid and recognized in the United States like any other religious marriage. The issues raised in the above cases are not the validity of religious marriages that take place in the United States, but rather the validity of a religious marriage that takes place in the United States and fails to comply with the state regulatory requirements, such as obtaining a marriage licence before the marriage is solemnized by an authorized religious figure. The validity of the religious marriages turns on whether the absence of the marriage licence renders the marriage void or voidable. While New Jersey and Michigan held that absence of the marriage licence rendered the marriage void, Tennessee and New York held that as long as the religious marriage was consistent with the parties' religion and was solemnized by a religious figure, then the marriage would be valid despite the lack of a marriage licence.

The New York voidable approach to resolving marriage validity issues is far more equitable in my opinion than New Jersey's void approach. Most significantly, the New York approach is more protective of vulnerable Muslim female immigrants. When the parties sign a marriage contract in the presence of two witnesses, live together as husband and wife, have children and financially support each other, the absence of a marriage licence should not invalidate their marriage. New Jersey and many other states recognize a cause of action called palimony for financial damages for breaching a written agreement to support your partner for life. Some states even recognize an oral agreement containing such a promise. Many states also recognize cohabitation between two people in a marriage-like arrangement as sufficient as an actual marriage when dealing with the question of terminating an alimony entitlement.

Most couples who fail to obtain a marriage licence ahead of the solemnization do not intend to circumvent or avoid the law. Whether it is ignorance or simple misinformation, the strong public policy in favor of validity of marriage as an institution with extensive financial and non-financial consequences, militates against the void approach.

Farraj raises a fascinating conflict of laws issue that cannot be overlooked. The majority and century-old principle that the law of the place of the marriage governs validity may be outdated in our mobile and transit society. Marital domicile might be closer to the physical and financial reality of the marriage under question, as opposed to a transit location selected for purposes of celebrating a marriage.

Finally, the cases above make it clear that while a religious marriage in the voidable jurisdictions is valid, religious divorces are not. In order to terminate a marriage, the parties must obtain a state-sanctioned dissolution. A state secular divorce however does not dissolve a marriage religiously. In Muslim-majority countries, secular divorces are not necessarily recognized, thus the marriage subsists. A devout Muslim woman is unable to remarry unless and until she has a valid religious divorce. If she does, her marriage will be religiously void and she will be committing adultery. If she predeceases her former husband, her husband will be considered the legally surviving husband entitled to inherit in her native Muslim country. The situation is even more complicated for Muslim women who visit their native country often. For example, several Muslim countries, such as Lebanon, Syria and Jordan, subject wives to travel restrictions.

Many husbands, out of vindictiveness, utilize the religious divorce as a sword to extract financial leverage in the divorce settlement or simply to make the wife's remarriage unlikely. For example, in *Hammoud v. Hammoud* (2012),[47] the husband refused to grant his wife a religious divorce despite the court's encouragement. The trial court acknowledged that it did not have 'authority to compel to religious divorce' but found that the wife's inability to remarry without a religious divorce was a relevant factor to be considered in favor of her spousal support claim. The appellate court reversed the spousal support award for various reasons, including that the open-ended duration of the spousal support award 'was structured to pressure [the husband] to agree to an Islamic divorce'.

Having handled many cases in which the husband utilized the religious divorce as a sword to extract financial leverage in the divorce settlement, it is clear to me that the issue of religious divorce for a women is not so simple. Many Michigan attorneys confirm that trial judges informally use the spousal support award to pressure husband to grant their wives religious divorces (Khatib forthcoming).[48] Unfortunately, only New York has a law that assists litigants to secure religious divorces. New York law requires a party seeking a divorce to include in his or her complaint a clause that states that he or she shall remove any barriers to the other spouse's remarriage. This in effect translates into requiring the filing party to grant the other spouse a religious divorce.[49] When a spouse fails to cooperate or facilitate in the wife obtaining a religious divorce, the defaulting party may be ordered by the court to obtain the religious divorce. While this law appears to require a secular court to engage in compelling religious divorces, the law has been challenged but found to be constitutional. In most states, it is extremely difficult for a woman to obtain a religious divorce without her husband's consent. Ohio, for example, will not even enforce a settlement agreement providing for the granting of a religious divorce on unconstitutional entanglement grounds.[50] The New Jersey Appellate Court recently held that a court is only authorized to direct the parties to obtain a religious divorce if their settlement agreement provided for it. Otherwise, the court has no authority to direct either party to cooperate to obtain a religious divorce (*Lowy v. Lowy*, A-472–10 App.Div. 2011; Awad and Popescu 2009; Awad 2012a).[51]

Religious-rearing and custody

In the following cases the courts refused to engage in a doctrinal evaluation of the parties' religious child-rearing disagreements. In *Jabri v. Jabri* (1993),[52] the father was a Muslim and the mother a Christian. They had four children. The trial court allowed the father to visit with the children and raise them in his Islamic faith, to the extent that the children were willing to visit with him and learn about Islam. The Appellate Court affirmed that decision, stating that unless the parties had a written agreement regarding religious-rearing, the custodial mother could determine the religious upbringing of the children.

Similarly, in *Najmi v. Najmi* (2008),[53] the father was Muslim while the mother was Christian. After the divorce, the trial court granted the wife custody of their child and permitted her to relocate to another state over the husband's objection that the move would prevent him from introducing his child to Islam. The Appellate Court affirmed that decision and summarized the law relating to religious-rearing disputes, stating that:

> A domestic relations court may consider the religious practices of the parents in order to protect the best interest of a child. However, the United States Constitution flatly prohibits a trial court from ever evaluating the merits of religious doctrine or defining the contents of that doctrine. Furthermore, custody may not be denied to a parent solely because she will not encourage her child to salute the flag, celebrate holidays, or participate in extracurricular activities.

The *Najmi* approach – i.e. the court has no authority to decide religious-rearing disputes on doctrinal grounds – is almost uniform around the country. The court only weighs in when the religious-rearing dispute impacts on the best interests of the children. Moreover, the court will always defer to the parent of primary residence or the physical custodian in connection with religious instructions, with the proviso that the children should also be exposed to the other parent's religion. However, if there is an agreement about religious-rearing, unless it violates public policy or is detrimental to the best interests of the children, the agreement would likely stand. Also, the history or status quo of the religious-rearing during the time the parties were an intact family would be relevant to the court.

Foreign custody decree

In the majority of reported and unreported cases, if the foreign custody decree is not based on the best interests of the child, our courts are reluctant to grant them comity. For example, in *Charara v. Yatim* (2010),[54] the court refused to recognize a Lebanese child custody determination because it was decided under law that was not in substantial conformity with Massachusetts's best interests standard but was rather based on a presumption in favor of the father. In *Hosain v. Malik*[55] and *S.B. v W.A.* (2012),[56] the court found that the foreign custody decrees were based on the child's best interests; therefore, they were granted comity. In *Hosain*, the parties married in Pakistan and had a daughter. In 1990, they separated and the wife moved to the United States, taking their daughter with her. The husband filed a lawsuit against the wife for custody of their daughter. She was represented by counsel in the Pakistani custody hearing, although she refused to appear in person. The Pakistani judge awarded custody to the husband. Meanwhile, the wife filed in Maryland for custody of their daughter and for a restraining order against the husband. The trial court held that the circuit court did not have jurisdiction and granted comity to the Pakistani custody decision. The Appellate Court affirmed that decision, finding that the Pakistani Court did apply the best interests of the child standard and that Pakistani law applied to the case was not contrary to Maryland public policy.

Analysis

Islamic law on custody[57] has very limited application in domestic cases. The determination of custody under state law is governed by the best interests standard. While culture and religion may be a factor, the best interests of the child is the overriding determinant. The religious-rearing jurisprudence around the United States is not uniform, but the decisions in *Najmi* and *Jabri* are a fair, general articulation of the law – that is, the court does not engage in doctrinal preferences or evaluations. The parent of primary residence receives deference in connection with religious instruction, but the other parent's involvement is not per se precluded. Rather, the decisions are fact specific. However, Islamic custody law comes into focus and dispute when foreign custody decrees are involved. The Uniform Child Custody Jurisdiction Enforcement Act provides the general standard for recognition of foreign divorce decrees. The recognition of a foreign custody decree will turn on whether the child's 'habitual residence' or 'home state' was in the foreign country, whether the parties were afforded notice and due process, whether the court applied the best interests standard and whether the foreign child custody law violates fundamental principles of human rights. Short of these factors being fulfiled, American courts are disinclined to recognize foreign Muslim custody decrees. While the traditional age- and gender-specific criteria survive in some Muslim countries, the trend in the Muslim world is in the direction of a form of best interests standard or combination of best interest and indigenous cultural traditions. In *Hosain* and *S.W.*, the court found that the foreign custody decree was based on the best interests of the child. In *S.W.*, the New York court found that Abu Dhabi applied the best interests of the child when awarding the mother custody. In *Hosain*, the Maryland court found that the Pakistani custody decree was based on best interests.

The other issue involving Islamic custody pertains to the Hague Convention on the Civil Aspects of International Child Abduction.[58] With the exception of Morocco and Turkey, no other Muslim countries have acceded to the Hague Convention. If a child is not returned after a visit in a Muslim country, without the Hague Convention the left-behind parent does not have a civil remedy to secure the return of his or her child back to the United States. However, setting a bright line rule that a child travelling to visit a Muslim country with a parent will not be returned is not logical. Bright line rules lead to injustice as they are not based on the unique facts of every case. Providing guidelines and permitting judges to weigh all of the admissible evidence is the fair approach to resolve these very private and emotional issues.

Many cases demonstrate that American judges thoughtfully craft guidelines in order to avoid bias and scapegoating an entire religious tradition when addressing issues of child abductions.

Abouzahr v. Abouzahr (2003),[59] for example, articulates an approach that is anchored in the facts of the case rather than in bright line rules. In this case, the husband was a Lebanese Muslim and the wife was an American Catholic. They had one child. The husband was a physician and moved back to live in Lebanon. The parties divorced and entered into a property settlement agreement, which permitted the husband to bring his daughter to Lebanon to visit for one month during the summer because he would be moving back to Lebanon permanently. After the divorce, the wife claimed that she discovered that Lebanon is not a signatory to the Hague Convention for the Civil Aspects of International Child Abduction and that Lebanese Islamic family law would favor the husband because she was not Muslim. She claimed that due to child's age, Lebanese law would grant custody to the husband and therefore the child should not be permitted to travel to Lebanon. The trial court held in favor of the husband, stating that it was in the child's best interest to see her father and her extended family in Lebanon. The Appellate Court affirmed the trial court's decision, noting that courts should consider several factors when deciding whether to permit or restrain out-of-country visitation. Most important, the fact that the country where the child will visit is a non-signatory to the Hague Convention was found not to be a per se prohibition to visitation abroad. Furthermore, the court held that:

> [i]n addition to the laws, practices and policies of the foreign nation, a court may consider, among other things, the domicile and roots of the parent seeking such visitation, the reason for the visit, the safety and security of the child, the age and attitude of the child to the visit, the relationship between the parents, the propriety and practicality of a bond or other security and the character and integrity of the parent seeking out-of-country visitation as gleaned from past comments and conduct.

Islamic law of inheritance

In *Alkhafaji v. Tiaa-Cref* (2010),[60] the issue in dispute was the proper beneficiary of a decedent's retirement certificate. The decedent agreed in his divorce settlement with his second wife to list his son with her and two children from a previous marriage as beneficiaries. The decedent married for a third time and listed his third wife and all his biological children as beneficiaries and directed that his estate be distributed according to Islamic law. After the decedent's death, his third wife sent a copy of his will to the pension administrator. The court found that the will was a sufficient written notice to effectuate the change in his life insurance and his pension was distributed in accordance with Islamic law (Khan 2007 and Hallaq 2009).[61] The trial court decision was reversed and the matter was remanded for further proceedings.

To the best of my knowledge, this is the only decision involving Islamic law of inheritance. I have consulted or worked on cases involving Islamic inheritance, but none resulted in published decisions because they all settled. This area is likely to surface in litigation with the growing demand among Muslim Americans for estate-planning instruments compliant with shari'a.

Conclusion

The globalization of domiciles, marriages, divorces, corporations and commercial transactions requires American courts to regularly interpret and apply foreign law – including Islamic law – to everything from the recognition of foreign divorces and custody decrees, the validity of marriages, the enforcement of money judgments or the elements of damages in a commercial dispute to negligence matters. The diversity of America as an immigrant experiment requires courts to take into account specific cultural and religious traditions, not as a replacement for American law, but as an aid to better understand the context of a dispute and contract for effective adjudication. The intersection of religious law and secular law has profound consequences for so many Americans. Secular courts need to better understand the religious and cultural context of the litigants' demands and disputes in order to better fashion creative remedies to protect litigants. The flexibility and creativity of the American judiciary, as demonstrated in the above cases, continues to enrich this evolving jurisprudence.

'The Life of the law has not been logic', Oliver Wendell Holmes, Jr. insightfully and famously said, '[i]t has been experience'. This is the true essence of the common law. More lawyers and judges around the country are becoming knowledgeable about and familiar with Islam, Islamic law and the laws of Muslim countries. With judges equipped with this knowledge, we can expect the law governing Muslim marriage contracts to become more consistent and uniform with the simple contract theory that preserves both the 1,400-year-old *mahr* tradition, yet does not foreclose a wife's claims for modern alimony and equitable distribution. While religious divorces in the United States will not legally dissolve a marriage, religious divorces rendered abroad will continue to be subject to public policy and due process constraints coupled with an evolving jurisprudence providing more judicial guidance on how to resolve jurisdiction where parties have multiple residences in different countries.

Courts, like in *Hammoud*, and legislators, as it happened with the New York Get law, must make/interpret law to protect Muslim women from husbands who withhold religious divorces out of vindictiveness or for financial blackmail. It is also important that Muslims include religious-rearing issues in their marriage contracts and/or settlement agreements. An increasing number of Muslim countries around the world are also considering joining the Hague

Convention and reforms around the Muslim world are moving toward incorporating the best interests of the child standard to determine custody disputes. A religious marriage without a marriage licence should not be rendered void, but states should consider adopting a New-York-style law that validates religious marriages without marriage licences, which is consistent with the strong public policy presumption of marriage validity.

The activity in the next decade will be dynamic and engaged. Our courts must be equipped with the cultural and religious context in order to adjudicate disputes fairly and equitably. The cases discussed above demonstrate the dynamic American judicial interpretative discourse that already exists and which is not based on ideological or bright line rules, but rather on a thoughtful case-by-case analysis of matters and a fidelity to our constitution. The proponents of the anti-shari'a legislation seek to halt this progress. As I explained in the introduction, the anti-shari'a legislation that has become law will not survive constitutional scrutiny. So, while it may slow the progress of an American judiciary seeking information in order to effectively and fairly adjudicate disputes, it will not stop it.

Notes

1 I would like to thank Elisa Giunchi for her comments on earlier drafts and for her patience with me despite my numerous requests for deadline extensions. Thanks also go to Nancy Zalusky Berg, Esq. for reading an earlier draft. And, thanks also to Rania Mustafa for helping with the citations and bibliography. Of course, any errors and mistakes are my own.

2 Anti-shari'a proponents cite a New Jersey case claiming that the judge allowed a Muslim husband to argue that he did not rape his wife because he is entitled to sex upon demand. This interpretation violates Islamic law, which forbids rape. Furthermore, like the laws in the majority of countries around the world, Islamic law provides either spouse with a ground for divorce in the case of sexual desertion. That would be the remedy for sexual desertion, not rape. In *S.D. v. M.J.R.*, 2 A.3d 412 (App.Div. 2010), the Appellate Court reversed the decision, finding that trial court misinterpreted the New Jersey sexual assault statute. The court found that defendant knew that his wife did not want to have intercourse, which was sufficient to violate the sexual assault statute. See my commentary on this case: Awad 2010b.

3 The original version of the anti-shari'a bill expressly targeted Muslims. After the Oklahoma Federal Court held that the anti-shari'a bill was unconstitutional, the anti-shari'a movement crafted a neutral foreign law ban statute.

4 The Qur'an is the Muslim Holy Scripture – like the New Testament for Christians or the Old Testament for the Jews. It is a compilation of revelations – the Word of God – received by the Prophet Mohammad from the Archangel Gabriel over a 23-year period beginning in 610 AD. The Sunna is the prophetic example embodied in the sayings and conduct of the Prophet Mohammad, as to what he promoted, what he allowed and what he prohibited; this was preserved in a narrative form that became known as *hadith*.

5 After the two primary sources of Islamic law, the Qur'an and the Sunna, the two main secondary sources of Islamic law are: *ijma* (consensus of the scholars and jurists, and sometimes the entire community) and *qiyas* (reasoning by analogy to one of the higher sources). A Muslim jurist would first rely on the primary sources to reach a legal opinion or ruling on a particular matter. The process of analytical

legal reasoning that is used to deduce or derive the law from the sources is called *ijtihad*. Ijtihad literally means to exert, strive, and/or endeavor. A jurist would utilize *ijtihad* by engaging and exerting his independent intellectual faculties and reasoning based on the express scriptures and/or spirit of the scriptures to reach a legal or theological ruling. In the classical period, when an issue arose that was not expressly addressed in the foundational texts, or when the foundational texts were subject to varying interpretations, a methodology to utilize the foundational texts and the sanctioned interpretive tools evolved into a sophisticated jurisprudential system. Today, there are four schools in Sunni law – Hanafi, Maliki, Shafi'i and Hanbali. See Hallaq 2009.

6 Until the rise of the nation-state model post colonialism, the jurist had exclusive authority to determine shari'a, and this body of law was communitarian and decentralized. The independence of the jurists and their exclusive authority to determine the Divine Will acted as the pre-modern separation of powers in the Muslim Empire. For a fascinating study of pre-modern Islamic governance and separation of power, see generally Hallaq 2012.

7 For a general introduction to classical Islamic law on marriage and divorce see Awad 2013: 625–30; Awad and Mawla 2013: 219–25; Nasir 2002 and Hibri 2005.

8 2010 WL 1189383 (Va. App.) (unpublished).

9 666 So.2d 246 (Fla. App. 2 Dist., 1996).

10 388 A.2d 1000 (N.J. Superior Court, 1978).

11 261 S.W.3d 190 (2008).

12 139 Wn. App. 1066.

13 A marital agreement entered in contemplation of marriage is governed by a less onerous standard than a marital agreement entered post-marriage. Post-marital agreements are called mid-marriage agreements or postnuptial agreements and are generally more difficult to enforce, but the trend around the United States is in favor of enforceability as long as additional requirements, such as advice of counsel, full complete financial disclosures, fair and equitable at time of execution and not unconscionable at time of enforcement. See, e.g., *Pacelli v. Pacelli*, 725 A.2d 56 (New Jersey Superior Court Appellate Division, 1999), *Ansin v. Craven-Ansin*, 929 N.E.2d 955 (Massachusetts Supreme Court, 2010) and *Bedrick v. Bedrick*, 17 A3d 17 (Connecticut Supreme Court, 2011).

14 2008 WL 2698679 (Ohio App.10 Dist.) (unpublished).

15 2001 WL 1518116 (Ohio App.6 Dist.) (unpublished).

16 For the first time on appeal, in *Zawahiri*, the wife raised the argument that her Islamic marriage contract was not a prenuptial agreement, but a simple contract. Because she failed to raise that argument at the trial level, the court held that she had waived her right to raise it on appeal.

17 204 Cal.App.3d 1387 (Cal. App. 4th dist. 1988).

18 88 Cal. App.4th 398 (2001).

19 2006 WL 1134034 (Va. Cir. Ct.) (unpublished).

20 127 Misc.2d 1013, 488 N.Y.S.2d 123 (1985).

21 355 N.J. Super. 305, 810 A.2d 93 (2002).

22 154 Wash. App. 609, 226 P.3d 787 (2010).

23 1995 WL 507388 (N.Y. Sup. Ct. Kings Cnty) (unpublished).

24 (Docket No. A-5191–08T3) (unpublished).

25 Uniform Premarital Agreement Act, 9C U.L.A. 43 (2001).

26 2004 WL 1752957 (Ohio App.8 Dist.) (unpublished).

27 A valid marriage contract under the laws of most Muslim majority countries requires an offer of marriage and acceptance of marriage before two witnesses. The majority of Muslim majority countries provide that the representatives of the couple by proxy can enter into a marriage on the behalf of the bride or groom or dissolve or consent to the dissolution of the marriage in behalf of either party.

28 2009 WL 930007 (Mich. App.)
29 See generally, Awad and Mawla 2013.
30 2009 WL 2709948 (Ohio App.3 Dist.) (unpublished).
31 38 Misc.3d 780, 959 N.Y.S.2d 802 (2012).
32 The judge focused on the issues before her rather than considering the entire body of Islamic law or the laws of Muslim countries. While some parts of Islamic law would violate public policy, the court explained, none of those issues were implicated in the litigation between the parties.
33 2005 WL 564191 (App.Div) (unpublished).
34 The three-menstrual-cycle period is called the *'iddah*, or waiting period, which the Qur'an defines specifically as three successive menstrual cycles (2:228). On *'iddah*, see Awad 2013.
35 *Matter of Hassan*, 11 I & N Dec. 179 (1965).
36 2001 WL 842023 (Ohio App.5 Dist.) (unpublished).
37 931 A.2d 1123 (App.Div., 2006).
38 2007 WL 4170868 (Ohio App.2 Dist.) (unpublished).
39 6 Misc. 2d 905 (Fam.Ct. 1974).
40 384 N.J. Super 339 (2006).
41 2006 WL 736561 (Mich. App.) (unpublished).
42 429 S.E.2d 626 (1993).
43 719 S.E.2d 192 (2011), reversed 731 S.E.2d 404 (2012).
44 23 Misc.3d 1109 (2009).
45 A marriage contract can be absolutely null/void or relatively null/voidable. In the void situation, no rights arise therefrom. Incestuous marriages, and certain family-degree-related marriages (affinity and consanguinity) are absolutely void. Polygamous marriages are void. In the voidable situation, all marital rights arise therefrom until the voidable marriage is dissolved legally. In other words, failure to comply with a condition of a contract does not automatically render the marriage invalid/void. The invalidity must be adjudicated by a court of law. Voidable marriage contracts include those with defects of consent and other formalities of a contract. Unless the law specifically states that absence of a formality renders a marriage contract void, the marriage would be voidable. If she wishes to dissolve it, then the marriage will be dissolved on the grounds of the spouse being underage at the time of marriage.
46 257 F.2d 306 (2nd Cir. 1958).
47 2012 WL 752044 (App.Div) (unpublished).
48 For a fascinating study based on interviews with a Michigan attorney regarding Islamic law in the family trial litigation, see generally Khatib (forthcoming).
49 In 1983, New York State passed a removal of barriers to marriage law. While the Jewish *Get* was the impetus behind the lase, the law applies to all faiths. New York Domestic Relations Law §253. The mother has a presumption of *hadana* until the child reaches a certain age, ranging from 7 years to 12 years. The law provides that that prior to the court granting a New York civil divorce, both parties to the divorce will take all steps possible to remove any barriers to the other person's remarriage. In effect, this law means that the parties must religiously divorce either before or shortly after obtaining a civil divorce. If a party fails to remove the barriers to remarriage, the aggrieved party has a civil remedy to compel the other party's cooperation to remove the barrier to remarriage. There is no other state with such legislation.
50 *Steinberg v. Steinberg*, 1982 WL 2446 (Ohio App. 1982) (unpublished).
51 See generally Awad 2012a; Awad and Popescu 2009.
52 193 A.D. 782 (App.Div. 1993).
53 2008 WL 4023719 (Ohio App. 9 Dist.) (unpublished).
54 78 Mass.App.Ct. 325 (Mass.App.Ct. 2010).

55 671 A.2d 988 (1996).
56 38 Misc.3d 780 (2012).
57 Classical Islamic law divides custody into three types of guardianship. The first type is guardianship for rearing purposes, which is called *hadana*. The second type is guardianship over the child's person, which is called *al-wilaya alla al-nafs*. The third type is guardianship over the child's money/property, which is called *al-wilaya alla al-mal*. The mother has a presumption of *hadana* until the child reaches a certain age. Except in very limited circumstances, the second and third types of guardianship, by operation of law, are the sole right of the father. As legal guardian over the child's person, the father has the authority to make decisions relating to the child's marriage, education and rearing. As guardian over the child's property, he has the authority to make decisions relating to the management of the child's property and finances from investing, to executing contracts on his/her behalf, to spending his/her money. It is important to note that there is some overlap between guardianship over the child's person and rearing. In other words, the mother has certain rights that come within the realm of guardianship over the person because the child lives with her, i.e. she is the residential custodian. But the mother does not have the authority to authorize marriage, travel, relocation, education and other related matters. Today the custody laws of many Muslim countries, such as Pakistan, Morocco and United Arab Emirates, are rapidly evolving and incorporating best interest factors.
58 Hague Convention on the Civil Aspects of International Child Abduction, opened for signature Oct. 25, 1980, 19 I.L.M. 1501.
59 361 N.J. Super. 135 (App. Div. 2003).
60 LLC, 2010 WL 1435056 (unpublished).
61 Islamic law of succession and inheritance is, in essence, an intestacy inheritance regime. The estate of a decedent is distributed according to a fixed-share formula consistent with the Qur'an. For a good English language source on this topic, see generally Khan 2007. Islamic law provides a list of the legal heirs of the decedent's estate. The legal heirs all take in accordance with their predetermined share as set forth in the Qur'an. A decedent is not permitted to deviate from this fixed-share system. In other words, a last will and testament would not be valid if it deviated from the fixed-share system. The only exception from this rule is that a decedent is entitled to bequeath up to one third of his estate to a non-legal heir.

Bibliography

Awad, A. (2002) 'Court enforces mahr provision in Muslim marriage contract', *New Jersey Law Journal*, 9 September, 1–6.

——(2010a) 'Oklahoma amendment is unconstitutional: Barring court from considering Sharia law violated the supremacy clause & the first amendment', *National Law Journal*, 15 November.

——(2010b) 'Religion-based claim in abuse case wisely pierced by appeals court', *New Jersey Law Journal*, 17 September.

——(2011) 'Appeals court had the chance to do right by a wife and children – But declined it', *North Carolina Lawyers Weekly*, 26 December.

——(2012a) 'Chipping away at divorce quagmire for Muslim and Jewish women', *New Jersey Law Journal*, 13 February.

——(2012b) 'Negative connotations surrounding Sharia must be dispelled', *Jurist-Sidebar*, 2 February.

——(2012c) 'The true story of Sharia in American courts', *The Nation Magazine*, 2 July.

——(2013) 'Marriage', subentry on historical practice and legal foundations, in N. DeLong-Bas (ed.), *The Oxford Encyclopedia of Islam and Women*, New York: Oxford University Press, 625–30.

Awad, A. and Hany, M. (2013) 'Divorce', subentry on historical practice and legal foundations, in N. DeLong-Bas (ed.), *The Oxford Encyclopedia of Islam and Women*, New York: Oxford University Press, 219–24.

Awad, A. and Michael, R. (2010) 'Iflas and Chapter 11: classical Islamic law and modern bankruptcy', 44 *International Lawyers*, 975: 976–78.

Awad, A. and Popescu, R. (2006) 'Declaring Muslim marriages void will have ruinous effect on wives', *New Jersey Law Journal*, 20 November.

——(2009) 'Remove remarriage barriers for Muslim, Jewish women,' *New Jersey Law Journal*, 13 April.

Cahn II, C. (1992) 'Estate planning to avoid complications of remarriage', 19 *Est. Plan*, 268.

Elliot, J. (2011) 'What sharia law actually mean', *Salon.com*, 26 Feb., 2011 (interview with Abed Awad). Available online at www.salon.com/2011/02/26/sharia_the_real_story/ (accessed 30 May 2013).

Esposito, J.L. and Delong-Bas, N.J. (2001) *Women in Muslim Family Law*, Syracuse, NY: Syracuse University Press.

Hallaq, W.B. (2009) *Sharī'a: Theory, Practice, Transformations*, Cambridge and New York: Cambridge University Press.

——(2012) *The Impossible State: Islam, politics, and modernity's moral predicament*, New York: Columbia University Press.

Hibri, A.Y. (2005) 'The nature of the Islamic marriage: sacramental, covenantal, or contractual?' in J. Witte, Jr and E. Ellison (eds), *Covenant Marriage in Comparative Perspective*, Grand Rapids, MI: WB Eerdmans.

Khan, H. (2007) *The Islamic Law of Inheritance*, Oxford: Oxford University Press.

Khatib, I. (forthcoming) 'Shari'ah law and American family courts: judicial inconsistency on the talāq and mahr issues in Wayne County, Michigan', *Journal of Law in Society*, 14(1).

Marston, A.A. (1997) 'Planning for love: the politics of prenuptial agreements', 49 *Stan. L. Rev.*, 887.

Nasir, J.J. (2002) *The Islamic Law of Personal Status*, The Hague New York: Kluwer Law International.

Pew Research Center (2007) 'Muslim American: middle class and mostly mainstream', 13 September. Available online at http://pewresearch.org (accessed 30 May 2013).

Quraishi, A. (2004) 'No altars: an introduction to Islamic family law in US courts', in N. Syeed-Miller (ed.), *Women's Rights and Islamic Family Law: perspectives on reform*, London and New York: Zed Books.

——(2012) 'Rumors of the Sharia threat are greatly exaggerated: what American judges really do with Islamic family law in their courtrooms', 57 *New York Law School Law Review*, 2: 245–57.

Wajaht, A. (2011) 'Fear, Inc.: The roots of the Islamophobia network in American', in F. Patel, M. Duss and A. Toh (eds), *Foreign Law Bans Legal Uncertainties and Practical Problems*, New York: Brennan Center. Available online at www.brennancenter.org/sites/default/files/publications/Foreign%20Law%20Bans.pdf (accessed 4 June 2013).

Younger, J.T. (1992) 'Perspectives on ante-nuptial agreements: an update', *Journal of American Academy of Matrimonial Lawyers*, 42: 1–44.

Zakaria, R. (2013) 'Sharia law ban and Muslim wives: Muslim women in Kansas are hit by the Sharia law ban, as they are unable to claim compensation from their estranged men', *Al-Jazeera English*, 16 February. Available online at www.aljazeera.com/indepth/opinion/2013/02/201321174724878286.html (accessed 30 May 2013).

Glossary

agunah/agunoh (pl.)	'chained' woman; a Jewish woman who is entitled to a *get* but her husband refuses to grant it
amrikan shariat	American *shari'a*
angrezi shariat	British *shari'a*
Beth Din/Battei Din (pl.)	Jewish tribunal
darar	harm
darura	necessity
dayanim	Jewish judges
du'a	prayer of supplication
fatwa	non binding religious response by a *mufti*
faskh	annulment of marriage
get	Jewish divorce
hadana	mother's custody of children
hadith	saying, action or decision attributed to the Prophet
'idda	the period of time after divorce when the wife must refrain from remarrying and she is entitled to maintenance
ijab	offer
ijma	consensus (one of the sources of Islamic law)
ijtihad	interpretative effort, individual juristic reasoning
kafala	form of guardianship of children which does not create a full parental relationship between child and guardian
ketubah/ketubot (pl.)	Jewish marriage contract
khul'	divorce initiated by the female spouse with the consent of the husband in return for compensation
laiklik	secularism

madhhab	legal school
mahr	dower
mamzer/mamzerin (pl.)	Jewish children whose divorced mother has not received a *get*
maqasid al-shari'a	objectives of shari'a
maslaha	common good
mu'akhkhar al-sadaq	deferred dower
mubarat	divorce with the consent of both spouses, at the initiative of the husband or both
mujtahid	a learned Muslim who practices *ijtihad*
nafaqa	maintenance
nikah	religious marriage
nusyuz	disobedient
qabul	acceptance
qadi	judge
qiwama	protection; guardianship
qiyas	analogy (one of the sources of Islamic law)
sadaq	nuptial gift
shari'a	Islamic law; God's will as expressed in the Qur'an and Sunna
shiqaq	discord
tafriq	form of divorce in which the court intervenes
talaq	unilateral divorce by the husband
talaq al-bid'a	innovatory *talaq*: the triple *talaq* that is allowed by *fiqh*
talaq i-tafwid	delegated divorce
talaq-ul- bid'a	innovatory talaq
talfiq	combination of opinions from different *madhhab*
tamkin	submission
'ulama'	religious scholars
vaad	council of rabbis
wali	guardian, male legal representative
wilaya	guardianship
al-wilaya alla al-nafs	guardianship over the child's person
al-wilaya alla al-mal	guardianship over the child's money/property
zina	illicit sexual relationship, between individuals who are not validly married to each other

Index

For Product Safety Concerns and Information please contact our EU representative GPSR@taylorandfrancis.com
Taylor & Francis Verlag GmbH, Kaufingerstraße 24, 80331 München, Germany

www.ingramcontent.com/pod-product-compliance
Ingram Content Group UK Ltd.
Pitfield, Milton Keynes, MK11 3LW, UK
UKHW022128190926
475702UK00013B/1694
9780415788007